EVERYMAN'S LIBRARY
EDITED BY ERNEST RHYS

POETRY & THE DRAMA

THREE DRAMAS
BY BJÖRNSTJERNE BJÖRNSON · TRANS-
LATED BY R. FARQUHARSON SHARP

BJÖRNSTJERNE BJÖRNSON, born in Österdal, Norway, in 1832, the son of a pastor. In 1852 graduated from University of Oslo. Spent 1860–3 in Italy, and on return was made manager of the theatre at Oslo. Travelled on Continent, 1868–76. Made director of the Bergen Theatre, 1897. Died in 1910.

THREE DRAMAS
THE EDITOR—THE BANKRUPT—THE KING

BJÖRNSTJERNE BJÖRNSON

GREENWOOD PRESS, PUBLISHERS
WESTPORT, CONNECTICUT

Library of Congress Cataloging in Publication Data

Bjørnson, Bjørnstjerne, 1832-1910.
  Three dramas: The editor--The bankrupt--The king.

  "Originally published in 1914."
  Reprint of the 1924 ed. published by Dent, London and
Dutton, New York, which was issued as no. 696 of Every-
man's library: Poetry & the drama.
  I. Title.
PT8816.A3S5 1974   839.8'2'26   73-17654
ISBN 0-8371-7260-8

Originally published in 1914 by J.M. Dent & Sons Ltd, London;
E.P. Dutton & Co., Inc., New York

Reprinted in 1974 by Greenwood Press,
a division of Williamhouse-Regency Inc.

Library of Congress Catalog Card Number 73-17654

ISBN 0-8371-7260-8

Printed in the United States of America

INTRODUCTION

THE three plays here presented were the outcome of a period when Björnson's views on many topics were undergoing a drastic revision and he was abandoning much of his previous orthodoxy in many directions. Two of them were written during, and one immediately after, a three years' absence from Norway—years spent almost entirely in southern Europe.[1] For nearly ten years previous to this voluntary exile, Björnson had been immersed in theatrical management and political propagandism. His political activities (guided by a more or less pronounced republican tendency) centred in an agitation for a truer equality between the kingdoms of Sweden and Norway, his point of view being that Norway had come to be regarded too much as a mere appanage of Sweden. Between that and his manifold and distracting cares as theatrical director, he had let imaginative work slide for the time being; but his years abroad had a recuperative effect, and, in addition, broadened his mental outlook in a remarkable manner. Foreign travel, a wider acquaintance with differing types of humanity, and, above all, a newly-won acquaintance with the contemporary literature of other countries, made a deep impression upon Björnson's vigorously receptive mind. He browsed voraciously upon the works of foreign writers. Herbert Spencer, Darwin, John Stuart Mill, Taine, Max-Müller, formed a portion of his mental pabulum at this time—and the result was a significant alteration of mental attitude on a number of questions, and a determination to make the attempt to embody his theories in dramatic form. He had

[1] Further details respecting Björnson's life will be found in the Introduction to *Three Comedies by Björnson*, published in Everyman's Library in 1912.

gained all at once, as he wrote to Georg Brandes, the eminent Danish critic, "eyes that saw and ears that heard." Up to this time the poet in him had been predominant; now it was to be the social philosopher that held the reins. Just as Ibsen did, so Björnson abandoned historical drama and artificial comedy for an attempt at prose drama which should have at all events a serious thesis. In this he anticipated Ibsen; for (unless we include the satirical political comedy, *The League of Youth*, which was published in 1869, among Ibsen's " social dramas ") Ibsen did not enter the field with *Pillars of Society* [1] until 1877, whereas Björnson's *The Editor, The Bankrupt*, and *The King* were all published between 1874 and 1877. Intellectual and literary life in Denmark had been a good deal stirred and quickened in the early seventies, and the influence of that awakening was inevitably felt by the more eager spirits in the other Scandinavian countries. It is amusing to note, as one Norwegian writer has pointed out, that this intellectual upheaval (which, in its turn, was a reflection of that taking place in outer Europe) came at a time when the bulk of the Scandinavian folk " were congratulating themselves that the doubt and ferment of unrest which were undermining the foundations of the great communities abroad had not had the power to ruffle the placid surface of our good, oldfashioned, Scandinavian orthodoxy." Björnson makes several sly hits in these plays (as does Ibsen in *Pillars of Society*) at this distrust of the opinions and manners of the larger communities outside of Scandinavia, notably America, with which the Scandinavian countries were more particularly in touch through emigration.

Brandes characterises the impelling motive of these three plays as a passionate appeal for a higher standard of truth—in journalism, in finance, in monarchy: an appeal for less casuistry and more honesty. Such a motive was characteristic of the vehement honesty of Björnson's own character; he must always, as he says

[1] Published in *The Pretenders and Two Other Plays*, in Everyman's Library, 1913.

in one of his letters, go over to the side of any one whom
he believed to "hold the truth in his hands."

The Editor (Redaktören) was written while Björnson
was in Florence, and was published at Copenhagen in
1874. It was at first not accepted for performance at
Christiania or Copenhagen, though an unauthorised per
formance of it was given at one of the lesser Christiania
theatres in 1875. Meanwhile a Swedish version of it
had been produced, authoritatively, at Stockholm in
February of that year. The play eventually made its
way on the Norwegian and Danish stage; but, before
that, it had been seen in German dress at Munich and
Hamburg. As an inevitable result of his recent activities
as a political speaker and pamphleteer, Björnson had
come in for a good deal of vituperation in the press, a
fact which no doubt added some gall to the ink with
which he drew the portrait of the journalist in this play.
The Stockholm critics, indeed, had condemned *The
Editor* as merely a pamphleteering attack on the editor
of a well-known journal. In answer to this criticism
Björnson wrote from Rome in March, 1875: " It is said
that my play is a pamphleteering attack on a certain
individual. That is a deliberate lie. I have studied
the journalist type, which is here represented, in many
other countries besides my own. The chief characteristic of this type is to be actuated by an inordinate
egotism that is perpetually being inflamed by passion;
that makes use of bogeys to frighten people, and does
this in such a way that, while it makes all its honest
contemporaries afraid of any freedom of thought, it
also produces the same result on every single individual
by means of reckless persecution. As I wished to por-
tray that type, I naturally took a good deal of the
portrait from the representative of the type that I
knew best; but, like every artist who wishes to produce
a complete creation, I had to build it up from separate
revelations of itself. There can, therefore, be no
question of any individual being represented in my play
except in so far as he may partially agree with the type."

However much Björnson may have written *The*

Björnson's Plays

Editor with a " purpose," his vivid dramatic sense kept
him from becoming merely didactic. The little tragedy
that takes place amongst this homely group of people
makes quite a moving play, thanks to the skill with
which the types are depicted—the bourgeois father and
mother, with their mixture of timidity and self-interest;
the manly, straightforward young politician, resolute to
carry on the work that has sapped his brother's life;
the warped, de-humanised nature of the journalist; the
sturdy common-sense of the yeoman farmer; and the
doctor, the " family friend," as a sort of mocking
chorus. Besides its plea for a higher regard for truth,
the play also attacks the precept, preached by worldly
wisdom, that we ought to harden our natures to make
ourselves invulnerable; a proposition which was hateful
to one of Björnson's persistently impressionable and
ingenuous nature. The fact remains, as Brandes grimly
admits, that " nowadays we have only a very qualified
sympathy with public characters who succumb to the
persecution of the press." Brandes sees in the play,
besides its obvious motive, an allegory. Halvdan Rejn,
the weary and dying politician, is (he says) meant for
Henrik Wergeland, a Norwegian poet-politician who had
similar struggles, sank under the weight of similar
attacks, died after a long illness, and was far higher
reputed after his death than during his life. In Harald
Rejn, with his honest enthusiasm and misjudged
political endeavours, Brandes sees Björnson himself;
while the yeoman brother, Haakon, seems to him to
typify the Norwegian people.

The Bankrupt (*En Fallit*: literally *A Bankruptcy*)
was partly written in Rome, partly in Tyrol, and published at Copenhagen in 1875. It was a thing entirely
new to the Scandinavian stage for a dramatist to deal
seriously with the tragi-comedy of money, and, while
making a forcible plea for honesty, to contrive to
produce a stirring and entertaining play on what might
seem so prosaic a foundation as business finance. Some
of the play's earliest critics dismissed it as " dry,"
" prosaic," " trivial," because of the nature of its

subject; but it made a speedy success on the boards, and very soon became a popular item in the repertories of the Christiania, Bergen and Copenhagen theatres. It was actually first performed, in a Swedish translation, at Stockholm, a few days before it was produced at Christiania. Very soon, too, the play reached Berlin, Munich, Vienna, and other German and Austrian theatres. It was played in Paris, at the Théâtre Libre in 1894. The character of Berent, the lawyer, which became a favourite one with the famous Swedish actor Ernst Possart, was admittedly more or less of a portrait of a well-known Norwegian lawyer, by name Dunker. When Björnson was writing the play, he went to stay for some days with Dunker, who was to instruct him as to the legal aspect of bankruptcy. Björnson took the opportunity of studying the lawyer as well as the law.

The King (*Kongen*) was written at Aulestad, the Norwegian home in which Björnson settled after his return from abroad, and was published at Copenhagen in 1877. It is perhaps not surprising that the play, with its curious blend of poetry and social philosophy, and its somewhat exuberant (though always interesting) wordiness, was not at first a conspicuous success on the stage; but the interest aroused by the published book was enormous. It was widely read and vigorously discussed, both in Scandinavia and abroad; and while, on the one hand, it brought upon Björnson the most scurrilous abuse and the harshest criticism from his political opponents, on the other hand a prominent compatriot of his (whose opinion was worth having) gave it as his verdict, at a political meeting held soon after the play's publication, that " the most notable thing that has happened in Norway of late—or at any rate, one of the most notable—in my opinion is this last book of Björnson's—*The King*."

The idea of a " democratic monarchy "—a kind of reformed constitutional monarchy, that should be a half-way house on the road to republicanism—was not entirely new; Björnson's success was in presenting the problem as seen from the *inside*—that is to say, from the king's point of view. His opponents, of course, branded him as a red-hot republican, which he was not. In a preface he wrote for a later edition of the play, he says that he did not intend the play mainly as an argument in favour of republicanism, but " to extend the boundaries of free discussion "; but that, at the same time, he believed the republic to be the ultimate form of government, and all European states to be proceeding at varying rates of speed towards it.

The King is composed of curiously incongruous elements. The railway meeting in the first act is pure comedy of a kind to compare with the meeting in Ibsen's *An Enemy of Society ;* the last act is melodrama with a large admixture of remarkably interesting social philosophy; the intervening acts betray the poet that always underlay the dramatist in Björnson. The crudity, again, of the melodramatic appearance of the wraith of Clara's father in the third act, contrasts strangely with the mature thoughtfulness of much of the last act and with the tender charm of what has gone before. And—strangest incongruity of all in a play so essentially " actual "—there is in the original, between each act, a mysterious " mellemspil," or " interlude," in verse, consisting of somewhat cryptic dialogues between Genii and Unseen Choirs in the clouds, between an " Old Grey Man " and a " Chorus of Tyrants " in a desolate scene of snow and ice, between Choruses of Men, Women, and Children in a sylvan landscape, and so forth—their utterances being of the nature of the obscurest choruses in the Greek dramatists, but for the most part with a less obvious relevance to the play itself. Such a device leads the present-day reader's thoughts inevitably to the use made of the " unseen chorus," in a similar way, by Thomas Hardy in *The Dynasts ;* but Hardy's interludes are closely relevant to his drama and help it on its way, which Björnson's do not. They have been entirely omitted in the present translation, on the ground of their complete superfluity as well as from the extreme difficulty of retaining their " atmosphere " in translation.

None of the three plays in the present volume have

Introduction   xiii

previously been translated into English. German, French, and Swedish versions of *The Editor* are extant; German, Swedish, Finnish, French, and Hungarian of *The Bankrupt ;* French and Spanish of *The King*.

R. FARQUHARSON SHARP.

The following is a list of the works of Björnstjerne Björnson:—

DRAMATIC AND POETIC WORKS.—Mellem Slagene (Between the Battles), 1857. Halte-Hulda (Lame Hulda), 1858. Kong Sverre (King Sverre), 1861. Sigurd Slembe (Sigurd the Bastard), 1862; translated by W. M. Payne, 1888. Maria Stuart i Skotland, 1864; translated by A. Sahlberg, 1912. De Nygifte (The Newly-Married Couple), 1865; translated by T. Soelfeldt, 1868; by S. and E. Hjerleid, 1870; as A Lesson in Marriage, by G. I. Colbron, 1911. Sigurd Jorsalfar (Sigurd the Crusader), 1872. Redaktören (The Editor), 1874. En Fallit (A Bankruptcy), 1874. Kongen (The King), 1877. Leonarda, 1879. Det ny System (The New System), 1879. En Hanske, 1883; translated as A Gauntlet, by H. L. Brækstad, 1890; by Osman Edwards, 1894. Over Ævne (Beyond our Strength), Part I., 1883; translated as Pastor Sang, by W. Wilson, 1893; Part II., 1895. Geografi og Kærlighed (Geography and Love), 1885. Paul Lange og Tora Parsberg, 1898; translated by H. L. Brækstad, 1899. Laboremus, 1901; translation published by Chapman and Hall, 1901. Paa Storhove (At Storhove), 1904. Daglannet, 1904. Naar den ny Vin blomstrer (When the Vineyards are in Blossom), 1909. The Newly-Married Couple, Leonarda, and A Gauntlet, translated by R. Farquharson Sharp (Everyman's Library), 1912.

Digte og Sange (Poems and Songs), 1870; Arnljot Gelline, 1870.

FICTION.—Synnöve Solbakken, 1857; translated as Trust and Trial, by Mary Howitt, 1858; as Love and Life in Norway, by Hon. Augusta Bethell and A. Plesner, 1870; as The Betrothal, in H. and A. Zimmern's Half-hours with Foreign Novelists, 1880; also translated by Julie Sutter, 1881; by R. B. Anderson, 1881. Arne, 1858; translated by T. Krag, 1861; by A. Plesner and S. Rugeley-Powers, 1866; by R. B. Anderson, 1881; by W. Low (Bohn's Library), 1890. Smaastykker (Sketches), 1860. En glad Gut, 1860; translated as Ovind, by S. and E. Hjerleid, 1869; as The Happy Boy, by R. B. Anderson, 1881; as The Happy Lad (published by Blackie), 1882. Fiskerjenten, 1868; translated as The Fisher Maiden, by M. E. Niles, 1869; as The Fishing Girl, by A. Plesner and F. Richardson, 1870; as The Fishing Girl, by S. and E. Hjerleid, 1871; as The Fisher Maiden, by R. B. Anderson, 1882. Brude-Slaatten, 1873; translated as The Bridal March, by R. B. Anderson, 1882; by J. E. Williams, 1893. Fortællinger (Tales), 1872. Magnhild, 1877; translated by R. B. Anderson, 1883. Kaptejn Mansana, 1879; translated as Captain Mansana by R. B. Anderson, 1882.

Det flager i Byen og paa Havnen (Flags are Flying in Town and Port), 1884; translated as The Heritage of the Kurts, by C. Fairfax, 1892. Paa Guds Veje, 1889; translated as In God's Way, by E. Carmichael, 1890. Nye Fortællinger (New Tales), 1894; To Fortællinger (Two Tales), 1901; Mary, 1906. Collected edition of the Novels, translated into English, edited by E. Gosse, 13 vols., 1895-1909.

[See Life of Björnson by W. M. Payne, 1910; E. Gosse's Study of the Writings of Björnson, in edition of Novels, 1895; H. H. Boyesen's Essays on Scandinavian Literature, 1895; G. Brandes' Critical Studies of Ibsen and Björnson, 1899.]

CONTENTS

THE EDITOR

A PLAY IN FOUR ACTS

DRAMATIS PERSONÆ

EVJE, a prosperous distiller.
MRS. EVJE.
GERTRUD, their daughter, engaged to HARALD REJN.
The DOCTOR.
The EDITOR.
HAAKON REJN, a yeoman farmer.
HALVDAN REJN } his brothers.
HARALD REJN
The DOCTOR'S ASSISTANT.
INGEBORG, maid to the Evjes.
JOHN, coachman to the Evjes.
HALVDAN REJN'S HOUSEKEEPER.
HALVDAN REJN'S MAID.
A Lamplighter.

The action takes place in a town in Norway.

THE EDITOR

ACT I

(SCENE.—*The breakfast-room at the* EVJES' *house. A glass-cupboard, in two partitions, stands against the left-hand wall, well forward. On the top of it stand a variety of objects. Beyond it, a stove. At the back of the room, a sideboard. In the middle of the room a small round folding table, laid for four persons. There is an armchair by the stove; a sofa on the right; chairs, etc. A door at the back of the room, and another in the left-hand wall. There are paintings on the walls, and the general impression of the room is one of snug comfort.* EVJE, MRS. EVJE, *and* GERTRUD *are seated at the table.* INGEBORG *is standing by the sideboard. Breakfast is proceeding in silence as the curtain rises.* INGEBORG *takes away* EVJE'S *cup and re-fills it. As she brings it back to him, a ring is heard at the bell.* GERTRUD *gets up.*)

Evje. Sit still; John will go to the door. (GERTRUD *sits down again. Directly afterwards, another ring is heard.*)

Mrs. Evje. What can John be doing?

Ingeborg. I will go. (*Goes out. She comes back, showing in* HARALD REJN, *who hangs up his hat and coat in the hall before coming in.*)

Harald. Good morning!

Evje and Mrs. Evje. Good morning! (HARALD *shakes hands with them.*)

Harald (*to* GERTRUD, *who is sitting on the right*). Good

3

morning, Gertrud! Am I a bit late to-day? (GERTRUD, *who has taken his hand, looks lovingly at him but says nothing.*)

Mrs. Evje. Yes, I suppose you have been for a long constitutional, although the weather is none of the best.

Harald. It is not; I expect we shall have a thick fog by the afternoon.

Evje. Did you have breakfast before you went out?

Harald. I did, thanks. (*To* INGEBORG, *who has come forward with a cup of coffee.*) No, thank you. I will sit down here while you are finishing. (*Sits down on the sofa behind* GERTRUD.)

Mrs. Evje. How is your brother Halvdan?

Harald. A little better to-day, thanks—but of course we cannot build on that.

Evje. Is your eldest brother coming to see him?

Harald. Yes, we expect him every day. Probably his wife has come with him, and that has been the reason of the delay; she finds it difficult to get away.

Mrs. Evje. Halvdan so often talks of her.

Harald. Yes, I believe she is the best friend he has.

Evje. No wonder, then, that she wants to come and say good-bye to him. By the way, have you seen how the paper bids him good-bye to-day?

Harald. Yes, I have seen it.

Mrs. Evje (*hurriedly*). I hope Halvdan has not seen it?

Harald (*smiling*). No, it is a long time now since Halvdan read a newspaper. (*A pause.*)

Evje. Then I suppose you have read what they say about you too?

Harald. Naturally.

Mrs. Evje. It is worse than anything they have said about you before.

Harald. Well—of course, you know, my election meeting comes on this evening.

Evje. I can tell you it has upset *us*.

Mrs. Evje. Day after day we wake up to find our house invaded by these abominations. That is a nice thought to begin your day's work with!

Harald. Is it so indispensable, then, to educated people to begin their day by reading such things?

Mrs. Evje. Well—one must have a paper.

Evje. And most people read it. Besides, one can't deny that a lot of what is in it is true, although its general tendency is to run everyone down.

Harald (getting up). Quite so, yes. (*Leans over* GER-TRUD's *shoulder.*) Gertrud, have you read it?

Gertrud (does not look at him, and hesitates for a moment; then says gently): Yes.

Harald (under his breath). So that is it! (*Walks away from her.*)

Evje. We have had a little bit of a scene here, I must tell you.

Harald (walking up and down). Yes, I can understand that.

Evje. I will repeat what I have said already: they write about *you*, and *we* have to suffer for it.

Mrs. Evje. Yes, and Gertrud especially.

Gertrud. No—I don't want anyone to consider me in the matter at all. Besides, it is not what they say of you in the paper that hurts me—. (*Stops abruptly.*)

Harald (who has come up to her). But what your parents are feeling about it? Is that it? (GERTRUD *does not answer.*)

Evje (pushing back his plate). There, I have finished! (*They rise from the table.* MRS. EVJE *helps* INGEBORG *to clear away the things, which* INGEBORG *carries out of the room.*)

Mrs. Evje. Couldn't you wash your hands of politics, Harald? (GERTRUD *goes out to the left.*)

Evje (who has followed GERTRUD *with his eyes).* We cannot deny that it pains us considerably that in our old age our peaceful home should be invaded by all this squabbling and abomination.

Mrs. Evje (who rung for INGEBORG *to move the table).* You have no need to do it, either, Harald! You are a grown man, and your own master. (INGEBORG *comes in.* HARALD *helps her to move the table.*)

Evje (to his wife). Don't let Ingeborg hear. Come along, we will go into my room.

Mrs. Evje. You forget, all the windows are open there. I have had the fire lit here, so that we could stay here.

Evje. Very well—then we will sit here. (*Sits down by the fire.*) Will you have a cigar?

Harald. No, thanks. (INGEBORG *goes out.*)

Evje (taking a cigar and lighting it). As my wife said just now—couldn't you wash your hands of politics, Harald? You, who have both talent and means, need not be at a loss for a vocation in life.

Harald (sitting down on the sofa). If I have any talent, it is for politics—and so I intend to devote my means to that.

Evje. What do you propose to gain by it?

Harald. What any one who believes in a cause hopes to gain—that is to say, to help it on.

Evje. And to become a cabinet minister?

Harald. I certainly can't do that any other way; well, I admit—that *is* my idea.

Evje. You will not be elected now.

Harald. That we shall see.

Evje. But suppose you are not re-elected to-morrow?

Harald. Then I must find some other way.

Evje. Always with the same object?

Harald. Always with the same object. (EVJE *sighs.*)

Mrs. Evje (who has taken her sewing and sat down by the fire). Oh, these politics!

Harald. At any rate, they are the most prominent factors in life just now.

Evje. We do not suppose we can exercise any influence over you. But at any rate it is possible that you yourself have not considered the position into which you have put the whole of us. (*Both he and his wife avoid looking at* HARALD *during this discussion.*)

Mrs. Evje. Say what you really mean, dear—that he is making us all thoroughly unhappy, and that is the truth!

Harald (*getting up, and walking up and down*). Well, look here—I have a proposal to make. It is, that you should abandon all opposition to Gertrud's marrying me at once. To-day again my brother has expressed the wish that we should be married by his bedside, so that he should be able to take part in it. I scarcely need add how happy it would make me.

Evje. But whether she is here at home or married to you, you know, her parents' distress would be just as great every time their child was persecuted.

Mrs. Evje. Surely you can appreciate that!

Harald. But what answer am I to give to my brother's request?—most likely the last he will ever—. (*Stops.*)

Evje (*after a pause*). He is very kind to wish it, as he always is. Nothing would make us happier; but we who are her parents do not consider that you could make our daughter happy as long as you remain in politics and on the lines on which you are now travelling.

Harald (*after a pause, during which he has stood still*). That is to say, you contemplate breaking off our engagement?

Evje (*looking at him quickly*). Far from it!

Mrs. Evje (*at the same time*). How can you say such a thing?

Evje (*turning towards the fire again*). We have spoken about it to Gertrud to-day—as to whether it would not be possible to induce you to choose some other career.

Mrs. Evje. You understand now, why you found

Gertrud upset. You must listen to us now, as she did, in all friendliness.

Evje (getting up and standing with his back to the fire). The first thing I do in the morning is to read my paper. You know what was in it to-day—the same as is in it now every day.

Mrs. Evje. No, I am sure it has never been as bad as to-day.

Harald (walking up and down again). The election is just at hand!

Evje. Well—it is just as painful to us, her father and mother, whether it is before or after the election. We are not accustomed to associate with any one who has not first-class credentials—and now we have to endure seeing doubt cast upon our own son-in-law's. Do not mis-understand me; to my mind, for credentials to be first-class they must not only actually be so, but must also be considered to be so by people in general. (HARALD *begins to walk up and down again.*) The second thing I do in the morning is to open my letters. Amongst to-day's were several from friends we had invited to a party we thought of giving—if, that is to say, your brother's illness took no sudden turn for the worse. No fewer than ten of them refuse our invitation—most of them making some excuse, and a few with a little more show of a real reason; but one of them speaks straight out, and I have his letter here. *(Takes it from his pocket.)* I have kept it for you. It is from my father's old friend, the bishop. I haven't my spectacles—and for me to have mislaid my spectacles will show you what a state of mind I am in. I don't think I have done such a thing for—. Here, read it yourself! Read it aloud!

Harald (taking the letter). " My dear Mr. Evje. As you are my poor dear friend's son, you must listen to the truth from me. I cannot willingly come to your house while I might meet there a certain person who, certainly, is one of you, but nevertheless is a person whom I cannot hold in entire respect."

Mrs. Evje. Well, Harald, what do you think our feelings must be when we read things like that?

Evje. Do not imagine that, in spite of that, *we* do not hold you in entire respect. We only ask you to ensure our daughter's happiness. You can do that with a word.

Mrs. Evje. We know what you are, whatever people say—even if they are bishops. But, in return, you ought to have confidence in our judgment; and our advice to you is, have done with it! Marry Gertrud at once, and go away for your honeymoon; by the time you come back, people will have got something else to talk about—and you will have found something else to occupy you as well.

Evje. You must not misunderstand us. We mean no coercion. We are not insisting on this alternative. If you wish to be married, you shall—without feeling yourself obliged to change your vocation for *our* sakes. We only want to make it clear that it would pain us—pain us very deeply.

Mrs. Evje. If you want to take time to think it over, or want to talk it over with Gertrud or with your brother, do! (GERTRUD *comes in and goes about the room looking for something.*)

Evje. What are you looking for, dear?

Gertrud. Oh, for the—.

Mrs. Evje. I expect it is the newspaper; your grandfather has been asking for it.

Evje. Surely there is no need for *him* to read it?

Mrs. Evje. He asked me for it, too. He knows quite well what has made us all unhappy.

Evje. Can't you tell him? No, that wouldn't do.

Mrs. Evje (*to* GERTRUD). I suppose you have had to confess to him what is the matter?

Gertrud (*trying to conceal an emotion that is almost too much for her*). Yes. (*Finds the paper, and goes out.*)

Mrs. Evje (when GERTRUD *has gone).* Poor child!

Evje. Does not what she is carrying to him, with all that it says about you and about your brother, seem to you like an omen? I will tell you how it strikes me. Your brother is a very much more gifted man than I am; and although it is true, as that paper says, that nothing of all that he has worked for has ever come to anything, still perhaps he may nevertheless have accomplished more than either you or me, although we have done a good deal between us to increase the prosperity of our town. I feel that to be so, although I cannot express what I mean precisely. But consider the reputation he will leave behind him. All educated people will say just what that paper says to-day—and to-morrow he will be forgotten. He will scarcely find a place in history, for history only concerns itself with the great leaders of men. What does it all come to, then? Neither present nor posthumous fame; but death—death all the time. He is dying by inches now, dying of the most horrible persecution; and the emotion that his end will cause among a few individuals cannot be called posthumous fame. (HARALD *begins to speak, but checks himself.)* Can *you* hope to make a better fight of it? You think you are stronger? Very well; perhaps you may have the strength to endure it until other times come and other opinions with them. But there will be one by your side who will not have the strength to endure it. Gertrud is not strong—she could never stand it; indeed now—already—. *(Is stopped by his emotion.)*

Mrs. Evje. She hides it from you, but she cannot hide it from us. Besides, a friend of ours—our dear doctor— said only yesterday—. *(Breaks off in tears.)*

Evje. We never told you, but he warned us some time ago; we had no idea it was so serious, or that it had anything to do with this. But yesterday he frightened us; he said she—. Well, you can ask him yourself. He will be here directly. (HARALD *fills a glass of water and raises it to his lips, but sets it down again untasted.*)

Mrs. Evje (going to him). I am so sorry for you, Harald! To have this come on you just now—when your splendid brother is at the point of death, and you yourself are being persecuted! (*A ring is heard at the bell.*)

Evje. But it should be a warning to you! Sometimes a single movement will change the course of a whole life.

Mrs. Evje. And do have a little confidence in us! (*A ring is heard again.*)

Evje. What on earth has become of John to-day? That is the second time the bell has rung.

Mrs. Evje. One of the maids is opening the door, I can hear.

Evje. I expect it is the doctor.

Mrs. Evje. Yes, it is he—I know his ring. (*A knock is heard at the door.*)

Evje. Come in! (*The* DOCTOR *comes in.*)

The Doctor. Good morning! (*Lays down his hat and stick.*) Well, so I hear John has been up to his pranks again? The rascal is in bed.

Evje and Mrs. Evje. In bed?

The Doctor. Came home at four o'clock in the morning, drunk. Ill to-day, naturally. Ingeborg asked me to go in and see him.

Evje. Well!—I am determined to put an end to it!

Mrs. Evje. Yes, I have never been able to understand why you were so lenient with John.

Evje. He has been with us five years; and, besides, it makes people talk so, if you have to send your servants away.

Mrs. Evje. But surely this sort of thing makes them talk much worse!

Evje. Well—he shall leave this very day.

The Doctor (to HARALD*).* How are you, Rejn?—Oho! I understand. I have come at an inopportune moment with my complaints of John? You have all got something more serious on your minds?

Mrs. Evje. Yes, we have had it out, as we agreed yesterday.

The Doctor. You must forgive me, my dear Rejn, for having told my old friends the whole truth yesterday. She (*pointing to* MRS. EVJE) was an old playfellow of mine, and her husband and I have been friends from boyhood; so we have no secrets from each other. And Gertrud's condition makes me very uneasy.

Harald. Why have you never told me that before?

The Doctor. Goodness knows I have often enough given her parents hints that she was not well; but they have only made up their minds that her happiness in her engagement would quite cure her. They are a considerate couple, these two dear people, you know; they didn't want to seem interfering.

Harald. Their consideration—which I appreciate and have lately had constant reason to be grateful for—has all at once become a more powerful weapon than open opposition. It makes a duty of what I should otherwise have felt to be unfair coercion. But now the situation is such that I can neither go forward nor back. After what I have gone through, you must see that I cannot withdraw on the very eve of the election—and after the election it will be too late. On the other hand—(*with emotion*)—I cannot, I dare not, go on with it if it is to cost me—. (*Breaks off.*)

Evje (*standing in front of the fire*). There, there! Take time to think it over, my dear boy; talk it over with her and with your brother.

The Doctor (*who has sat down on a chair to the left, a little away from the others*). I have just been to see your brother. A remarkable man! But do you know what occurred to me as I sat there? He is dying because he *is* a man. The only people that are fit for political life nowadays are those whose hearts have been turned to stone. (*Picks up something from the table and gets up.*) Ah, just look here! Here is a fine specimen of petrifaction. It is a fragment of palm leaf of some kind, found impressed in a bit of rock from Spitzbergen. I sent it you myself, so I know it. That is what you have to be like to withstand arctic storms!—it will take no harm. But your brother—well, his life had been like that of the original palm tree, with the air sighing through its branches; the change of climate was too sudden for him. (*Goes up to* HARALD.) You have still to try it. Shall you be able to kill all the humanity that is in you? If you can make yourself as insensate a thing as this stone, I daresay you will be able to stand the life. But are you willing to venture upon political life at such a price? If you are—so be it; but remember that in that case you must also kill all humanity in Gertrud— in these two—in every one that is dear to you. Otherwise no one will understand you or follow you. If you cannot do that, you will never be more than a dabbler in politics —a quarter, an eighth part, of a politician—and all your efforts, in what you consider your vocation, will be pitiable!

Mrs. Evje (*who has been occupied at the back of the room, but now sits down by the fire*). That is quite true! I know cases of petrifaction like that—and God preserve anyone that I love from it!

Evje (*coming forward, towards* HARALD). I don't want to say anything to hurt your feelings—least of all just now. But I just want to add my warning, because I believe I have discovered that there is a danger that persecution may make you hard.

Harald. Yes! —but do you suppose it is only politics that offer that dangerous prospect?

The Doctor. You are quite right! It is all the cry nowadays, " Harden yourself! " It isn't only military men and doctors that have to be hardened; commercial men have to be hardened, civil servants have to be hardened, or dried up; and everybody else has to be hardened for life, apparently. But what does it all mean? It means that we are to drive out all warmth from our hearts, all desire from our imaginations. There is a child's heart at the bottom of every one of our hearts—ever young, full of laughter and tears; and that is what we shall have killed before we are " fitted for the battle of life," as they put it. No, no—that is what we ought to preserve; we were given it for that! (HARALD *hides his face in his hands, and sits so for some time.*)

Mrs. Evje. Any mother or any wife knows that.

Evje (standing with his back to the fire). You want to bring back the age of romance, doctor!

The Doctor (with a laugh). Not its errors—because in those days unclean minds brought to birth a great deal that was unclean. (*Seriously.*) But what is it, when all is said and done, but a violent protest on the part of the Teutonic people against the Romanesque spirit and school —a remarkable school, but not *ours.* To us it seems a barren, merely intellectual school—a mere mass of formulas which led to a precocious development of the mind. And that was the spirit it bred—critical and barren. But these schools of thought are now all we have, and both of them are bad for us! They have no use for the heart or the imagination; they do not breed faith or a longing for high achievement. Look at *our* life! Is *our* life really our own?

Mrs. Evje. No. You have only to think of our language, our tastes, our society, our—

The Doctor (interrupting her). Those are the externals of our life, merely the externals! No, look within—look at such a view of life as we were talking about, clamouring for " hardening "—is that ours? Can we, for all our diligence, make as much way in it as, for instance, a born Parisian journalist?—become like a bar of steel with a point at each end, a pen-point and a sword-point? *We*

Harald. —expressed your abhorrence of certain political tendencies with which neither you nor I have any sympathy—which affront our ideas of humane conduct. You do not feel called upon to enter actively into the lists against them; but why do you try to prevent those who do feel so called upon? You lament the existing state of things—and yet you help to maintain it, and make a friend of the man who is its champion!

The Doctor (*turning his head*). Apparently we are on our defence, Evje!

Harald. No—I am. I was told a little while ago that I was in a fair way to become hardened and callous, and that I must abandon my career—and that I must do so for Gertrud's sake, too, because she would never be able to share the fight with me. I was told this at one of the bitterest moments in my life. And that made me hesitate for a moment. But now I have turned my face forward again, because you have enlightened me! (*A short, sharp cough is heard in the hall.*)

Mrs. Evje (*getting up*). That is he! (*A knock is heard at the door; the* DOCTOR *gets up and pushes his chair back. The* EDITOR *comes in.*)

The Editor. Good morning, my children! How are you?

Mrs. Evje (*sitting down*). I did not hear the bell.

The Editor. I don't suppose you did—I came in by the back door. I took you by surprise, eh? Discussing me, too—what? (*Laughs.*)

Evje. You have given us enough reason to, to-day, any way.

The Editor. Yes, haven't I? Such a thing for a man to do to his best friends—eh?

Evje. That is true.

The Editor. To his old schoolfellows—his neighbours—eh? I expect it has disturbed your natural moderation—eh?

C 696

Evje. I pride myself on my moderation.

The Editor. As much as on your brandy!

Evje. Are you going to begin your nonsense again?

The Editor. Good-morning, Doctor! Have you been making them a fine speech this morning?—about my paper? or about humanity?— romanticism? or catholicism?—eh? (*Laughs.*)

The Doctor (*laughing*). Certainly one of us two has made a fine speech this morning!

The Editor. Not me; mine was made yesterday!—How is your hall-porter?

The Doctor (*laughing*). Quite well, I am ashamed to say.

The Editor. There's a faithful subscriber to my paper, if you like! (*The* DOCTOR *laughs.*) Well, Mrs. Evje, I can give you news of your man, Master John!

Mrs. Evje. Can you? It is more than I can.

The Editor. Yes—he is in bed still. That is why I came in the back way—to enquire after his health.

Mrs. Evje. But how—?

The Editor. How is he after last night?

Mrs. Evje. Really, I believe you know everything. We had no idea he was out last night.

The Editor. Oh, that is the very latest intelligence! He has been figuring as a speaker—he was drunk, of course—before the Association founded by his master's future son-in-law. , And he made a most effective speech —indeed, the speakers at that Association always make most effective speeches! It was all about a Sliding Scale of Taxation, Profit-Sharing for Workers, the necessity for a Labour majority in Parliament, etc., etc.,—all the usual Socialist rhodomontade. You see how infectious intellectual ideas are!

Evje. Well!—I shall turn him out of the house to-day!

The Editor. But that is not in accordance with your love of moderation, Evje!

Evje. It is a scandal.

The Editor (to EVJE). But not the worst. Because, if you want to avoid that sort of thing, there are others you must turn out of the house. (*Glances towards* HARALD.)

Evje. You seem determined to quarrel to-day?

The Editor. Yes, with your " moderation."

Evje. You would be none the worse of a little of it.

The Editor. " Brandy and Moderation " is your watchword—eh?

Evje. Do stop talking such nonsense!—I know one thing, and that is that you seem to find the brandy from my distillery remarkably to your taste!

The Doctor (interrupting them). When you are in these provoking moods there is always some grievance lurking at the back of your mind. Out with it! I am a doctor, you know; I want to get at the cause of your complaint!

The Editor. You were not very successful in that, you know, when you said my maid had cholera, and she really only was—. (*Laughs.*)

The Doctor (laughing). Are you going to bring that story up again? Every one is liable to make mistakes, you know—even you, my boy!

The Editor. Certainly. But before making a mistake this time—ahem!—I wanted first of all to enquire whether—

The Doctor. Ah! now it is coming!

The Editor —whether you have any objection to my mentioning John in my paper?

Mrs. Evje. What has John to do with us?

The Editor. Just as much as the Association, where he delivered his speech, has; it—ahem!—is one of the family institutions!

Evje. I have had no more to do with making John what he is than I have had with making that Association what it is.

The Editor. Your future son-in-law made the Association what it is, and the Association has made John what he is.

The Doctor. Or, to put it the other way round: John is Mr. Evje's servant; John has become an active member of the Association; therefore Mr. Evje is a patron of the Association.

The Editor. Or this way: John, being the well-known Mr. Evje's servant, has for that reason become an active member of the Association which—as he expressed it— his employer's future son-in-law " has had the honour to found! "

Mrs. Evje. Surely you never mean to put that in the paper?

The Editor (laughing). They are John's own words.

Mr. Evje. Of course, he would never put a tipsy man's maunderings into the paper. *(To his wife.)* Don't you understand that he is joking?

The Editor (clearing his throat). It is already in type.

The Doctor. Oh, nonsense!

The Editor. The scene afforded an opportunity for an extremely amusing sketch, without mentioning any names.

Mr. Evje. I sincerely hope that—

The Doctor (to EVJE*).* Oh, he is only teasing you! You know him.

The Editor. What do you think of this? " Those who indirectly support so dangerous an institution will have to face exposure."—I quite agree with it.

Mrs. Evje (getting up). What do you mean? Do you mean that my husband—?

The Editor. A little fright will be a good discipline for him!

Evje. Is what you quoted meant as an accusation against us—whether you are serious or whether you are joking?

The Doctor. He is only trying to frighten you with a bogey; it is not the first time, you know!

Evje. Yes, but what have *I* to be frightened of? *I* don't belong to the Association.

The Editor. But persons who do belong to it frequent your house. A man is known by the company he keeps.

Mrs. Evje. I really begin to think he *does* mean it seriously.

The Editor. It is too ugly a thing to jest about, you mean?

Evje. Is it possible that you seriously mean to allude to John as my servant?

The Editor. Isn't he your servant?

Evje. And to put that in the paper for every one to read?

The Editor. No—only for those who read the paper.

Evje. And you have come here to tell us that?

The Editor. Do you suppose I would do it without telling you?

Mrs. Evje. It is perfectly shameless!

The Editor. It certainly is.

Evje. Is it your intention to quarrel with me?

The Editor. Of course!

Evje. With your own schoolfellow?—one who has been a true friend to you in all your ups and downs? It is abominable!

The Editor. Perhaps it was to ensure my holding my tongue that you have been my friend!

Mrs. Evje. You *couldn't* behave in such a fashion to a friend!

The Editor (*drily*). To my own brother, if he stood in my way!

Harald (*to himself*). This is too much! (*Comes forward.*) Is your hatred for me so bitter that on my account you must persecute even my future parents-in-law, your own old friends?

The Editor (*who, as soon as* HARALD *came forward, has turned away to the* DOCTOR). Have you heard how people are being beaten up to go to the meeting of electors to-night? The last political speeches of the campaign must be made with red fire burning at the wings! (*Laughs.*)

Mrs. Evje (*coming up to him*). No, you are not going to get out of it by changing the subject. Is it really your intention to put my husband in your paper?

The Editor. He is putting himself there.

Evje. I, who all my life have avoided being drawn into any political party?

The Doctor. What has Evje to do with Harald Rejn's politics?

The Editor. He endorses them!

Mrs. Evje. No!—a thousand times no!

Evje. Why, only to-day—

The Doctor. I can bear witness to that!

The Editor. It is no use protesting!

Evje. But you must believe our protestations!

The Editor. Bah! You will see something more to-morrow—

Evje. Something more?

Mrs. Evje. Against my husband?

The Editor. That scandal about the Stock Exchange Committee. No less than three Letters to the Editor about it have been lying in my pigeon-holes for some time.

Evje (*in bewilderment*). Are you going to put nonsense of that sort in your paper? The most respected men on the Exchange—?

Mrs. Evje. Members of the Committee—?

The Editor. They are only respected men so long as they respect themselves. When their chairman enters into connections which offend public opinion, the whole crew of them must be made to feel what sort of a man it is they are associating with.

The Doctor. So on Mr. Rejn's account you are going to expose Evje, and on Evje's account the Stock Exchange Committee? I suppose my turn will come soon!

The Editor. It will come.

The Doctor. Indeed!

The Editor. The letters that have been sent to me are all from highly respected men. That shows that public opinion has turned round; and public opinion must be obeyed! (*Throws out his hands.*)

Evje (in a troubled voice). It is quite true that I have noticed in several little ways that their temper—. (*Looks round him, and checks himself. Then speaks more confidently.*) But it was just at such a time that I looked for help from you, my friend. That is why I did not bother myself much about it.

The Editor (to EVJE). But you know it is you that are attacking me now!

Evje. I?

Mrs. Evje. He?

The Editor. And, besides, I have no choice in the matter. You have made your bed, and must lie on it.

Evje (growing angry again). But do you really mean that you don't feel yourself how shocking such behaviour to an old friend is?

The Editor. " Old friend," " old schoolfellow," " neighbour,"—out with the whole catalogue!

Mrs. Evje. I am sure you don't deserve to be either one or the other! (*The* EDITOR *laughs.*) Think what you wrote to-day about Halvdan Rejn, who is dying. A man could only write that who—who—

The Editor. Well?—who?

Mrs. Evje. Who has not an atom of heart.

The Editor. Ha, ha! " The natural affections!"— " family considerations!" Truth, my dear lady, has no family ties; it has no respect even for a " dying man."

Mrs. Evje. Yes, indeed—every decent man has some respect for suffering, and even wicked men are silent in the presence of death!

The Editor. "Sufferer "—" dying man "—" martyr," I suppose! Oh, we know all that old story!

Harald (coming forward). Let me tell you that you are a—person with whom I will not condescend to argue. (*Walks away from him.*)

The Editor (who has at once crossed the room). This theatrical flaunting of the " dying man " before people's eyes, that a calculating brother has permitted himself, is of course what is really shocking in the whole affair. But I will tear the mask off him.

The Doctor (following him). Listen to me, now; listen! We are gentlefolk, you know! And even if Mr. Rejn has let himself be so carried away as to mention his dying brother on a public occasion—well, I am not going to say that I approve of it, but surely it is excusable and—

Harald (coming forward). I want none of your defence, thank you!

The Doctor. The one of you is just as mad as the other! (*To the* EDITOR.) But what has all this to do with Evje, seeing that, after all, the whole of this affair of the Rejns'—

Evje (to the EDITOR, *eagerly*). I give you my word of honour that I have never approved of Harald's utterances about his brother, either. I am a man of moderation, as you know; I do not approve of his politics. Only to-day—

Mrs. Evje. And what on earth have politics to do with the Stock Exchange Committee?

The Doctor. Or with Evje's coachman!

Evje. You might just as well take it into your head to write about my clerks, or my workmen, or—

The Doctor. His carpenters, or his brewers—or his horses!

The Editor (stands suddenly still and says, drily): You may assure yourselves that things are quite sufficient as they are! (*Begins to button up his coat.*)

Evje. Is it so bad as all that!

Mrs. Evje. Good gracious!—what is it then?

The Editor (*taking up his hat*). You will be able to read it to-morrow, together with some more about the " dying man." Good-bye!

Evje.   } (*together.*) But before you go—
Mrs. Evje }

The Doctor. Hush, hush! Let us remember we are gentlefolk! What will you bet that the whole thing is not just a bogey to frighten you?

The Editor (*holding out his hand towards the* DOCTOR). I hold Mr. Evje's position in the town in the hollow of my hand!

Evje (*fuming*). Is your object to ruin *that*, then?

Mrs. Evje. You will never succeed in that!

The Doctor. Hush, hush! let us remember we are gentlefolk!

Evje. In my own house—my old schoolfellow—that he should have the audacity—!

The Editor. I have told you the truth openly. And, as far as that goes, you have stood more than that from me in your own house, my boy. Because the misfortune is that you are a coward.

Evje. I a coward?

The Doctor (*laughing*). Hush, hush! Let us remember we are gentlefolk!

Evje. Yes, I have been weak enough to be afraid of scandal, especially in the newspapers, it is true; that is why I have put up with you too long! But now you shall see that I am not a coward. Leave my house!

Mrs. Evje. That's right!

The Doctor. But you must part like gentlefolk, you know.

The Editor. Pooh! You will be sending me a message directly, to call me back!

Evje. You have the face to say that?

Mrs. Evje (to EVJE). Come, dear, don't provoke him any more!

The Editor (turning to go). You daren't do otherwise.

The Doctor. But part like gentlefolk—!

Evje (following the EDITOR). No, as sure as I live—

The Editor. You will be sending a message to call me back! Ha, ha, ha!

Evje. Never, never!

Mrs. Evje. My dear—!

The Editor. Yes, you will—directly—this very day! Ha, ha, ha!

The Doctor. Don't part like that! Part like gentle—

Evje. No, I tell you!

The Editor (laughing all the time). Yes!

Mrs. Evje. My dear—remember you may bring on one of your attacks!

The Editor (at the door). You are too much of a coward! Ha! ha! *(Goes out.)*

Evje (in a rage). No!

The Editor (sticking his head in at the door). Yes! *(Goes away.)*

The Doctor. What a visit! I cannot help laughing, all the same! Ha, ha, ha, ha!

Evje. Do you dare to laugh at that?

The Doctor. "Old schoolfellows "—ha, ha! "Moderation "—ha, ha! "The same party "—ha, ha, ha!

Mrs. Evje. Oh, my husband is ill!

Evje (faintly). Yes—a little water!

Mrs. Evje. Water, water, Harald!

The Doctor. One of his attacks—that is another affair altogether. Here *(takes a bottle from his pocket)*—smell this! That's it! Now, a little water! *(Gives him some.)* No danger this time. Cheer up, old boy!

Evje. What a scandal!

Mrs. Evje. Yes, you will never be able to bear it, dear; I told you so.

Evje. To think of *my* name appearing in the papers, when all my life I have—

Mrs. Evje. —done everything you could to keep clear of such things! And you such a dear, good, upright man!—Oh, these politics are the curse of the world!

The Doctor (laughing). As I told you, you must go through a special process of hardening before you can stand them.

Evje. And think of public opinion—my position—my connections! It is more than I can bear!

Mrs. Evje (to the Doctor). I am sure the first time he reads something about himself in the paper, it will make him really ill! He won't be able to stand it, I know.

The Doctor. Oh, he will get over it.

Mrs. Evje. No, he won't. I am frightened at the mere thought of it. He will never be able to bear it, never!

Evje. When all my life I have tried to keep clear of such things—!

Mrs. Evje. And now in your old age, though you deserve it no more than a child does, to be dragged into it! If I could prevent that, I would willingly take on my own shoulders whatever—

Evje. No, no—not you! Not you!

The Doctor. But the thing is not necessarily done because he threatened he would do it.

Evje. Do you think—?

The Doctor. He is so dreadfully hot-headed, but I am sure he will think twice—

Mrs. Evje. —before he attacks a lifelong friend! Yes, that is so, isn't it!

Evje. Do you really think that there is any possibility then—?

The Doctor. I really can't say!

Mrs. Evje. Nothing in the world is impossible!

Evje. We were both so hot-headed.

The Doctor. Yes, it will have to be a more peaceable conversation than that of a few minutes ago!

Evje. I don't know how it is—there is something so provoking about him.

Mrs. Evje. Yes, and you have not been very well lately, either. I have often said so to you.

Evje. No, I haven't. It has been just one thing after another! And all my life I have tried to keep clear of such things!

The Doctor. I will tell you what, old friend; I am sure the best thing to do would be—

Evje. What?

The Doctor. I am sure you will not be easy in your mind until someone has talked to him.

Mrs. Evje. Yes, couldn't that be done? Good gracious, *that* is not sending a message to him!

Evje. But who would—? (*A short silence.*)

The Doctor. I don't know who would be best.

Mrs. Evje. All our old friends have deserted us; we shall soon have none.

The Doctor. Well, at all events, you have me.

Evje. Would you really be willing to—? Do you mean it? (*Grasps his hand.*)

The Doctor. Of course I will! He can't eat me!

Mrs. Evje. How good you are! Of course you only need tell him—what is quite true—that my husband would never be able to bear it! He, who all these years—

Evje. —have put up with an incredible amount for his sake, both from himself and from others!

Mrs. Evje. Yes, that is true! And now you will go, dear friend—our only friend!—and talk to him quite amicably and sensibly, won't you?

Evje. But don't delay! He is so hot-headed that we must find him before—

The Doctor. Oh, I will find him; he is always about the town.

Evje. And tell him—ask him—

The Doctor. Oh, I know what to say to him.

Mrs. Evje. That is right!

Evje. Thank you! I shall never forget how, at a moment when everything threatened to overwhelm me, you were the only one to stand by me! Ah, I feel as if a load had fallen off my shoulders! I feel all at once quite happy again!

The Doctor. That's right. You pull yourself together! I will see to everything else.

Evje. Thanks, thanks! But make haste!

The Doctor. I am off! My hat? (*Turns, and sees* HARALD, *and says to himself:*) A-ha! *He* looks as if he had had about enough of this. It would have been a joke to—

Evje. Oh, do make haste, my friend!

The Doctor. Yes, yes—if only I could find my hat.

Mrs. Evje. It is on the table.

The Doctor. So it is!

Evje. Good luck to you!

Mrs. Evje. And do it very tactfully!

The Doctor (*meaningly*). And I hope you three will enjoy yourselves! (*Goes out.*)

Evje. What a morning!

Mrs. Evje. We, who have always endeavoured to take everything quietly and indulgently—

Evje. Yes, and to conduct our family affairs peaceably and affectionately! (*Jumps up and turns to* HARALD.) The whole thing is *your* fault!

Mrs. Evje. Yes, it is Harald's fault! From the day this unfortunate engagement came about, we have scarcely had a moment's peace here.

Evje. No, no, that is not the case! We must be reasonable. At first, when Mr. Rejn had a fine future before him, when people vied with one another to catch him, then the engagement was an honour to us as well as to our daughter. But from the moment he took up these wretched politics—that is to say, from the time his brother fell ill—well, he can see for himself what the result has been to us!

Mrs. Evje. And he certainly must admit that it is not what we have deserved; indeed it is more than a respected and well-bred family can put up with.

Harald. I quite agree that it is more than a respected and well-bred family *ought* to put up with.

Mrs. Evje. Oh, so *you* feel that too?

Harald. Certainly. And the only excuse I can see is that there are many more in the same case. It is only in that way that such things become possible.

Evje. I do not understand. Many more like—?—like whom?

Harald. Like you!

Mrs. Evje. In what respect?

Harald. I will explain. Most of the successful politicians nowadays have not gained their position by means of any greatness of their own, but by the pitiable weakness of others. Another age will form a different estimate of them—see them in their proper perspective, and find them to be much smaller men!

Evje. But what has that to do with us?

Harald. Well, just try to size up that man whom a little while ago you turned out of your house and afterwards sent a message to—

Evje. We sent *no* message to him!

Mrs. Evje. A friend of ours has gone to talk to him. That is quite a different thing!

Harald. Well, take his measure by yours and yours by his! He went away, and he will come back like a conquering hero. Will that be thanks to his greatness, or his talent—to the loftiness of his opinions or his feelings? No; it will be thanks to your pitiable weakness.

Mrs. Evje. Upon my word!

Evje. Well, I—!

Harald. Do you think any one who has any pluck in his disposition would consent to be a party to such a contemptible state of things? Think of your own daughter, educated by that good old man who lies in there, but an obedient child to you; think how she must be perpetually torn between what she loves and respects and what she sees going on here! No wonder she is ill! But remember this—she is not ill because she sticks to me; she is ill because of your pitiable weakness!

Mrs. Evje. How can you dare to say such things! So you too—!

Evje. Such an absolute want of respect!

Harald. Listen to me, once for all. I intend, God helping me, to take up the fight that has killed my brother, the noblest man I know! And Gertrud is going to take up *her* share in the fight, as I do mine. But to come to this house as long as *he* comes here—to go through what I have gone through to-day—sullies my self-respect to such an extent, and offends my better feelings so deeply, that either he never sets foot here again, or I do not!

Evje and Mrs. Evje. But—!

Harald (quietly). When I came here to-day, I thought we should be able to arrange matters without my speaking out; but there is nothing else for it, so good-bye! (*Goes out. A moment's silence follows.*)

Mrs. Evje. Is *he* giving *us* our dismissal? Or does he not really mean to break with us?—My dear, what is the matter? (*Goes to her husband's side.*)

Evje (without moving). Tell me, my dear—am I a bad man?

Mrs. Evje. You, a bad man?

Evje. Because, if I were not a bad, wicked man, they could not behave in such a way to me, one after the other.

Mrs. Evje. But, my dear, you are the best and dearest and most considerate of men! And they are shameless traitors to you, my dear husband!

Evje. But how on earth, then, could it come about that I, who all my life have tried to keep clear of such things—for I have, haven't I?

Mrs. Evje. Every one knows that, that knows anything about you.

Evje. How could it come about that in my old age I should be despised and forsaken by everybody? Surely it is no crime to want to live in peace, apart from all that sort of thing?

Mrs. Evje. No, indeed; that is what all decent people want to do.

Evje. Yes, I thought so too. But now you see!

Mrs. Evje. But *you* have been dreadfully unfortunate.

Evje. Why should I have been just the one to be dreadfully unfortunate? Most people escape such things altogether.

Mrs. Evje (starting). Here is Gertrud.

Evje. Poor child!

Mrs. Evje. What on earth are we to say to her?

Evje. Be careful, my dear! be careful! (GERTRUD *comes in quietly and comes forward to them.*)

Gertrud. Did I see Harald go away?

Mrs. Evje. Yes, my child, he—he went away.

Gertrud. Without saying good-bye to me?

Evje. That's true, he didn't say good-bye to you.

Mrs. Evje. Were you expecting him to come into grandfather's room to say good-bye to you?

Gertrud. Yes. Tell me how things went here?

Evje. Why were you not here, dear?

Gertrud (in astonishment). I here? You said you did not want me to be present—

Evje. I remember, yes; we thought it would not be advisable.

Gertrud (still speaking quietly, but in growing alarm). But how did things go, then?

Evje. How did they go? Badly.

Mrs. Evje (hurriedly). That is to say, he did not behave at all well. You must prepare yourself for the worst, my child!

Gertrud. Is it something very bad, then?

Evje. You know he is a little hasty just now, when he has so much on his hands. He lacks a proper sense of moderation—but he will learn it, sure enough.

Gertrud (almost inaudibly). But what does it mean? Is he never coming back?

Evje. Never coming back? What an extraordinary question! Of course he will come back. He was only a little over-hasty, you know—

Gertrud. And said he would never come back?

Mrs. Evje. Come, come, my dear—you mustn't be alarmed.

Evje. He talked such a lot, you know, that we must not attach any particular importance to anything he said.

Gertrud. So that is how it is!

Mrs. Evje. We must make allowances for all that he is going through just now—

Evje (suddenly). My child, you look so pale—

Mrs. Evje (going to her). Gertrud!

Gertrud (with a quiet movement of protest). I must give grandfather his drink; that was really what I came for. And that was how I happened to see Harald through the window. I will take grandfather his drink. (*The curtain falls as she goes out of the room.*)

ACT II

(SCENE.—*A street in the "villa quarter" of the town. Between it and another street running parallel with it in the background, are two houses standing in gardens, half of the façade of one of them projecting into the stage on the right. On the left a third street runs at right angles to the others, to the back of the stage. The left side of this third street opens on to a well-wooded park. The house in the foreground on the right is in two stories. There is a narrow strip of garden in front of it, enclosed by an iron railing with a gate in it. The gate is standing open. The entrance door to the house is immediately behind this gate. There is light in a small window by the door; the ground floor windows are in darkness; in those of the upper floor, light is visible through heavy curtains. It is a wintry evening, and everything is swathed in an unusually thick fog, in which the gas lamps in the streets show dimmer and dimmer as they recede in the distance. As the curtain goes up, a lamplighter is seen descending his ladder from a lamp-post, where he has just lit the lamp at the corner of the house.*)

The Lamplighter (as he reaches the ground). It's all one whether the lamps are lit or not, in such a fog as this.

(MRS. EVJE *is seen drawing back the curtain at a window on the first floor. She opens the window and looks out.*)

Mrs. Evje. The fog is so thick, my dear, that I can't see across the street.

Evje (coming to the window, with fur coat and cap on). So it is!—Well, so much the better, my dear! (*They withdraw into the room; the window is shut and the curtains drawn. Two passers-by come along the street from the right, talking.*)

34

First Passer-by. The Land of Fogs—the old idea of the Land of Fogs was that of a vision of confused and faint sensation, with the light of the intelligence dimmed and blurred like these gas lamps in the fog.

Second Passer-by. It would be that, if our hearts did not often act as guiding lights to our befogged intelligences. Look at this house behind us—the brandy distiller's. The devilish workings of his intelligence have befogged the whole country—befogged it with brandy—and some such guiding light is much needed there.

First Passer-by. Ah, well,—the old idea of the Land of Fogs was that fogs were—. (*The sound of their conversation dies away as they pass into the park on the left.* GERTRUD, *closely veiled and wrapped in furs, comes slowly out of the park. She stops at the corner and looks down the street, then passes slowly along to the right, looking up at the house as she goes. She is scarcely out of sight when the house-door opens and* EVJE *comes out.*)

Evje. This is about the time he comes home—I daren't go to his house and ask for him; I don't know if he would admit me. I daren't trust to the Doctor alone.—This uncertainty is dreadful! (*He starts at seeing* GERTRUD, *whom he does not recognise in the fog, walking towards him. She turns suddenly and walks back the way she came.*) Who was that? She gave me quite a fright in this fog! Her furs seemed rather like—no, no, it couldn't be. I must not let any one recognise me. (*Puts up the high collar of his coat, so that only his nose is visible.*) Both of them called me a coward, but they are very much mistaken. It is not cowardice for a man who is respected and honoured to try and avoid scandal. Hm! Naturally those who trade in scandals think otherwise!—To act without attaching weight to the opinion of others, to disregard one's own predilections, to put up with being laughed at—all for the sake of preventing a scandal—that is to be strong and courageous. And it is admirable, too;

for it *is* admirable to act fearlessly in the interest of one's family, and of one's business, and of propriety. *(Starts as he hears his door opened.* JOHN *has come along the street and gone into the house.)* Is that some one coming out of my house? No, it is a man going in. And then to think of Harald Rejn beginning that nonsense about my being a coward, because I refused to become a party man! Every one ought to take sides in politics—that is their cry. Hm! I should say it required rather more courage nowadays to *refrain* from taking sides. *(Starts again.)* Who is that? Oh, only that woman again. She is waiting for some one too. I expect we shall both catch bad colds. *(Walks up and down.)* It is an odd sensation to be walking up and down on the watch outside one's own house. Cowardice? Pshaw! To let one's self be abused in a public street without stirring a finger to prevent it, *that* would be cowardice. I only hope he has not gone round the other way? There is much more traffic in that street, and some one might easily—. I think I will take a turn towards the town, and turn back when I am a little way from here; it will look less suspicious. I *must* catch him, because his paper will be going to press. *(Looks up at his house.)* My poor wife, sitting up there dreadfully alarmed on my account! *(Goes out to the right. As soon as he has gone, the house-door opens and* JOHN *comes warily out.)*

JOHN. So he has gone out, has he! Oh, well, he is bound to come in again! I will wait and catch him, that I will! Tra, la, la, la, la! I can play about here in the fog till he comes back; I have nothing to lose! And it will be best to catch him in the street; he will make less fuss, and can't run away from me! Tra, la, la, la, la! *(Lounges out to the right. A moment later,* HARALD *comes out of the park. He is dressed much as* EVJE *is, but has not his coat-collar turned up.)*

Harald. There is a light in her window! Then she is

alone in her room.   What am I going to do now?   Twice already I have come to look at that light; now I have seen it—and must go away!   Good-bye, my darling! Be patient, and wait!   I know your thoughts are with me now; and I know you feel that mine are with you! (*As he turns away from the house he sees the veiled figure of* GERTRUD, *who, as soon as she has come nearer, rushes to him, throws up her veil, and falls into his arms in a glad embrace.*)

Gertrud. I was certain that, if you could not go into the house again, you would be out here!   I knew you would not go away from me, dear!

Harald. No—neither now nor ever.

Gertrud. And, while I was walking up and down here in the fog, I felt that though there might be all this gloom and cold around us outside, there was the brightness and warmth of certainty in our hearts.

Harald. Yes, our love is the one certainty for me! Fog may obscure the goal I aim at, the road I have to tread, the very ground I stand on; doubts may even for a while attack my faith; but my love for you shines clear through it all!

Gertrud. Thank you, my darling!   If that is so, there is nothing that we cannot overcome!

Harald. Of course, you know what took place to-day?

Gertrud. I can guess.

Harald. Is it true that you are ill?   Why did you never tell me?

Gertrud. No, the doctor is not telling the truth; I am not ill!   Even if I were, what matter?   I should go on living as long as I could—and should have done my duty before I gave in!

Harald. That is the way to look at it!

Gertrud. But I am not ill!   I suffer, it is true—and am likely to—every time you are persecuted, or my parents on my account.   Because *I* have drawn them into all

this that they are so unfitted for, and that is why it pains
me so to see how unprepared it finds them—most of all
when, out of tenderness for me, they try to conceal it.
But I can't alter things. We are fighting for a cause that
you believe to be right, and so do I; surely that is better
than never to suffer at all in any good cause. Try me!
Let me share the fight with you! I am not weak; it is
only that my heart is sore for those I love.

Harald. You splendid, loyal creature!—and you are
mine! (*Embraces her.*)

Gertrud. You should hear what grandfather says!

Harald. Yes, how is the dear old gentleman?

Gertrud. Pretty well, thanks, though he never gets out
now. But he is following your work, and he says that
what you are aiming at is right, if you ask for God's guid-
ance on your way. Harald—you will always be the same
as you are now—good and genuine—won't you, dear?
Not like the rest of them—nothing but bitterness and
malice, always talking of principles and consequences and
all the rest of it, and always attacking others? If one were
obliged to be like that, it would be a curse to be a
politician.

Harald. I will be what you make me! I think that
behind every man's public life you can see his private life
—whether he has a real home, and what it is like, or
whether he only has a place he lives in—that is to say,
no real home.

Gertrud. With God's help I shall try to make a bright,
snug and cosy home for you! And this fog is delightful,
because it only makes the thought of such a home all the
cosier and snugger! It makes us seem so alone, too;
no one is out driving or walking; and we can talk as loud
as we please, because the fog deadens the sound of our
voices. Oh, I feel so happy again now! Do you know,
I think it is rather nice to be persecuted a little; it makes
our meetings so much more precious!

Harald. But, you know dear, to meet you like this— and just now—

Gertrud (as they walk up and down together). Yes, of course! I had altogether forgotten how much you have to bear just now; I have been chattering away—. Oh, I don't know how I could feel so happy, because I am really dreadfully distressed. But, you know, I sit the whole day beside grandfather, thinking, without even being able to talk. I generally read aloud to him; now and then he makes a remark, but he really lives more in the next world than in this one now. (*They hear a cough in the distance, and give a start, because they recognise it. The* EDITOR *and* EVJE, *walking along together,* EVJE *apparently talking very earnestly, are seen, indistinctly through the fog, in the street running parallel with the one* HARALD *and* GERTRUD *are in.* JOHN *is seen following them cautiously. They disappear into the park.*)

Harald. I hear the enemy! I am sure I caught a glimpse of him over there through the fog, talking to another man.

Gertrud. Is he always about the streets even in weather like this?

Harald. Well, we won't let him disturb us. (*They begin walking up and down again in front of the house.*)

Gertrud. Do you know whom I met out here? Father!

Harald. Really? Then it is as I thought; the other man over there was your father!

Gertrud. Do you think it was? Poor father!

Harald. Yes, he is weak.

Gertrud. But you must be good to him. He is so good himself. Think how mother loves him; she is absolutely wrapped up in him, because he is so good!

Harald. He is a good man, and an able man. But, but, but—

Gertrud. They have lived a very tranquil life. We of the younger generation try to undertake heavier duties and greater responsibilities than the older generation did. But we must not be angry with them.

Harald. I am afraid it is only too easy to feel angry with them.

Gertrud. No, do as grandfather does! If he thinks any one is going to be amenable to it, he talks to them quietly; if not, he only behaves affectionately to them. Do you understand, dear?—just affectionately.

Harald. Well, to-day—ought I to have put up with their allowing themselves to be treated in such an unseemly way, and their treating me in such an unseemly way?

Gertrud. Was it really as bad as that?

Harald. You would not believe what it was like, I assure you!

Gertrud (standing still). Poor father! Poor father! (*Throws her arms round* HARALD'S *neck.*) Be good to them, Harald!—just because of their faults, dear! We are their children, you know, and it is God's commandment, even if we were not their children.

Harald. If only I could take you up in my arms and carry you off home with me now! Your love takes possession of my heart and my will, and purifies both of them. I am at a crisis in my life now—and now you should be on my side!

Gertrud. Listen!—to begin with, I will go with you to your meeting to-night!

Harald. Yes, yes,—I will come and fetch you!

Gertrud. Down at the door here!

Harald. Yes!

Gertrud. And, in the next place, I am going to walk into the town with you now.

Harald. But then I shall have to see you home again.

Gertrud. Do you object?

Harald. No, no! And you shall teach me a lot of things on the way!

Gertrud. Yes, you will be so wise before we get back!
(*They go out to the right.*)

(*The* EDITOR *and* EVJE *come out of the park.* JOHN
*follows them, unseen by them, and slips past them
to the right when they stop for a moment. The
following conversation is carried on in hurried
tones, and every time the* EDITOR *raises his voice*
EVJE *hushes him, and speaks himself in a persistently lowered voice.*)

Evje. But what concern of yours—or of the public's—
are my private affairs? I don't want to have anything
to do with politics.

The Editor, Well, then, you ought not to have had anything to do with *him.*

Evje. When I first made his acquaintance he was not a
politician.

The Editor. Then you ought to have dropped him when
he became one.

Evje. Ought I to have dropped you too, when you
became one?

The Editor. Let me repeat, for the last time, that we are
not talking about me!

Evje. Hush, hush! What a fellow you are! You get
into a rage if any one chaffs you. But *you* want to hit
out at everybody all round!

The Editor. Do you suppose I am myself?

Evje. Who the devil are you, if you are not yourself?

The Editor. I am merely the servant of the public.

Evje. The public executioner, that is to say?

The Editor. Well, yes, if you prefer it. But you shall
pay for that word some day.

Evje. There—you see! Always talking of paying for
things!—of revenge!

The Editor. You shall pay for it, I tell you!

Evje. You are absolutely mad!—Poof! I am sweating
as if it were the dog days! (*Changes his tone.*) Think of

the time when we used to go to school together—when you never could go to bed without first coming to thank me for the jolly times we were having together!

The Editor. None of that nonsense! I am accustomed to be hated, despised, spit upon, scourged; if any one speaks kindly to me, I do not trust them!

Evje. You must trust me!

The Editor. No—and, besides, I observed very clearly to-day that you had counted on having me in reserve if ever you got into a scrape.

Evje. Well, who doesn't count on his friends? Doesn't every one take them into his reckoning?

The Editor. I don't; I have no friends.

Evje. Haven't you me? Do you think I would leave you in the lurch?

The Editor. That is hypocrisy! At times when I have needed it, the very last thing you have thought of has been to give me any help!

Evje. Have I not helped you?

The Editor. That is hypocrisy, too—to pretend you think I am speaking of money. No; when I have been accused of being dishonourable—of lying—you, the " old schoolfellow," the " old friend," the " neighbour," have never once had the courage to come forward on my behalf.

Evje. I never meddle with politics.

The Editor (*with rising temper*). More hypocrisy! Another of your damned evasions!

Evje. Hush, hush, hush!

The Editor. You try to excuse yourself with a lie! You are doubly a traitor!—And then you expect me to have compassion on you!

Evje. As sure as I stand here, I have never thought of deserting you, however bad things were.

The Editor. And you have the face to take credit to yourself for that? It is all calculation from beginning to end! You thought it would be the best way of making me remember your loyalty, and reward you for it.

Evje. This is abominable!

The Editor. Oh, you are cunning enough! You represent wealth of another kind, which at first was not entirely irreproachably come by—

Evje. There you go again!

The Editor. —and want to give it the *cachet* of good society; so you take care to keep friends with a newspaper that may be able to give you a helping hand in gaining what you want. Can you deny it?

Evje. There may be a slight tinge of calculation even in our highest purposes. But the misfortune about you is that you can see nothing but the calculation, though it may be only an infinitesimal part of the whole thing.

The Editor. Oho—I have had experience of you!

Evje. Then you must have had experience of your party's loyalty, too.

The Editor. My party's loyalty!

Evje. Well, after all, it keeps you where you are to-day.

The Editor. *It* keeps me there?

Evje. And you have friends in that party—myself amongst others—who certainly would rather stand outside altogether, but nevertheless give you their advice and support when you are in difficulties. You cannot deny that.

The Editor. I have friends in the party? Oh yes; and if we lose a fight these fine counsellors are the first to run away! They are always egging me on and egging me on; but only let public opinion once get tired of me, and they will throw me overboard without more ado! By that sort of treachery they manage to fill the sails of the party craft with a new breeze—and leave me to shift the best way I can!—they, for whom I have fought with all my might and main! I despise my opponents—they are either scoundrels and thieves, or they are blockheads and braggarts. But my supporters are lick-spittles, fools, cravens. I despise the whole pack of them, from first to last! If any one would give me the assurance that if, as a pledge that I would never use a pen again, I were to chop off my right hand I should thereby gain the prospect of a peaceful life a thousand miles away from here, I believe I would do it!— I despise the whole pack of them—oh, how I despise them!

Evje. But this is horrible! Do you find no comfort in religion? Or, at all events, you have your paper!

The Editor. My paper, yes—but what good do you suppose that is to me? And do you think I give the impression of being a religious man?

Evje. Then what do you work for?

The Editor. Perhaps you think I work for your sake?— or for the sake of prosperity, or order, or whatever it is you cowards and self-seekers like to imagine it is that you personify? No, the whole human race is not worth the powder and shot that they are holding at each other's heads.

Evje. Then why do you come and almost threaten my life, if the whole thing seems so worthless to you?

The Editor. Do you seriously suppose that I would give in, so as to spare you or some other shopkeeper?—so that you should be able to say triumphantly, "You see he didn't dare! He didn't dare to quarrel with Capital!"— or, "You see he has given in—he has turned tail!" No; what I should like to do would be to lay a mine underground, and blow myself and the whole lot of you sky high!

Evje. And I and all the happiness of my family life are to be sacrificed in order that you shall not have to give in on a side issue of no importance!—Oh, I am chilled to the bone!

The Editor. Ha, ha! It is good to hear you speaking like yourself again, because it reminds me that it is time to put an end to this solemn nonsense! (*Looks at his watch.*) A quarter past! You must be quick!

Evje. Are you really in earnest?

The Editor. I often play off jokes on you, it is true. But I don't know how you will like this one to-morrow morning.

Evje. Then let me tell you that I solemnly refuse! I will not break off the engagement! Put me in your paper, if you like; I am a free man.

The Editor. Bah! nobody is that. Then you refuse? Good-bye! (*Walks away from* EVJE.)

Evje (*going after him*). No, no—where are you going?

The Editor (*stopping*). Nowhere—or rather, I am going home.

Evje. But you won't really do what you said?

The Editor. Ha! ha! ha! (*Moves away.*)

Evje (*following him*). No, listen! Listen to me for a minute!

The Editor (*turning back*). Do you think I have time to stop at all the stations your vanity or your fright will invent on the way? (*Moves away.*)

Evje. You mad creature—listen to me! (*The* EDITOR *stops.*) Tell me exactly what you mean to do?

The Editor. Fiddlesticks! (*Moves on.*)

Evje (*following him*). Do you mean to put in the paper that I have broken off this match?

The Editor (*stopping*). Better than that—I shall spread the news in the town; then it will get about, and all the journalists will get hold of it.

Evje. Give me a day or two to think it over!

The Editor. Oh, no—you are not going to catch me like that! It is election time, and the other side must be made to feel that all decent people have deserted them.

Evje. But it is a lie, you know!

The Editor. What is lying, and what is truth? But your resignation from the Stock Exchange Committee and your subsequent failure to be elected to any public position will be no lies, I can assure you! Public opinion is not to be trifled with, you know!

Evje. And this from you!

The Editor. Bah! Public opinion is a very faithless friend.

Evje. But who, after all, constitute public opinion?

The Editor. Oh, no—you are not going to lead me into a trap again! Besides—it would be very difficult to say exactly who does constitute it.

Evje. This is really—! Then you won't put that in the paper?

The Editor. The news of a broken engagement travels quickest by foot-post—ha, ha, ha! (*Coughs; then adds seriously:*) But won't you, of your own accord, break off what are really absolutely inadmissible relations with a man who scandalises all your acquaintances?

Evje. Lay the blame on me, of course! I know his credentials are no longer first class; but my daughter— ah, you would not be able to understand that. The circumstances are quite exceptional, and—. Look here, shall we go up and talk it over with my wife?

The Editor. Ha, ha!—you turned me out of the house this morning!

Evje. Oh, forget all about that!

The Editor (*looking at his watch*). Half past! Now, without any more evasions—will you, or will you not?

Evje (*with a struggle*). No! I repeat, no! (*The* EDITOR *moves away.*) Yes, yes!—It nearly kills me to do it!

The Editor. "The Capitalist, secure in his position, who needs pay no regard to," etc., etc.—that is the "common form," isn't it, you man of first-class credentials? Ha, ha! Good-bye. I am going home to send the boy to the printers; he has waited long enough. (*Moves away.*)

Evje (*following him*). You are the cruellest, hardest, most reckless—

The Editor (*who has been laughing, suddenly becomes serious*). Hush! Do you see?

Evje (*turning round*). What? Where?

The Editor. Over there!

Evje. Those two?

The Editor. Yes—your daughter and Mr. Harald Rejn.

Evje. But he swore this morning that he would never set foot in my house again!

The Editor. But he will stay *outside* your house, as you see! These gentlemen of the Opposition, when they give any assurance, always do it with a mental reservation! You can't trust the beggars! Come round the corner. (*They do so.*)

Evje. An assignation in the street in the fog! To think my daughter would let herself be induced to do such a thing!

The Editor. Evil communications corrupt good manners! You are a mere bungler in delicate matters, Evje. You made a bad choice in that quarter!

Evje. But he seemed to be—

The Editor. Yes, yes, I know! A real gentleman would have guessed what he would develop into. He has a brother, you know! (HARALD *and* GERTRUD *come in slowly, arm-in-arm.*)

Gertrud. While your brother has been ill you have received many gratifying proofs of the good feeling and goodwill that there is in this town—haven't you?

Harald. Yes, I have. I have found no ill-will against him, nothing but kindness on all sides—with the exception of one person, of course.

Gertrud. But even he has a heart! It has often seemed to me as if I heard a cry of yearning and disappointment from it—and that just when he spoke most bitterly.

Harald. Yes, it needs no very sharp sight to see that he, who makes so many unhappy, is himself the unhappiest of all.

The Editor. What the deuce are they talking about?

Evje. We cannot hear from here. And the fog deadens their voices.

The Editor. Go a bit nearer, then!

Evje. Not before they separate. You only understand *him !*

Harald (to GERTRUD). What are you holding there?

Gertrud (who has taken off her glove and then a ring from her finger). The ring they gave me when I was confirmed. Give me your hand! No, take your glove off!

Harald. Do you want me to try your ring on? I shall not be able to get it on.

Gertrud. On the little finger of your left hand? Yes!

Harald (putting it on). So I can. Well?

Gertrud. You mustn't laugh at me. I have been beating up my courage to do this all this time. It was really why I wanted to walk a little farther with you first! I wanted to bring the conversation round to it, you see! I am so convinced that your happiness, and consequently mine, depends on your being able to be kind. You have got this meeting before you to-night. It will be a decisive moment for you. If you, when you are facing all this horrible persecution, can be a kind boy, you will win all along the line! *(Pulls at his buttons in an embarrassed way.)* So I wanted you to wear this ring to remind you. The diamonds in it sparkle; they are like my tears when you are hard and forget us two. I know it is stupid of me *(wipes her eyes hastily),* but now, when it comes to the point, I can't say what I—. But do wear it!

Harald (kissing her). I will wear it! *(Gently.)* Its pure rays shall shed a light on my life.

Gertrud. Thank you! *(Throws her arms round him and kisses him.)*

The Editor. What they are doing now is all right! Ha, ha, ha!

Evje. I won't stand it! *(The* EDITOR *coughs loudly.)* What are you doing? *(The* EDITOR *goes to the neighbouring house and rings the bell. The door is opened and he goes in, laughing as he goes.)*

Gertrud (who has started from HARALD'S *arms at the sound of the cough).* That is—!

Harald. It sounds like him! (*Turns, and sees Evje.*)

Gertrud. Father! (*Turns to run away, but stops.*) No, it is cowardly to run away. (*Comes back, and stands at* HARALD'S *side.* EVJE *comes forward.*)

Evje. I should not have expected my daughter, a well-brought-up girl, to make an assignation in the street with —with—

Gertrud. With her *fiancé.*

Evje. —with a man who has made a mock of her father and mother, and of his own doing has banished himself from our house.

Harald. From your house, certainly; but not from my future wife.

Evje. A nice explanation! Do you suppose we will consent to have as our son-in-law a man who spurns her parents?

Gertrud. Father!

Evje. Be quiet, my child! You ought to have felt that yourself.

Gertrud. But, father, you surely do not expect him to submit to your being abused and himself ill-treated in our house?

Evje. Are you going to teach your parents—?

Gertrud (putting her arm round his neck). I don't want to teach you anything; because you know yourself, dear, that Harald is worth far more—and far more to us—than the man who went away just now! (*At this moment the printer's boy, who has come out of the* EDITOR'S *house, runs past them towards the town.*)

Evje (seeing the boy, tries to get away). Go in now, Gertrud! I have something I wish to talk to Mr. Rejn about.

Gertrud. You have nothing to talk to Harald about that I cannot hear.

E 696

Evje. Yes, I have.

Harald. But why may she not hear it? What you want is to break off our engagement.

Gertrud. Father—! (*Moves away from him.*) Is that true?

Evje. Well—since it cannot be otherwise—it *is* true; that is to say, for the moment. (*Aside.*) Good Lord, they can make it up right enough when this is all over!

Gertrud (*who is standing as if thunderstruck*). I saw you with him!—Ah, that is how it is! (*Looks at her father, bursts into tears and rushes to the door of their house, pulls the bell and disappears into the house.*)

Evje. What is it? What is the matter with her?

Harald. I think I know. She realises that her life's happiness has been bought and sold. (*Bows to* EVJE.) Good-bye! (*Goes out to the right.*)

Evje (*after standing dumb for some moments*). Bought and sold? Some people take everything so dreadfully solemnly. It is only a manœuvre—to get out of this difficulty. Why is it that I cannot get free of it! They both of them exaggerate matters so absurdly; first of all this crazy fellow, and then Harald with his " Good-bye," spoken as if the ground were giving way beneath his feet! I—I—feel as if every one had deserted me. I will go in to my wife—my dear, good wife; she will understand me. She is sitting up there, full of anxiety about me. (*He turns towards his house ; but, on reaching the garden gate, sees* JOHN *standing there.*)

John (*touching his hat respectfully*). Excuse me, Mr. Evje—

Evje. You, John! Go away! I told you never to set foot in my house again.

John (*very respectfully*). But won't you allow me to stand outside your house either, sir?

Evje. No!

John (*standing in* EVJE'S *way, but still with a show of great respect*). Not at the door here?

Evje. What are you standing in my way for, you scoundrel?

John. Shall I assist you to call for help, sir? (*Calls out.*) Help!

Evje. Be quiet, you drunken fool! Don't make a disturbance! What do you want? Be quick!

John. I want, with all respect, to ask you, sir, why you have sent me away.

Evje. Because you are a swine that gets drunk and then talks nonsense. You don't know what a dilemma you have put me in.—Now go away from here, quietly!

John. I know all about it! I was following you and the Editor all the time, you know!

Evje. What?

John. These articles, that were to go in the paper— the printing was at a standstill, waiting for them.

Evje. Hush, hush, John! So you overheard that, did you? You are too clever; you ought never to have been a servant.—Now, be off with you! Here is a shilling or two for you. Good-bye.

John. Thank you very much, sir.—This was how it was, sir. You see, I thought of the number of times I had run over to the printer's with messages when that nice Editor gentleman was spending an evening with you —and so I thought I might just as well run over with this one.

Evje (*starting back in alarm*). What? What have you done?

John. Just to do you a good turn, sir, I ran along and told them they might print those articles.

Evje. What articles?

John. The ones about you, sir. "Print away," I said—and they printed away. By Jove, how they worked, and then off to the post with the papers!

Evje. You had the impudence, you—! Ah, it's not true! I saw the printer's boy myself, running to the office to countermand the instructions.

John. I caught him up outside here and told him that a message had been sent from Mr. Evje's house. And I gave him sixpence to go to the theatre with; but he must have had to run for it, to be in time, because I am sure it was after seven. Excuse me, sir, but it *is* after seven now, isn't it?

Evje. You scoundrel! You vindictive brute!

John. You can have a look at the paper, sir, if you like.

Evje. Have *you* got a copy?

John. Yes, sir, the first copy struck off is always sent to the Editor, so I volunteered to bring it to him. But you must be anxious to see it, sir! (*Holds it out to* EVJE.)

Evje (*snatching it from him*). Give it to me! Let me see—. (*Moves towards his door, but stops.*) No, my wife mustn't—. Here, under the gas-lamp! This filthy fog! I can't—. (*Feels in his pocket for his glasses, and puts them on.*) Ah, that's better! (*Holds the paper under the light.*) What a mischance! The blackguard—! Where is the article, then? Oh, here—I can't see properly, my heart is beating so!

John. Shall I run for the doctor, sir?

Evje. Will you go away, you—! (*Holds the paper first up, and then down, in his attempts to see better.*) Ah, here it is! "The Stock Exchange Committee"—oh! (*Lowers the paper.*)

John (*mimicking him*). Oh!

Evje (*trying to read*). What a vile thing to do!

John. Oh, go on! go on!

Evje (*as he reads*). This beats everything I ever—Oh!

John. Oh! We *are* in a bad way!

Evje (*wiping his forehead*). What a different thing it is to read libellous attacks on others—and on one's self!

(*Goes on reading.*) Oh! Oh! What horrible, revolting rascality! What is it he says here? I must read through it again! Oh, oh!

John. And often of a morning, when you have been reading the paper, I have heard you laughing till the bed shook under you!

Evje. Yes, I who have so often laughed at others! (*Reads.*) No, this is beyond belief! I can't read any more! This will ruin my position in the town; I can hear every one laughing at me—he knows all my weaknesses, and has managed to make it all so hideously ludicrous! (*Tries to go on reading.*) Why, here is some more! (*Reads.*) It begins even worse than the other! (*Lowers the paper, panting, then tries to go on reading.*) No, I can't—I can't! I must wait! Everything seems going round and round— and my heart is beating so violently that I know I shall have one of my attacks! What a devil it is that I have been making a friend of! What a creature to have broken bread with! — an unprincipled scoundrel! And the disgrace of it! — the disgrace! What will they say at the Exchange? What will—? I shall not dare to go out of my house, at least for some weeks! And then people will only say I have taken to my bed! Oh, oh! I feel as if it were the end of everything!

John (*solicitously*). Can I help you, sir?

Evje. Will you leave me alone—! No, I will have my revenge on him immediately! I will go and ring his bell, and go into his house and call him a scoundrel and spit in his face—! Did I bring my stick out with me? Where is my stick? I will send my man for it, and then I will thrash him round and round his own room!

John (*eagerly*). I will fetch it for you, sir!

Evje (*without hearing him*). No, it would only make more scandal!—How can I take my revenge? I must do him some injury—some real injury that will seem to poison his food for him and rob him of his rest. Scoundrels like that don't deserve sleep! It must be something, too, that will make his family every bit as unhappy as mine will be when they have read this—something that will make them hide their heads for shame—something that will make them terrified every time their door-bell rings, out of shame for what their servants may hear!— No, no, I am getting as evil-minded as he is, now!— What a horrible trade—for ever sowing the seeds of sin and reaping a crop of curses! Now I understand what Harald Rejn meant by saying that no one ought to give his help to such things!—Heavens, hear my vow: never again will I give my help to such things!—What am I to say to my wife—my dear, good wife, who has no suspicion how disgraced I am! And Gertrud, our good Gertrud —ah, at all events I can give her some pleasure at once. I cannot conceal it from them; but I will tell them myself, so that they shall not read it.

John. Is there anything else I can do for you, sir?

Evje (almost screaming at him). Once for all, can't you let me alone!

Mrs. Evje (leaning out of a window she has opened). The sound must have come from the street, all the same. Are you there, my dear?

Evje (drawing back in alarm). There she is! Shall I answer?

Mrs. Evje. Are you there, my dear?

Evje. Yes, dear, here I am!

Mrs. Evje. So you are! I heard your voice, and looked all over the house. What is the matter, dear?

Evje. Oh, I am so unhappy!

Mrs. Evje. Good heavens, are you, dear? Come along in—or shall I come down to you?

Evje. No, I will come in. Shut the window, or you will catch cold.

Mrs. Evje. Do you know, Gertrud is sitting up here, crying?

Evje. Good gracious, is she? I will come up—I will come up!

John. I will help him up, ma'am! (*Pretends to be doing so.*)

Mrs. Evje. Is that you, John?

Evje (*in a low voice*). Will you be off!

John. Yes, it is me, ma'am. He is so unwell.

Mrs. Evje. Is he! Heavens, it is one of his attacks! Help him, John!

Evje (*as before*). Don't you dare!

John (*who has rung the bell loudly*). I do hope you will soon be better, sir! (*Calls up to the window.*) I can leave him now, ma'am! (*To* Evje, *as he goes.*) This has been a bit of luck, for me; but you shall have some more of it! (*Disappears into the fog as* Evje *goes into his house. The two Passers-by, that were seen at the beginning of the scene, are now indistinctly seen returning along the street at the back.*)

First Passer-by. Well, the land of Fogs used to be thought by the ancients to lie in the north, where all confused ideas come from—

Second Passer-by (*who does not seem to be able to get a word in*). But, listen to me for a moment—do you think it means—?

Curtain

ACT III

(SCENE.—*A room in* HALVDAN REJN'S *house. He is lying, supported on pillows, on a sofa on the left-hand side of the room. There is a table in the background, and another near the sofa. A lamp is hanging from the ceiling, and another standing on the table at the back.* HAAKON REJN, *his dress proclaiming him to be a well-to-do yeoman farmer, is sitting on a chair by the sofa.*)

Halvdan. So she couldn't come?

Haakon. No; there are the youngsters, you know—she finds it difficult to get away.

Halvdan (*after a moment's silence*). Remember to thank her for all her kindness to me. The happiest moments of my life have been those Sundays and evenings that she and you and I spent together at your house. (*A pause.*)

Haakon. She wanted very much to know how you were feeling—whether you, who have suffered so much, are at peace now.

Halvdan. At peace? A man who has to die with all his work unfinished, cannot easily root out all thoughts of that from his heart.

Haakon. You should try to lay in God's hands all that you have striven for.

Halvdan. That is what I struggle daily to do. (*A pause.*)

Haakon. A sister of my wife's, who was a widow and badly off, died leaving three young children. But she was glad to die. "Their Heavenly Father will help them better when I am out of the way," she said. "I took up too much room," she said; "I know I have often stood in their way." (*A pause.*)

56

Halvdan. You tell that just as your wife would; she told me that story once.

Haakon. I was to tell you from her that she believes you are to die in order that what you have worked for may come to its fullest fruit. She thinks that when you are gone, people will appreciate better what your aims were.

Halvdan. There is some comfort in the thought that I may be dying in order that what I have loved may live. I have already given up happiness—even honour—for it; I gladly give my life for it now. (*A pause.*)

Haakon. Do you bear ill-will to any of those who have opposed you so cruelly?

Halvdan. To no one.

Haakon. Not even to those whose doing it is that you are lying here?

Halvdan. No, to no one. (*A pause.*)

Haakon. Could you bear to read something hateful about yourself to-day?

Halvdan. I don't know.

Haakon. Then you have not done with it all yet.

Halvdan. No, I know I have not. It is only sometimes that the busy world outside seems to me like a ship sailing idly before the wind. More often, I am back in the midst of it again—planning, hoping, praying! I am young, you know, and have had to suffer so much—there was so much I wanted to do. (*Lifts a handkerchief to his forehead.* HAAKON *helps him to wipe his face with it. A pause.*)

Haakon. But it must be a comfort to you, too, that Harald is taking up what you are laying down. There is good stuff in him.

Halvdan. Yes.

Haakon. And he never says more than is necessary. The country folk will understand him all the better for it.

Halvdan. I hope so. As soon as he comes into my

room I feel as if the atmosphere were charged with electricity—I feel as if I *must* have a part in what he is doing—and so I work, and tire myself out. Ah, it often seems very hard to have to die, and leave undone a great work that one has failed to accomplish!

Haakon. But you have made him what he is, you know —and many others.

Halvdan. I have started the fight, that is all. It is hard to have to desert at the beginning of it!—But God is good, and will understand; He will not be surprised at what my thoughts are full of, when I go to Him. (*A ring is heard at the bell.*)

Haakon. I expect that is Harald.

Halvdan. No, he never rings. Besides, I expect he is taking a walk, to think over what he is going to say to-night.

Haakon. Yes, I suppose it will be a big meeting. (*The* HOUSEKEEPER *comes in.*)

The Housekeeper. Mr. Evje is here, sir, asking for Mr. Harald. I told him we were expecting him every moment. Shall I ask him to come in?

Halvdan. Yes, show him in. (HAAKON *gets up, as* EVJE *is shown in.*)

Evje (*to* HALVDAN). Good evening! (*Sees* HAAKON.) Ah, good evening! So you have come? That is splendid. Is your wife with you?

Haakon. No, she couldn't leave the children.

Evje. I see. (*To* HALVDAN.) And how are you? About the same? Of course, yes. — Where is your brother?

Halvdan. He has his meeting to-night, you know.

Evje. His momentous meeting—I know! I am going to it myself!

Halvdan (*turns his face towards him*). You?

Evje. My object in coming here was to take him home with me, so that we could all go together to the meeting.

We mean to go on to the platform with him; I mean people to see that we are with him!

Halvdan (turning his face away). Really!

Evje (to HAAKON). You never answered my letter, Mr. Rejn.

Haakon. No, I knew I was coming in to town.

Evje. Well—will you sell?

Haakon. No.

Evje. But, my dear Mr. Rejn, you have not sold a single potato to my distillery for five years! And with a farm like yours! This year you had the best crop in the whole valley.

Haakon. Oh, yes—it wasn't so bad.

Evje. Not so bad! It was an extraordinary crop; and, everywhere else round about, the crops were very middling.

Haakon. Oh, yes—it might have been worse.

Evje (laughing). I should think so! But then why won't you sell? (*Turns to* HALVDAN.) I hope you will excuse our talking business in a sick-room; a business man has to seize every opportunity, you know! (*To* HAAKON.) You have never got higher prices elsewhere than you have from me.

Haakon. No, so I believe; but I have my own reasons.

Evje. Your own reasons? What are they?

Haakon. I had a servant once—it is about five years ago now — a good, capable fellow. He used to take potatoes for me to the distillery every day, and every evening came back drunk. So I spoke to him seriously about it; and his answer was: "How do you suppose our brandy-merchants are to grow rich, if chaps like me don't drink pretty hard?" You know the man; he went into your service afterwards. But from that day I have never sold a potato to a distillery.

Evje. But, my dear Mr. Rejn, we cannot be held

responsible for the use to which such rascals put God's gifts!

Haakon. No—no—I suppose not; still, I am not going to have anything more to do with it.

Evje (to HALVDAN). Do you think your brother will not be home before the meeting?

Halvdan. I should think he would; there is plenty of time yet.

Evje. There is; but I should have liked to take him home with me first. The fact is *(laughs)* I have promised my wife and daughter not to go home without him. You know what women are! Shall I just go into his room and wait for him? There is something I want to talk to him about, you know.

Halvdan. I don't think there is a fire in there.

Evje. Oh, well, never mind—I will sit here. I have got a newspaper to read, and you two must go on with your talk just as if I were not here! I shall hear nothing, because I have something to read that interests me. (*He pulls a chair up to the table on the right with its back to* HALVDAN. HAAKON *brings the lamp from the table at the back.*) Ah, thank you very much! Now, just talk away as if I were not here! (*Takes the paper from his pocket and sits down.*)

Haakon (sitting down again beside his brother). I should have liked to go to the meeting, too.

Halvdan. Of course you must go! You will hear Harald tell them how each nation has its own appointed task in the world; that is why it *is* a nation. But, as long as it does not realise the fact, its politics will be nothing but wrangling between the various class-interests —a haphazard struggle for power. Our nation has never got beyond that point! I have shouted myself to death over what is a mere market.

Evje (to himself, striking the table with his fist). The whole commercial community is insulted in this insult to me! I will stir them up at the meeting, and insist on our taking our revenge in common!

Haakon. I don't think things will be any better until we are better Christians. Men think of nothing nowadays but themselves and their position.

Evje (to himself). No, no—that wouldn't do. What would people say? They would only say I was badly hit by this.

Halvdan (half to himself). A Christian nation, thinking of nothing but its own interests—that is to say, power! Equality and Liberty have no meaning for it. Haakon, it surely will be bliss for a wounded soul to be taken into the Everlasting Love, high above all this so-called Christianity of the world! For my soul is sorely wounded!

Evje (to himself). If only I could strike him dead!

Halvdan. But may they all be forgiven!— You asked just now whether I could bear to read something hateful about myself to-day. I think I could.

Haakon. Then I can tell you the other message she gave me for you. I have been a little shy of telling you that. It was that you should remember that you must do more than forgive; you must pray for them. (*A pause.*)

Halvdan (with his hand over his eyes). I do.

Evje (crumpling up the paper and throwing it on the floor). No, I won't stand it! If the blackguard—. (*Gets up in alarm, as he realises what he has done, and is just going to pick up the paper ; but at that moment turns round facing the others, and lets it lie.*) No, I won't touch it again—never, as long as I live! (*To the others.*) You must forgive me, but I was reading something that upset me very much. Your brother will tell you all about it in the morning, no doubt. Poof—it is very warm in here! But, of course, that is natural in a sick-room. I don't think he can be coming now. I think, too, that I will go on, so as not to be late for the meeting; there is sure to be a difficulty in getting seats. I will get him to go home with me after the meeting, instead. That will be better, after all.

Haakon. I was thinking of going to the meeting. Would you mind if I went with you?—for I do not know the way myself.

Evje. You will come with me, Mr. Rejn? (*To himself.*) That will be splendid—to make my entrance in the company of one of our yeomen farmers! (*Aloud.*) By all means let us go together! I feel flattered by the opportunity, because I have always maintained that our yeomen are the pick of the nation. Well, then—(*to Halvdan*) I hope you will soon be feeling better, Mr. Rejn. God bless you!

Halvdan (*raising himself on his elbow, and looking at him with a smile*). Something must have gone amiss with you to-day.

Evje. Why do you say that?

Halvdan. Because as a rule you appear so composed—so aloof from all this squabbling.

Evje (*impetuously*). But, do what I like, I am not allowed to keep aloof from it! I have no greater wish in the world than to do so, I can assure you. Oh, well, your excellent brother—my future son-in-law, as I am proud to call him—he will tell you all about it. Good-bye! —and—and—God bless you!

Haakon. Shall I tell your housekeeper to come to you?

Halvdan. Oh, no; but you might tell her to come in a little while.

Haakon. Good-bye for the present, then!

Halvdan. Thank you for coming! Good-bye. (*Sinks back on to the sofa. The others go out,* HAAKON *turning round once at the door.*)

Halvdan. It is something in the paper that has disturbed his equanimity. What can it be? The same thing that made Harald so gloomy to-day, I wonder?

(*Gets half up.*) It is lying there.— No! What interest
have I in all their petty spite now? (*Sinks back again.*)
" Could you bear to read something hateful about yourself to-day? " Haakon asked. Then I suppose there is
something about me in it to-day. (*Puts his hand over his
heart.*) My heart doesn't seem to be beating any the
faster for my knowing that. (*Gets half up.*) There it
lies! (*Sinks back again.*) No, I am only trying to tempt
myself. All the same, I should like to know how many
stations I have passed on my journey to the great City of
Peace! Can their malice affect me still? Surely I have
passed *that* station?— It would be worth trying, to see.
There it lies! (*Takes up a stick that is standing by the
sofa.*) Surely I can get over there by myself? (*Gets
up from the sofa with the help of the stick, and smiles.*) I
have not much strength left. (*Takes a few steps.*) Scarcely
enough to get across the floor. (*A few more steps.*) To
think that I should have—so much vanity—my weak
point—. (*His breath fails him, but he gets as far as the
chair on which* EVJE *was sitting, and sits down.*) One
ought to have done with all that before the soul can get
quite away from the dust that—. (*Begins to rake the
paper towards him with his stick.*) And here am I, sitting
here raking more of it towards me!—No, let the thing lie!
I won't soil my wings any more.—Poor Harald! He has
to take up the burden now! What a horrible bungle it is,
that we should be brought into the world to give each
other as much pain as possible! (*Decidedly.*) Well, I
am going to see what legacy of unhappiness I am leaving
him! I want to have a vivid impression of the misery
I am escaping from. There is a certain comfort even in
that. (*Bends down and picks up the paper, rests for a
moment, and then unfolds the paper.*) But this is not
to-day's paper; it is dated for to-morrow! How can
Evje have got hold of it? Yes, here is the date—Sunday.
" Remember that thou keep holy the Sabbath Day! "

On that day men's souls should turn to God—and they offer Him *this!* It is after reading *this* that these fine ladies and gentlemen go to church! (*Pushes the paper away from him.*) Suppose these " Christians " were to be brought to judgment one day without warning?—Let us think of ourselves and not of others! (*Lets his eye rest on the paper.*) Does that mean me? (*Reads.*) " Not yet actually dead, but already canonised by a calculating brother—." (*Checks himself.*) God forgive them! (*Reads on.*) " His teachings will no doubt obtain him a pæan of praise, but this will be—or, at least, so it is to be hoped— from within the closely locked doors of the state's prisons and houses of correction "—(*checks himself a little*)— " for that is whither he leads his followers."—Good God, to think that they can say such things!—And yet, they said worse things of *Him!* Peace! (*Reads.*) " No doubt he talks against Socialism; no doubt he coquets with Christianity; but it is by these very means that he has become so expert a seducer of men's opinions—which was his aim all along." (*Puts his hands before his face.*) I should not have read it; forgive me! I am too weak still!—Ah! I feel—what is it? (*Puts his hands suddenly to his heart, still unconsciously grasping the newspaper in them.*) I must get into my room—get to bed! (*Gets up with the help of his stick.*) If only I can get there! Oh, I feel it coming on!—I must—. (*Tries to hurry, but when he is halfway across the floor he stumbles, throws out his hands but finds no support, staggers on for a few steps, and falls full length on the threshold of his bedroom, so that half his length lies within the door and half without. A moment later, the* HOUSEKEEPER *comes in.*)

The Housekeeper (*not observing that he is not still on the sofa*). Won't you go to bed now, sir? You can't stand so much in one day. (*Goes to the sofa.*) Where is he? Surely he has not tried to walk in alone? (*Hurries across to the bedroom door and almost falls over his body. She starts back with a scream.*) Where is—? (*Catches up the lamp, hurries back, and bends over him; then calls out, screaming:*) Help! Help! (*Rings the bell wildly. A* MAID *appears.*) Mr. Halvdan is lying here! Heaven knows whether he is dead or alive! Run for the Doctor! Leave the door open behind you, and beg the first man you meet in the street to come up here at once and help me. Tell them it is a matter of life and death!

Maid. Yes!

The Housekeeper. Hurry!

Maid (*going out*). Yes, yes!

The Housekeeper (*coming back into the room*). Is he alive or dead? I haven't the courage to find out. And both his brothers away! (*Cries.*) God grant some one comes soon!—Poor man, alone in his death as he was in his life! But what was he doing *there?* Why did he get up from the sofa? (*Sees the paper.*) Surely that can't be—? (*Puts the lamp on the floor and unfolds the paper.*) Yes, it is the paper, right enough! Who can have given it him? I can't look at it now; but if it is like the number I read the other day (*lets the paper fall, and gets up with the lamp*) then I understand everything —and may God requite those that do such things! (*The* EDITOR *rushes in.*)

The Editor. Is it here?

The Housekeeper (*holds the lamp to him, then starts back*). What do *you* want here?

The Editor. Where am I? A girl came running down the street and told me I must come up here and help some one that was dying. What do you want me to do? —or is it not here?

The Housekeeper. And it was *you* she met? It is the hand of God!

The Editor. What are you babbling about? If it is not here, say so at once.

The Housekeeper. Yes, it is here. There he lies!

F 696

The Editor. Then oughtn't we to get him into bed?

The Housekeeper. Yes. But do you know who it is you are helping?

The Editor (to himself). She is not very polite. (*Aloud.*) No; but what does that matter?

The Housekeeper. This much—that it is you that have killed him.

The Editor. I—? She is mad.

The Housekeeper. The man lying there is Halvdan Rejn. And he had been reading about himself in your paper.—Come, now, and carry him in. (*She goes into the bedroom with the lamp. Her voice is heard from inside the room.*) Now, take hold of him and lift him. You can think afterwards.

The Editor (stoops to lift the body, but gets up again). I don't think he is dead yet.

The Housekeeper. All the more reason to make haste.

The Editor (stoops down again, but gets up once more.) Let me take his head.

The Housekeeper. Why?

The Editor. So that—if he should open his eyes—

The Housekeeper. —he won't see you. (*Comes out of the bedroom*). Go in there, then, and take his head. (*He goes in.*) What was that?

The Editor (from inside the room). I slipped. There is something wet here.

The Housekeeper. Yes, he has had a hemorrhage. Carefully, now. (*They carry him in. The stage remains empty for a moment. Then the* EDITOR *comes back, wiping his forehead. He walks backwards and forwards, treading on the paper as he goes, but without noticing it.*)

The Editor. What a horrible thing to happen!—Newspapers are not meant for dying people.—It is not my fault.—Is this blood on my hand? It is! (*Wipes it with his handkerchief.*) And now it is on my handkerchief! (*Throws it away.*) No, it has my name on it. (*Picks it up again.*) No one can say it is my fault. (*Sits down, then gets up, wiping his forehead with his handkerchief without noticing what he is doing.*) Ah, I hope I haven't put blood on my forehead? I seem to feel it there! (*Feels with his hand to see if his brow is wet.*) No. (*Sits down, then gets up again.*) Let me get away from here. (*Stops.*) To think that I should be the one to come up!— that it should just happen to-night that I did not receive my paper, and so went out! It almost seems more than accident. Indeed, I often had a foreboding that it would happen. (*Stands opposite the bedroom door.*) But is he dead? I think I will go and fetch the Doctor. Oh no, of course the maid has gone for him. He hasn't long to live, anyway; I could see that. (*Walks forward, pointing with his finger.*) " There goes the man that killed Halvdan Rejn! And his punishment was that he had to lift up his bloodstained body himself." That is what they will say; and they will look at me as if—. (*Sits down.*) No, let me get away! (*Takes a few steps, then stops suddenly.*) That article in to-morrow's paper! It is worse than the others! (*Pulls out his watch.*) Too late— the post has gone! I would have given—. (*Checks himself.*) I have nothing worth giving. In the morning it will be known all over the town just as every one is reading my fresh article. There will be a riot; I shall be hunted like a wild beast. What shall I do? I might sneak out of the town? Then they will gloat over me! I won't allow them that pleasure! No, I cannot stay my hand after a failure; only after a victory. That is the cursed part of it—never, never to be able to end it. Oh, for some one that could end it—end it, end it! Oh, for one day of real peace! Shall *I* ever get that? (*Sits down.*) No, no, I must get away! (*Gets up.*) To-morrow must take care of itself. (*Starts.*) There is the paper he was reading! (*Steps over it.*) I will take it away— and burn it. (*Takes it up.*) I cannot burn it here;

some one might come. (*Is just going to put it into his pocket, as it is, but takes it out again to fold it better.*) A Sunday's paper, apparently! Then it is *not* to-day's? An old number, I suppose. Then the whole thing is a mistake! (*Sighs with relief.*) Let me look again! (*Opens the paper, tremblingly.*) I don't deserve it, but—. (*Reads.*) Sunday, the—. To-morrow's paper? *Here?* How in all the world did it get here? (*Appears horrified.*) Here are the articles about Evje! How on earth did they get in? Didn't I send a message? Didn't I write? This on the top of everything else! Are even my printers conspiring against me? Well, even if it ruins me, I shall go on! They shall find out what I can do. How on earth can I be expected to help it if a weak-minded fellow dies, or if my printers are drunk or my manager has delirium tremens! I shall pursue my end through all chances and in spite of all their tricks, and I shall crush them, crush them—I shall—. (*Gives way to a paroxysm of rage. At this moment the* MAID *comes in with the* DOCTOR'S ASSISTANT. *The* MAID *rushes into the bedroom. The* EDITOR *starts up.*) Who is that? What do you want?

The Doctor's Assistant (*coldly*). What do *you* want here?

The Editor. I? Oh, I was called up to help the sick man into his bed.

The Doctor's Assistant (*as before*). Ah!—so it was *you!* (*A pause.*)

The Editor. Have you ever seen me before?

The Doctor's Assistant. Yes. I have heard you grind your teeth before this. (*Goes into the bedroom.*)

The Editor (*after standing for a moment looking after him*). They will all look at me to-morrow like that—with those cold eyes. "Every man's hand against him, and his hand against every man;" there can only be one end to that. To-night, the meeting — and Harald Rejn will take them by storm. To-morrow, his brother's death— and my new article in the paper—and, in addition to that, those about Evje, who at present is only angry. And the election in two days! Oh, yes, he will be elected now. So I may as well give it all up at once. I would change places with any wolf that has a lair to hide in. Those cold eyes of his! (*Shudders.*) That is how every one will look at me to-morrow! They have pierced through my armour! (*The* DOCTOR'S ASSISTANT *comes back, and the* EDITOR *makes an effort to resume his former confident manner.*)

The Doctor's Assistant. I don't know whether you will be glad to hear that it is all over.

The Editor (*under his breath*). You brute!

The Doctor's Assistant. His old housekeeper does not feel equal to coming here to tell you what his last words were. They were: "Forgive him!" (*Goes out.*)

The Editor (*sitting down, then getting up again*). No, I mustn't be found here. (*Walks about the room on tiptoe, as if he were afraid of waking some one. When he comes opposite to the bedroom door, he turns towards it, stretches out his arms and says :*) Give me your forgiveness too!

ACT IV

(SCENE.—*A large and handsomely furnished sitting-room at the* EVJE'S. *The room is brightly lit and the fire burning. The entrance door is on the right, and beyond it a door leading to the dining-room.* INGEBORG *is busy taking the covers off the chairs, folding them carefully as she does so. After a little, the bell rings. She goes to open the door, and returns, showing in the* DOCTOR.)

The Doctor. Oho! Is it to be in here to-night?

Ingeborg (who has resumed her work of making the room ready). Yes, sir.

The Doctor. Where are they all?

Ingeborg. At the meeting, sir.

The Doctor. All of them?

Ingeborg. Yes, all of them. Miss Gertrud went first—

The Doctor. Yes, I saw her well enough!

Ingeborg. And then the master, and a farmer gentleman with him, came in to fetch the mistress.

The Doctor (to himself). Something has happened here, then. (*Aloud.*) Tell me, Ingeborg—has *he* been here again? You know who I mean. (*Coughs in imitation of the* EDITOR'S *cough.*)

Ingeborg. Oh, the Editor; no, sir.

The Doctor (to himself). I wonder what has happened. (*Aloud.*) Well, evidently there is to be a festivity here to-night; and, as I see the chairs are getting their covers taken off, I may as well take mine off too. (*Takes off his coat and gives it to* INGEBORG, *who carries it out.*) I don't blame Evje for wanting to celebrate Harald's success after a meeting like that! He is not exactly eloquent

in the ordinary sense of the word—doesn't bother about
his antitheses and climaxes and paradoxes, and all that
sort of nonsense; but he is a *man!*   He goes bail for what
he says, and he says what he likes—ha, ha!   And that
dear Gertrud, too! Follows him into the hall, and, as there
isn't a single seat left there, goes up on to the platform
among the committee, and sits there looking at him with
those trustful blue eyes of hers, as if there was no one
else in the room!   And *we* were all looking at *her!*   She
helped him more than ten good speakers would have done,
I am sure.   Her faith in him bred it in others, whether
they liked it or no.   She is one who would die for her
faith!   Yes, yes!   The man that gets her—.   (INGEBORG
comes back.) Well! (*Rubs his hands together.*) Look
here, Ingeborg. (*Very politely.*) Do you know what is
meant by the Rights of Man?

Ingeborg (*going on with her work*). No, sir.   Something
we have earned, I suppose.

The Doctor. Yes, you earn them every day.

Ingeborg. Our meals, perhaps?

The Doctor (*laughing*). No, it isn't something to eat,
unfortunately. (*Politely.*) Do you ever read papers,
Ingeborg?

Ingeborg. Papers?   Oh, you mean the price-lists they
leave at the kitchen door.   Yes, sir; every day, before
we go to market, I—

The Doctor. No, I don't mean papers of that sort.   I
mean—

Ingeborg. Oh, you mean the newspaper I take in to
master's room every morning.   No, sir, I don't read that.
I am told there are such horrors in it.

The Doctor. Quite so.   Don't you care to read about
horrors, then?

Ingeborg. Oh, we poor folk see enough of them in our
everyday lives, without reading about them! — But
perhaps the gentry enjoy it.

The Doctor. You are a very wise woman. Let me tell you, though, that there is a fight going on, about—oh, well, never mind what it is about. And the Editor and Mr. Rejn, who both come to this house, are the two chief fighters. Don't you want to know what they are fighting about?

Ingeborg (going on unconcernedly with her work). Oh, so they are fighting, are they? No, I don't care the least bit, sir!

The Doctor (to himself). Ha, ha—the difference between Ingeborg and me is that I am interested in the fight merely as a student of human nature, and she is not interested in it at all. I wonder which is farthest from any genuine belief in politics?—from our " duty as a citizen," as they call it? *(To* INGEBORG.) Ingeborg, do you know what your " duty as a citizen " means?

Ingeborg. My " duty as a citizen "? That means paying fines, doesn't it, sir?

The Doctor. Yes; and a very heavy fine, into the bargain!

Ingeborg. The master was fined because the pavement was not swept. John was ill.

The Doctor. Quite right, that was one of his duties as a citizen.—Tell me, Ingeborg, are they expecting a lot of people here to-night?

Ingeborg. No, sir, I have only laid table for quite a few.

The Doctor. And what are they going to have?

Ingeborg. Oh, one or two dishes and one or two sorts of wine—.

The Doctor. Aha! *(A ring is heard at the bell.* INGE-BORG *goes to the door.)* There they are! Now we shall have a fine time!

Ingeborg (coming back with a letter). It is a note for you, sir.

The Doctor. Oh, bother!

Ingeborg. The man who brought it was not sure whether you would be at the meeting or here.

The Doctor. How could he know—? (*Putting on his glasses.*) Oh, from my assistant—that is quite another thing. Of course he wants my help or my advice. Well, he shan't have it! I have run about quite enough to-day. Tell the messenger that I haven't time! I have my Duties as a Citizen to attend to! (*Calls after her.*) And my Manhood's Rights too! (*Opens the envelope.*) No, I won't read it; if I do, the matter will worry me all the evening. I know what I am. (*Puts the note in his pocket.*) I mean to enjoy this evening! (*Suddenly.*) I wonder how our friend the Editor is enjoying this evening! Was he at the meeting, I wonder? A remarkable personality — but malignity itself! Lion-hearted, though! He would fight till the last drop of his blood! But what is it, really, that he is fighting for? That question has always interested me, for I can't make it out. (*To* INGEBORG, *who has come back.*) Well?

Ingeborg. The messenger has gone.—Yes, sir, I told him everything you told me to.

The Doctor. Of course. You would! Why the deuce does any one pay any attention to what I say! (*The bell rings.*) Here they are at last! Now we shall have a delightful evening! (EVJE *and* MRS. EVJE *come in.*) I am first, you see!

Evje and Mrs. Evje. Were you at the meeting, too?

The Doctor. Where else should I be?

Evje. Did you see me?

Mrs. Evje. There were so many people there, dear.

Evje. But I was standing on a seat.

Mrs. Evje. Yes, he was standing on a seat!

The Doctor. There were plenty of people doing that.

Evje. I wanted to be seen!—There *have* been goings on here to-day, my friend!

Mrs. Evje. You will never guess what has happened!

The Doctor. Anyway I can see that something has happened.

Evje and Mrs. Evje. Oh—!

The Doctor. What is it, then?

Evje. Those articles will be in to-morrow's paper.

The Doctor. In the paper?—Yes, I didn't find him.

Evje. But I found him!

The Doctor (impatiently). Well?

Evje. I will tell you all about it another time. But I have read them—

Mrs. Evje. And he has told me all about them!

The Doctor. Are they very bad?

Evje. Oh—oh!

Mrs. Evje. Oh—oh—oh!

The Doctor (with a look of pleased curiosity.) As bad as all that?

Evje and Mrs. Evje. Oh—oh—oh—oh!

The Doctor. And *that* was why you went to the meeting!

Evje. Of course—tit for tat! It was my wife's idea.

Mrs. Evje. It was the obvious thing to do, dear.

Evje. Our whole family at the meeting!—So that all the town should know that it was nothing but the meanest political persecution because I had joined my son-in-law's party.

Mrs. Evje. We are party people now, you know!

Evje. Do you know, there is something exciting about being mixed up with such things—something invigorating, something—

The Doctor (stepping back). Are *you* bitten with it, too?

Evje. Yes, if I can't be left in peace, I shall become a party man.

The Doctor (enthusiastically). Did you see Gertrud?

Evje and Mrs. Evje (with emotion). Our Gertrud! Yes, indeed we did!

The Doctor. Did you see her coming in with him!

Evje and Mrs. Evje (as before). Yes, we saw her coming in with him!

The Doctor. I suppose you did not know she was going?

Evje and Mrs. Evje. Oh, yes!

Mrs. Evje. She had said she would go with us—

Evje. But when we went to fetch her, the bird had flown!

The Doctor. How pretty she looked, too! All the men were looking at her. And how she looked at him!

Mrs. Evje. It made me want to cry. I had quite a job to prevent myself.

Evje. You need not have minded, dear! God has given us great happiness. Her faith in him and her love shone so from her eyes that it went to my heart. I felt quite upset! (*Wipes his eyes.*)

The Doctor. And what about *him*—eh? I don't fancy any one will think about stopping *his* career. We have been a pack of fools.

Evje. That we have!

The Doctor. He is not exactly eloquent, but—

Evje. That is precisely what I was saying to my wife! He is not exactly eloquent, but he is—

The Doctor. —a man!

Evje. A man! My very words, weren't they, my dear?

Mrs. Evje. Yes.—And I say he is so strong a man that he can afford to be tender-hearted. For he certainly has been that.

Evje. Yes, he has been that!

The Doctor (laughing). In spite of his strength!

Evje. Oh, you may make the most of your—. Aha! (*Loud ringing at the bell is heard.*) Here they are!

Mrs. Evje. Let us go and meet them!

The Doctor. No; look here—let us wait for them at the other side of the room, so that they may make a triumphal progress up to us!

Evje and Mrs. Evje. Yes! (*They go to the opposite end*

of the room, while HARALD *comes in rather quickly, with* GERTRUD *on his arm. As they cross the room, the others cry out:* " Bravo! Bravo! " *and clap their hands.*)

Gertrud (*still holding to* HARALD'S *arm*). And he is my man! My man!

> (*Throws her arms round his neck, crying with happiness, and kisses him; then does the same to her mother, and then to her father, to whom she whispers:* Thank you!)

The Doctor. Oh—me too!

Gertrud (*after a moment's hesitation*). Yes—you too!

> (*The* DOCTOR *helps her to take off her cloak, and talks to her, whispering and laughing.*)

Harald (*shaking* EVJE'S *hand*). Good evening!

Evje. Forgive me!

Harald. With all my heart!

Mrs. Evje. And now everything is all right!

Harald. For good!

Evje and Mrs. Evje. For good!

Harald. And, thank you for coming to the meeting.

Evje. It was no more than our duty! Look here—did you see me?

Harald. The whole time! But, tell me, was it a delusion, or was it my brother Haakon that was standing on the floor beside you, rather in the shadow?

Evje and Mrs. Evje. It *was* he!

Evje. I fetched him from your brother Halvdan's.

Harald. I am so glad! It must have pleased Haakon. Gertrud and I at first thought of going in to see Halvdan before we came on here; but we saw all his lights were out. He must be asleep.

Evje. I can give you news of him. He is all right.

Harald. And Haakon?

Evje. Very well, too. A fine fellow! I wanted him to come home with us now; but he said he was tired after his journey.

Mrs. Evje (to INGEBORG, *who has come in from the dining-room*). Is it ready?

Ingeborg. Yes, ma'am.

Mrs. Evje. Then come along. (INGEBORG *opens the dining-room door.*)

The Doctor and Evje. Yes, come along!

The Doctor. But we must go ceremoniously! Let us make a little festivity of it to-night! You must head the procession, Evje—and then the two young people—

Gertrud (taking HARALD'S *arm*). Yes!

The Doctor. And Mrs. Evje and I will bring up the rear! (*Offers her his arm.*)

Evje. Forward! (*The bell rings. He stops.*) Who can it be—as late as this?

The Doctor. Probably some friends on their way back from the meeting.

Mrs. Evje. We must wait a moment! (*To* INGEBORG, *who is going to open the door.*) Put a leaf in the table, and lay places for as many as come.

Ingeborg. Yes, ma'am. (*The bell rings again, as she goes to open the door.*)

The Doctor. They are impatient! So much the better— it shows they are in a good humour after the meeting! (*A knock is heard at the door.*)

All. Come in! (*The* EDITOR *comes in, with no overcoat on, but wearing his hat, which he forgets to take off till he is well into the room. He goes straight up to* EVJE, *who has crossed over to the left-hand side of the room.*)

All (when they see him in the doorway). You! (GERTRUD *clings closer to* HARALD.)

The Editor. I wanted once more, as in the old days, not to go to bed without—this time it is not a question of thanking you for the happy time we have had together— but without begging your pardon ! (*He speaks quietly, but with suppressed emotion.*) There has been some unfortunate misunderstanding. Those articles have been

printed, in spite of my express instructions to the contrary—I do not know how.

Evje. I have read them.

The Editor. You have read them?

Evje. Yes, the copy of the paper that was meant for
you came into my hands.

The Editor. So that was it!—Forgive me, old friend!
Won't you give me your hand?

Mrs. Evje (coming forward). That he shall never do!

The Editor (glancing over his shoulder at her). Let no one
come between us at a moment like this! You don't
know—. A hundred times in my life I would have done
what I am doing now, had I not been afraid that people
would call it affectation on my part and repulse me.
Don't *you* do that!—least of all now! Give me your hand,
Evje! I beg you, in the sight and hearing of you all—.
(EVJE *seems to vacillate.*)

Mrs. Evje. No, you shan't!—not while he has anything
to do with a newspaper. Otherwise it will all begin over
again to-morrow. He is not his own master, you know.

The Editor. I have done with it all.

Mrs. Evje. Oh, you have said that so often! Nobody
believes it. No; when a man can push political hatred
so far as to write about an old friend, in whose house he
has been a daily guest, as if he were a criminal—and all
because he doesn't like his son-in-law, or his servant—one
doesn't shake hands with him the very day his attacks
appear in the paper.

The Editor (who, all the time, has kept his back turned to
MRS. EVJE, *and has not looked at her).* Evje, you are a
good-hearted fellow, I know. Don't listen to what others
say, now. This is a very bitter hour for me. You would
be doing a good deed! Give me your hand——or a word!
I am in such a state now that I must have visible signs of
some one's forgiveness, or I shall—!

Mrs. Evje (emphatically). Yes, a little repentance will

do you good! But it will do you no good if you obtain forgiveness easily! You want to learn, just for once, what it is to be wounded at heart. You are only accustomed to deal with people whom you can flog one day and have at your feet—either from fear or from vanity—the next. And have we—God forgive us!—ever thought seriously the worse of you for it? No; because we never understood what it was till we were hit by it ourselves. But that is all the more reason why we should do our duty now! Hatred shall be met with hatred!

The Doctor (at the back of the room, to GERTRUD *and* HARALD). She is her father's daughter, after all, when it comes to the point!

The Editor (turns upon MRS. EVJE, *with his fist clenched, but restrains himself from answering her*). Then you won't shake hands, Evje? Not a word of forgiveness?

Evje. I think my wife is right.

The Editor (controlling himself with difficulty). You are a weak man, I know—

Evje. What do you mean?

The Editor. —but do not be weak this time! If you knew everything, you would know you *must* not refuse me what I ask. There are others concerned—and for that reason—

The Doctor. Let us go!

Mrs. Evje. No, stay! He shall not have his way again.

The Editor. Well, of all—! It is certainly true that those who are hardest on sinners are those who have never been tempted themselves — and the most merciless creature in the world is an injured woman.

Mrs. Evje. Now he is coming out in his true colours!

The Doctor (not without glee). Yes, that he is!

The Editor (controlling himself once more). Evje—you, who know me, know what it must cost me to do this— and you can form some idea of the need I am in. I have never—

Evje. I believe you; but I never can feel sure what your next move will be. You have so many.

The Editor. My next move is to have done with it all, as sure as—

Mrs. Evje. Don't believe him! A man who can ask for your sympathy one moment and abuse you the next is not fit to promise anything—and certainly not fit to be forgiven, either.

The Editor (with an outburst of passion). Then may everything evil overtake me if I ever ask you or any one else for sympathy again! You have succeeded in teaching me that I can do without it! I can rise above your cowardly cruelty. (*To* EVJE.) You are a miserable, weak creature—and have always been, for all your apparent good-natured shrewdness! (*To* MRS. EVJE.) And as for you, who have often laughed so heartily at my so-called malice, and now all at once have become so severely virtuous—why, you are both like part-proprietors of my paper! You have taken all the profit you could from me, as long as it served your purpose—I have seen that for a long time! And all my pretended friends are like you—secret holders of shares in me, so as to secure their own safety and the persecution of others!—every bit as guilty as I am, only more prudent, more timid, more cowardly—!

Evje. Once more—leave this house, which you have outraged!

Mrs. Evje. And how dare you set foot in here again?

The Editor. No, I am not going until all the anger that is in my heart has turned into fear in yours! Because now I will *not* have done with it all! No—it is just through *his* death that respect for me will revive—it will be like a rampart of bayonets round me! " There goes one who can kill a man with a word, if he likes! " *That* will make them treat me respectfully!

Harald and the Doctor. What does he mean?

The Editor (as he hears HARALD'S *voice).* And you—you mountebank, who can stand up in public and seek applause before your brother's corpse is cold—don't come talking cant to me! You are more contemptible than I am! I couldn't have done that; I couldn't stand there, as you are doing now, impatient to get to your champagne and pretty speeches!—Oh, how I despise all such lying and heartlessness! (*They all look at him and at each other with a questioning expression.*)

Harald. Is my brother dead?

Mrs. Evje. Is his brother dead?

Gertrud. Good God, is Halvdan dead?

Evje. Is he dead? Impossible!

The Doctor. Is Rejn dead—and I—?

Evje. I saw him only a couple of hours ago, looking quite well.

The Editor (in a broken voice). Didn't you know ?

All (except the DOCTOR). No!

The Doctor. Ah, that letter, that letter! (*Looks in his pocket for it and his glasses.*)

The Editor. I am the wretchedest man alive! (*Sinks into a chair.*)

The Doctor. I had a letter from my assistant, but I have not read it!

Mrs. Evje. Read it, read it!

The Doctor (reading). "I am writing in great haste. As I expect you will be going to your old friends' after the meeting, and will meet Harald Rejn there, the task will probably fall to you of telling him—(*the* EDITOR *gets up to go, but stands still*)—that Halvdan Rejn died about eight o'clock of a fresh attack of hemorrhage! (HARALD *leaves* GERTRUD'S *side and comes forward, with a cry. The* EDITOR *steadies himself by holding on to the table.*) No one was with him; he was found lying across the threshold of his bedroom. A copy of the newspaper was lying on

G 696

the floor behind him." (HARALD, *with a groan, advances threateningly towards the* EDITOR.)

Gertrud. Harald, my ring!—my ring! (HARALD *stops, collects himself, buries his face in his hands and bursts into uncontrollable tears.* GERTRUD *puts her arms round him and holds him folded in them.*)

The Doctor (*laying a hand on* HARALD'S *arm*). " The old housekeeper told me he had only spoken two words, and they were ' Forgive him!' " (HARALD *bursts into tears.*)

The Doctor (*after waiting for a little*). " Apparently chance —or perhaps something else—decreed that the maid, who ran for help, should meet the very man. who had caused the tragedy, and that it should be *he* who helped the housekeeper to lay him on his deathbed." (*All look at the* EDITOR.)

Evje. That was why he came! (*A pause.*)

Gertrud. Harald! (HARALD, *who has turned away from her to struggle with his emotion, does not turn round.*) If *he* could forgive—

The Editor (*with a gesture of refusal*). No!

Gertrud (*quietly, to the* EDITOR). If you want to deserve it, make an end of all this!

The Editor. It is all at an end! (*To* MRS. EVJE.) You were right. I knew it myself, too. My armour is pierced through. A child might conquer me now—and this child has done so; for she has begged for mercy for me, and no one has ever done that before. (*Puts his hand over his eyes, turns away, and goes out. As he is going out the bell rings. A moment later,* INGEBORG *shows in* HAAKON REJN.)

Gertrud (*who has put her arms round* HARALD, *whispers*). Who is it?

Harald. My brother. (*Goes to meet* HAAKON *and throws himself into his arms.*) You had a talk with him this afternoon, then?

Haakon. Yes.

Mrs. Evje. Let us all go to him.

Evje and Gertrud. Yes.

Mrs. Evje (to INGEBORG). Bring in our cloaks and hats again, and afterwards clear the table. (INGEBORG *does so.*)

Harald (unable to control his emotion). Haakon, this is my future wife. (*Goes away from them.*)

Haakon. Well, my dear, your engagement has begun seriously; take all the future seriously, too.

The Doctor. You need not say that to *her*. What she needs is to take life more lightly.

Haakon. Oh, yes—if she lays everything in God's hands she can always take life lightly.

Mrs. Evje. It is our own fault, I expect, when we take it too lightly.

Evje. But sometimes we learn a lesson by that.

Haakon. Oh, yes. Well, we must stand by one another, we who take life in the same way.

Mrs. Evje. Shall we go, children?

Harald (to HAAKON). Will you bring Gertrud, Haakon? I would rather go alone. (*They go out. The curtain falls.*)

THE BANKRUPT

A PLAY IN FOUR ACTS

DRAMATIS PERSONÆ

HENNING TJÆLDE, merchant and brewer.

MRS. TJÆLDE, his wife.

VALBORG
SIGNE } their daughters.

LIEUTENANT HAMAR, engaged to Signe.

SANNÆS, Tjælde's confidential clerk.

JAKOBSEN, manager of Tjælde's brewery.

BERENT, a lawyer.

PRAM, a custom-house official.

An Agent.

The VICAR.

LIND
FINNE
RING
HOLM } Guests.
KNUTZON
KNUDSEN
FALBE

THE BANKRUPT

ACT I

(SCENE.—*A sitting-room in the* TJÆLDES' *house, opening on a verandah that is decorated with flowers. It is a hot summer's day. There is a view of the sea beyond the verandah, and boats are visible among the islands that fringe the coast. A good-sized yacht, with sails spread, is lying close up under the verandah on the right. The room is luxuriously furnished and full of flowers. There are two French windows in the left-hand wall; two doors in the right-hand. A table in the middle of the room; arm-chairs and rocking-chairs scattered about. A sofa in the foreground on the right.* LIEUTENANT HAMAR *is lying on the sofa, and* SIGNE *sitting in a rocking-chair.*)

Hamar. What shall we do with ourselves to-day?

Signe (*rocking herself*). Hm! (*A pause.*)

Hamar. That was a delicious sail we had last night. (*Yawns.*) But I am sleepy to-day. Shall we go for a ride?

Signe. Hm! (*A pause.*)

Hamar. I am too hot on this sofa. I think I will move. (*Gets up.* SIGNE *begins to hum an air as she rocks herself.*) Play me something, Signe!

Signe (*singing her words to the air she has been humming*). The piano is out of tune.

Hamar. Read to me, then!

Signe (*as before, looking out of the window*). They are swimming the horses. They are swimming the horses. They are swimming the horses.

Hamar. I think I will go and have a swim too. Or perhaps I will wait till nearer lunch-time.

Signe (as before). So as to have a better appetite—appetite—appetite.

(MRS. TJÆLDE *comes in from the right, walking slowly.*)

Hamar. You look very thoughtful!

Mrs. Tjælde. Yes, I don't know what to order.

Signe (as before). For dinner, I suppose you mean?

Mrs. Tjælde. Yes.

Hamar. Do you expect any one?

Mrs. Tjælde. Yes, your father writes to me that Mr. Finne is coming.

Signe (speaking). The most tiresome person possible, of course.

Mrs. Tjælde. How would boiled salmon and roast chicken do?

Signe. We had that the other day.

Mrs. Tjælde (with a sigh). There is nothing that we didn't. There is so little choice in the market just now.

Signe. Then we ought to send to town.

Mrs. Tjælde. Oh, these meals, these meals!

Hamar (yawning). They are the best thing in life, anyway.

Signe. To eat, yes—but not to cook; I never will cook a dinner.

Mrs. Tjælde (sitting down at the table). One could put up with the cooking. It's the having always to think of something fresh!

Hamar. Why don't you get a *chef* from one of the hotels, as I have so often advised you?

Mrs. Tjælde. Oh, we have tried that, but he was more trouble than it was worth.

Hamar. Yes, because he had no invention. Get a French *chef!*

Mrs. Tjælde. Yes, and have to be always beside him to

interpret!—But I am no nearer this dinner. And lately I have been finding such difficulty in getting about.

Hamar. I have never in my life heard so much talk about meals as I have in this house.

Mrs. Tjælde. You see, you have never been in a prosperous business-man's house before. Our friends are mostly business-men, of course—and most of them have no greater pleasures than those of the table.

Signe. That's true.

Mrs. Tjælde. Are you wearing *that* dress to-day?

Signe. Yes.

Mrs. Tjælde. You have worn a different one every day.

Signe. Well, if Hamar is tired of both the blue one and the grey one, what can I do?

Hamar. And I don't like this one any better than the others.

Signe. Indeed!—Then I really think you had better order me one yourself.

Hamar. Come to town with me, and I will!

Signe.[1] Yes, mother—Hamar and I have made up our minds that we must go back to town.

Mrs. Tjælde. But you were there only a fortnight ago!

Hamar. And it is exactly a fortnight too long since we were there!

Mrs. Tjælde (thoughtfully). Now, what *can* I order for dinner?

(VALBORG *comes into sight on the verandah.*)

Signe (turning round and seeing VALBORG). Enter Her Highness!

Hamar (turning round). Carrying a bouquet! Oho! I have seen it before!

Signe. Have you? Did *you* give it her?

Hamar. No; I was coming through the garden—and

[1] There would be nothing contrary to Norwegian ideas of propriety in Signe's proposal. In Norway an engaged couple could travel alone; and the *fiancée* would go to stay in the house of her future husband's relations.

saw it on the table in Valborg's summerhouse. Is it your birthday, Valborg?

Valborg. No.

Hamar. I thought not. Perhaps there is some other festivity to-day?

Valborg. No. (SIGNE *suddenly bursts out laughing.*)

Hamar. Why do you laugh?

Signe. Because I understand! Ha, ha, ha, ha!

Hamar. What do you understand?

Signe. Whose hands it is that have decked the altar! Ha, ha, ha!

Hamar. I suppose you think they were mine?

Signe. No, they were redder hands than yours! Ha, ha, ha, ha! (VALBORG *throws the bouquet down.*) Oh, dear me, it doesn't do to laugh so much in this heat. But it is delightful! To think he should have hit upon that idea! Ha, ha, ha!

Hamar (laughing). Do you mean—?

Signe (laughing). Yes! You must know that Valborg—

Valborg. Signe!

Signe. —who has sent so many distinguished suitors about their business, cannot escape from the attentions of a certain red pair of hands—ha, ha, ha, ha!

Hamar. Do you mean Sannæs?

Signe. Yes! (*Points out of the window.*) There is the culprit! He is waiting, Valborg, for you to come, in maiden meditation, with the bouquet in your hands—as you came just now—

Mrs. Tjælde (getting up). No, it is your father he is waiting for. Ah, he sees him now. (*Goes out by the verandah.*)

Signe. Yes, it really is father—riding a bay horse!

Hamar (getting up). On a bay horse! Let us go and say " how do you do " to the bay horse!

Signe. N—o, no!

Hamar. You won't come and say " how do you do " to

the bay horse? A cavalry officer's wife must love horses next best to her husband.

Signe. And he his wife next best to his horses.

Hamar. What? Are you jealous of a horse?

Signe. Oh, I know very well you have never been so fond of me as you are of horses.

Hamar. Come along! (*Pulls her up out of her chair.*)

Signe. But I don't feel the least interested in the bay horse.

Hamar. Very well, then, I will go alone!

Signe. No, I will come.

Hamar (*to* VALBORG). Won't you come and welcome the bay horse too?

Valborg. No, but I will go and welcome my father!

Signe (*looking back, as she goes*). Yes, of course—father as well. (*She and* HAMAR *go out.*)

> (VALBORG *goes to the farthest window and stands looking out of it. Her dress is the same colour as the long curtain, and a piece of statuary and some flowers conceal her from any one entering the room.* SANNÆS *comes in, carrying a small saddle-bag and a cloak, which he puts down on a chair behind the door. As he turns round he sees the bouquet on the floor.*)

Sannæs. There it is! Has she dropped it by accident, or did she throw it down? Never mind—she has had it in her hands. (*Picks it up, kisses it, and is going to take it away.*)

Valborg (*coming forward*). Leave it alone!

Sannæs (*dropping the bouquet*). You here, Miss Valborg—? I didn't see you—

Valborg. But I can see what you are after. How dare you presume to think of persecuting me with your flowers and your—your red hands? (*He puts his hands behind his back.*) How dare you make me a laughing-stock to every one in the house, and I suppose to every one in the town?

Sannæs. I—I—I—

Valborg. And what about me? Don't you think I deserve a little consideration? You will be turned out of the house before long, if you do not take care—! Now be quick and get away before the others come in. (SANNÆS *turns away, holding his hands in front of him, and goes out by the verandah to the right. At the same moment* TJÆLDE *is seen coming at the other end of the verandah, followed by* HAMAR *and* SIGNE.)

Tjælde. Yes, it is a fine horse.

Hamar. Fine? I don't believe there is its equal in the country.

Tjælde. I dare say. Did you notice that he hadn't turned a hair?

Hamar. What glorious lungs! And such a beauty, too—his head, his legs, his neck—! I never saw such a beauty!

Tjælde. Yes, he is a handsome beast. (*Looks out of the verandah at the yacht.*) Have you been out for a sail?

Hamar. I was sailing among the islands last night, and came back this morning with the fishing-boats—a delightful sail!

Tjælde. I wish I had time to do that.

Hamar. But surely it is only imagination on your part, to think that you never have time?

Tjælde. Oh, well, perhaps I have time but not inclination.

Signe. And how do things stand where you have been?

Tjælde. Badly.

Valborg (*coming forward*). Welcome home, father!

Tjælde. Thank you, dear!

Hamar. Is it not possible to save anything?

Tjælde. Not at present; that is why I took the horse.

Hamar. Then the bay horse is the only thing you get out of the smash?

Tjælde. Do you know that I might say that horse has cost me three or four thousand pounds?

Hamar. Well, that is its only defect, anyway! Still, if the worst comes to the worst, and you can afford it—the horse is priceless! (TJÆLDE *turns away, puts down his hat and coat and takes off his gloves.*)

Signe. It is beautiful to see your enthusiasm when you talk about horses. I rather think it is the only enthusiasm you have.

Hamar. Yes, if I were not a cavalry officer I should like to be a horse!

Signe. Thank you! And what should I be?

Valborg. "Oh, were I but the saddle on thy back! Oh, were I but the whip about thy loins!"

Hamar. "Oh, were I but the flowers in thy—." No, "hand" doesn't rhyme!

Tjælde (*coming forward, meets* MRS. TJÆLDE, *who has come in from the right.*) Well, my dear, how are you?

Mrs. Tjælde. Oh, I find it more and more difficult to get about.

Tjælde. There is always something the matter with you, my dear! Can I have something to eat?

Mrs. Tjælde. Yes, it has been standing waiting for you. Here it comes. (*A maid brings in a tray which she lays on the table.*)

Tjælde. Good!

Mrs. Tjælde. Will you have a cup of tea?

Tjælde. No, thank you.

Mrs. Tjælde (*sitting down beside him and pouring him out a glass of wine*). And how have things gone with the Möllers?

Tjælde. Badly. I told you so already.

Mrs. Tjælde. I didn't hear you.

Valborg. I had a letter to-day from Nanna Möller. She

tells me all about it—how none of the family knew anything about it till the officers of the courts came.

Tjælde. Yes, there must have been a dreadful scene.

Mrs. Tjælde. Did he tell you anything about it?

Tjælde (as he eats). I didn't speak to him.

Mrs. Tjælde. My dear! Why, you are old friends!

Tjælde. Bah! Old friends! He sat looking as if he had taken leave of his senses. Besides, I have had enough of that family. I didn't go there to hear them talk about their troubles.

Signe. I suppose it was all very sad?

Tjælde (still eating). Shocking!

Mrs. Tjælde. What will they have to live on?

Tjælde. What is allowed them by their creditors, of course.

Signe. But all the things they had?

Tjælde. Sold.

Signe. All those pretty things—their furniture, their carriages, their—?

Tjælde. All sold.

Hamar. And his watch? It is the most beautiful watch I have ever seen—next to yours.

Tjælde. It had to go, of course, being jewellery. Give me some wine; I am hot and thirsty.

Signe. Poor things!

Mrs. Tjælde. Where are they going to live now?

Tjælde. In the house of one of the skippers of what was their fleet. Two small rooms and a kitchen.

Signe. Two small rooms and a kitchen! (*A pause.*)

Mrs. Tjælde. What do they intend to do?

Tjælde. There was a subscription started to enable Mrs. Möller to get the job of catering for the Club.

Mrs. Tjælde. Is the poor woman going to have more cooking to do!

Signe. Did they send no messages to us?

Tjælde. Of course they did ; but I didn't pay any attention to them.

Hamar (who has been standing on the verandah). But Möller—what did he say? What did he do?

Tjælde. I don't know, I tell you.

Valborg (who has been walking up and down the room during the preceding conversation). He has said and done quite enough already.

Tjælde (who has at last finished eating and drinking, is struck by her words). What do you mean by that, Valborg?

Valborg. That if I were his daughter I would never forgive him.

Mrs. Tjælde. My dear Valborg, don't say such things!

Valborg. I mean it! A man who would bring such shame and misery upon his family does not deserve any mercy from them.

Mrs. Tjælde. We are all in need of mercy.

Valborg. In one sense, yes. But what I mean is that I could never give him my respect or my affection again. He would have wronged me too cruelly.

Tjælde (getting up). Wronged you?

Mrs. Tjælde. Have you finished already, dear?

Tjælde. Yes.

Mrs. Tjælde. No more wine?

Tjælde. I said I had finished. Wronged you? How?

Valborg. Well, I cannot imagine how one could be more cruelly wronged than to be allowed to assume a position that was nothing but a lie, to live up to means that had no real existence but were merely a sham—one's clothes a lie, one's very existence a lie! Suppose I were the sort of girl that found a certain delight in making use of her position as a rich man's daughter—in using it to the fullest possible extent; well, when I discovered that all that my father had given me was stolen—that all he had made me believe in was a lie—I am sure that then my anger and my shame would be beyond all bounds!

Mrs. Tjælde. My child, you have never been tried. You don't know how such things may happen. You don't really know what you are saying!

Hamar. Well it might do Möller good if he heard what she says!

Valborg. He has heard it. His daughter said that to him.

Mrs. Tjælde. His own daughter! Child, child, is that what you write to each other about? God forgive you both!

Valborg. Oh, He will forgive us, because we speak the truth.

Mrs. Tjælde. Child, child!

Tjælde. You evidently don't understand what business is—success one day and failure the next.

Valborg. No one will ever persuade me that business is a lottery.

Tjælde. No, a sound business is not.

Valborg. Exactly. It is the unsound sort that I condemn.

Tjælde. Still, even the soundest have their anxious moments.

Valborg. If the anxious moments really foreshadow a crisis, no man of honour would keep his family or his creditors in ignorance of the fact. My God, how Mr. Möller has deceived his!

Signe. Valborg is always talking about business!

Valborg. Yes, it has had an attraction for me ever since I was a child. I am not ashamed of that.

Signe. You think you know all about it, anyway.

Valborg. Oh, no; but you can easily get to know a little about anything you are fond of.

Hamar. And one would need no great knowledge of business to condemn the way Möller went on. It was obvious to every one. And the way his family went on, too! Who went the pace as much as the Möllers? Think of his daughter's toilettes!

Valborg. His daughter is my best friend. I don't want to hear her abused.

Hamar. Your Highness will admit that it is possible to be the daughter of a *very* rich man without being as proud and as vain as—as the lady I am not allowed to mention!

Valborg. Nanna is neither proud nor vain. She is absolutely genuine. She had the aptitude for being exactly what she thought she was—a rich man's daughter.

Hamar. Hás she the " aptitude " for being a bankrupt's daughter now?

Valborg. Certainly. She has sold all her trinkets, her dresses—every single thing she had. What she wears, she has either paid for herself or obtained by promising future payment.

Hamar. May I ask if she kept her stockings?

Valborg. She sent everything to a sale.

Hamar. If I had known that I would certainly have attended it!

Valborg. Yes, I daresay there was plenty to make fun of, and plenty of idle loafers, too, who were not ashamed to do so.

Mrs. Tjælde. Children, children!

Hamar. May I ask if Miss Nanna sent her own idleness to the sale with her other effects?—because I have never known any one with a finer supply of it!

Valborg. She never thought she would need to work.

Tjælde (coming forward to VALBORG). To take up the thread of what we were saying: you don't understand what a business-man's hope is from one day to the other—always a renewed hope. That fact does not make him a swindler. He may be unduly sanguine, perhaps—a poet, if you like, who lives in a world of dreams—or he may be a real genius, who sees land ahead when no one else suspects it.

Valborg. I don't think I misunderstand the real state

of affairs. But perhaps you do, father. Because is not what you call hope, poetry, genius, merely speculating with what belongs to others, when a man knows that he owes more than he has got?

Tjælde. It may be very difficult to be certain even whether he does that or not.

Valborg. Really? I should have thought his books would tell him—

Tjælde. About his assets and his liabilities, certainly. But values are fluctuating things; and he may always have in hand some venture which, though it cannot be specified, may alter the whole situation.

Valborg. If he undeniably owes more than he possesses, any venture he undertakes must be a speculation with other people's money.

Tjælde. Well—perhaps that is so; but that does not mean that he steals the money—he only uses it in trust for them.

Valborg. Entrusted to him on the false supposition that he is solvent.

Tjælde. But possibly that money may save the whole situation.

Valborg. That does not alter the fact that he has got the use of it by a lie.

Tjælde. You use very harsh terms. (MRS. TJÆLDE *has once or twice been making signs to* VALBORG, *which the latter sees but pays no attention to.*)

Valborg. In that case the lie consists in the concealment.

Tjælde. But what do you want him to do? To lay all his cards on the table, and so ruin both himself and the others?

Valborg. Yes, he ought to take every one concerned into his confidence.

Tjælde. Bah! In that case we should see a thousand failures every year, and fortunes lost one after the other everywhere! No, you have a level head, Valborg, but

your ideas are narrow. Look here, where are the newspapers? (SIGNE, *who has been talking confidentially to*
HAMAR *on the verandah, comes forward.*)

Signe. I took them down to your office. I did not
know you meant to stay in here.

Tjælde. Oh, bother the office! Please fetch them for
me. (SIGNE *goes out, followed by Hamar.*)

Mrs. Tjælde (*in an undertone to* VALBORG). Why will
you never listen to your mother, Valborg? (VALBORG
*goes out to the verandah; leans on the edge of it, with her head
on her hands, and looks out.*)

Tjælde. I think I will change my coat. Oh no, I will
wait till dinner-time.

Mrs. Tjælde. Dinner! And here I am still sitting here!

Tjælde. Are we expecting any one?

Mrs. Tjælde. Yes, have you forgotten?

Tjælde. Of course, yes.

Mrs. Tjælde (*going out*). What on earth am I to order?

> (TJÆLDE *comes forward as soon as he is alone, sits
> down on a chair with a weary, harassed expression,
> and buries his face in his hands with a sigh.* SIGNE
> *and* HAMAR *come back, she carrying some news-
> papers.* HAMAR *is going out to the verandah
> again, but* SIGNE *pulls him back.*)

Signe. Here you are, father. Here are—

Tjælde. What? Who?

Signe (*astonished*). The newspapers.

Tjælde. Ah, yes. Give them to me. (*Opens them
hurriedly. They are mostly foreign papers, in which he
scans the money articles one after another.*)

Signe (*after a whispered conversation with* HAMAR).
Father!

Tjælde (*without looking up from the papers*). Well?
(*To himself, gloomily.*) Down again, always down!

Signe. Hamar and I want so much to go into town
again to Aunt Ulla's.

Tjælde. But you know you were there only a fortnight ago. I received your bills yesterday. Have you seen them?

Signe. No need for that, father, if *you* have seen them! Why do you sigh?

Tjælde. Oh—because I see that stocks keep falling.

Signe. Pooh! Why should you bother about that? Now you are sighing again. I am sure you know how horrid it is for those you love not to have what they want. You won't be so unkind to us, father?

Tjælde. No, my child, it can't be done.

Signe. Why?

Tjælde. Because—because—well, because now that it is summer time so many people will be coming here whom we shall have to entertain.

Signe. But entertaining people is the most tiresome thing I know, and Hamar agrees with me.

Tjælde. Don't you think I have to do tiresome things sometimes, my girl?

Signe. Father dear, why are you talking so solemnly and ceremoniously? It sounds quite funny from you!

Tjælde. Seriously, my child, it is by no means an unimportant matter for a big business house like ours, with such a wide-spread connection, that people coming here from all quarters should find themselves hospitably received. You might do that much for me.

Signe. Hamar and I will never have a moment alone at that rate.

Tjælde. I think you mostly squabble when you are alone.

Signe. Squabble? That is a very ugly word, father.

Tjælde. Besides, you would be no more alone if you were in town.

Signe. Oh, but it is quite different there!

Tjælde. So I should think—from the way you throw your money about!

Signe (laughing). Throw our money about! What else have we to do? Isn't that what we are for? Daddy, listen—dear old dad—

Tjælde. No, dear—no.

Signe. You have never been so horrid to me before.

Hamar (who has been making signs to her to stop, whispers). Can't you be quiet! Don't you see he is put out about something?

Signe (whispering). Well, you might have backed me up a little.

Hamar (as before). No, I am a bit wiser than you.

Signe (as before). You have been so odd lately. I am sure I don't know what you want?

Hamar (as before). Oh, well, it doesn't matter now— because I am going to town alone.

Signe (as before). What are you going to do?

Hamar (going). I am going to town alone. I am sick of this!

Signe (following him). Just you try! (*Both go out by the verandah, to the right.* TJÆLDE *lets the newspapers fall out of his hands with a heavy sigh.*)

Valborg (looking in from the verandah). Father! (TJÆLDE *starts.*) There goes Mr. Berent, the lawyer from Christiania.

Tjælde (getting up). Berent? Where? On the wharf?

Valborg. Yes. (*Comes back into the room.* TJÆLDE *looks out of the window.*) The reason I told you was because I saw him yesterday at the timber-yard, and a little while before that, at the brewery and at the works.

Tjælde (to himself). What can that mean? (*Aloud.*) Oh, I know he is very fond of making little trips to all sorts of places in the summer. This year he has come here— and no doubt he likes to see the chief industries of the place. There is not much else here to see! But are you sure it is he? I think—

Valborg (looking out). Yes, it is he. Look now, you know his walk—

Tjælde. —and his trick of crossing his feet—yes, it is he. It looks as if he were coming here.

Valborg. No, he has turned away.

Tjælde. All the better! (*To himself, thoughtfully.*) Could it possibly mean—? (SANNÆS *comes in from the right.*)

Sannæs. Am I disturbing you, sir?

Tjælde. Is that you, Sannæs? (SANNÆS, *as he comes forward, sees* VALBORG *standing by the farther window. He appears frightened and hides his hands quickly behind his back.*) What do you want? (VALBORG *looks at* SANNÆS, *then goes on to the verandah and out to the right.*) What is it, man? What the deuce are you standing there for?

Sannæs (bringing his hands from behind his back as soon as VALBORG *has passed him, and looking after her.*) I didn't like to ask you, before Miss Valborg, whether you are coming down to your office to-day or not.

Tjælde. Have you gone mad? Why on earth shouldn't you ask me that before Miss Valborg?

Sannæs. I mean that—if not—I should like to speak to you here, if it is convenient.

Tjælde. Look here, Sannæs, you ought to try and get rid of your shyness; it doesn't suit a business man. A business man should be smart and active, and not let his wits go wool-gathering because he finds himself in the same room with a woman. I have often noticed it in you. —Now, what is it? Out with it!

Sannæs. You are not coming to the office this morning, sir?

Tjælde. No, there is no post goes out before this evening.

Sannæs. No. But there are some bills of exchange—

Tjælde. Bills? No.

Sannæs. Yes, sir—that fourth one of Möller's that was protested, and the big English one.

Tjælde (angrily). Have they not been met yet? What does this mean?

Sannæs. The manager of the bank wanted to see you first, sir!

Tjælde. Have you gone crazy—? *(Collects himself.)* There must be some misunderstanding, Sannæs.

Sannæs. That is what I thought; so I spoke about it to the chief clerk, and to Mr. Holst as well.

Tjælde. And Mr. Holst said—?

Sannæs. The same thing.

Tjælde (walking up and down). I will go and see him—or rather, I *won't* go and see him; because this is evidently something that—. We have some days' grace yet, haven't we?

Sannæs. Yes, sir.

Tjælde. And still no telegram from Mr. Lind?

Sannæs. No, sir.

Tjælde (to himself). I can't understand it. *(Aloud.)* We will negotiate this matter direct with Christiania, Sannæs. That is what we will do—and leave these little local banks alone in future. That will do, Sannæs! *(Makes a gesture of dismissal. Then says to himself :)* That damned Möller! It has made them all suspicious! *(Turns round and sees* SANNÆS *still there.)* What are you waiting for?

Sannæs. It is settling day—and I have no money in the safe.

Tjælde. No money in the safe! A big business like this, and nothing in the safe on settling day! What kind of management is that, I should like to know? Must I teach you the A B C of business over and over again? One can never take a half day off, or hand over the control of the tiniest part of the business—! I have no one, absolutely no one, that I can rely on! How have you let things get into such a state?

Sannæs. Well, there was a third bill, which expired to-day—Holm and Co., for £400. I had relied upon the bank, unfortunately—so there was nothing for it but to empty the safe—here and at the brewery as well.

Tjælde (walking about restlessly). Hm—hm—hm!— Now, who can have put that into Holst's head?—Very well, that will do. (*Dismisses* SANNÆS, *who goes out but comes back immediately.*)

Sannæs (whispering). Here is Mr. Berent!

Tjælde (surprised). Coming here?

Sannæs. He is just coming up the steps! (*Goes out by the further door on the right.*)

Tjælde (calls after him in a whisper). Send up some wine and cakes!—It is just as I suspected! (*Catches sight of himself in a mirror.*) Good Lord, how bad I look! (*Turns away painfully from the mirror ; looks in it again, forces a smile to his face, and so, smiling, goes towards the verandah, where* BERENT *is seen coming in slowly from the left.*)

Tjælde (greeting BERENT *politely but with reserve).* I feel honoured at receiving a visit from so distinguished a man.

Berent. Mr. Tjælde, I believe?

Tjælde. At your service! My eldest daughter has just been telling me that she had seen you walking about my property.

Berent. Yes; an extensive property—and an extensive business.

Tjælde. Too extensive, Mr. Berent. Too many-sided. But one thing has led to another. Pray sit down.

Berent. Thank you; it is very warm to-day. (*A maid brings in cakes and wine, and puts them on the table.*)

Tjælde. Let me give you a glass of wine?

Berent. No, thank you.

Tjælde. Or something to eat?

Berent. Nothing, thank you.

Tjælde (taking out his cigar-case). May I offer you a cigar? I can answer for their quality.

Berent. I am very fond of a good cigar. But for the moment I will not take anything, thank you! (*A pause.* TJÆLDE *takes a seat.*)

Tjælde (in a quiet, confidential voice). Have you been long here, Mr. Berent?

Berent. Only a day or two. You have been away, have you not?

Tjælde. Yes—that unhappy affair of Mr. Möller's. A meeting of creditors after the sale.

Berent. Times are hard just now.

Tjælde. Extraordinarily so!

Berent. Do you think that Möller's failure will bring down any more firms with it—besides those we know of already, I mean?

Tjælde. I don't think so. His—his misfortune was an exceptional case in every respect.

Berent. It has made the banks a little nervous, I hear.

Tjælde. I dare say.

Berent. Of course you know the state of affairs here better than any one.

Tjælde (with a smile). I am very much indebted to you for your flattering confidence in me.

Berent. I suppose all this might have a bad effect upon the export trade of this part of the country?

Tjælde. Yes—it is really hard to tell; but the important thing certainly is to keep every one on their legs.

Berent. That is your opinion?

Tjælde. Undoubtedly.

Berent. As a general rule a crisis of this sort shows up the unsound elements in a commercial community.

Tjælde (with a smile). And for that reason this crisis should be allowed to take its natural course, you mean?

Berent. That is my meaning.

Tjælde. Hm!—In some places it is possible that the dividing line between the sound firms and the unsound may not be very distinct.

Berent. Can there really be any danger of such a thing here?

Tjælde. Well—you are expecting too much of my knowledge of affairs; but I should be inclined to think that there may. (*A pause.*)

Berent. I have been instructed by the banks to prepare an opinion upon the situation—a fact which I have, so far, only confided to *you.*

Tjælde. I am much obliged.

Berent. The smaller local banks here have combined, and are acting in concert.

Tjælde. Indeed? (*A pause.*) I suppose you have seen Mr. Holst, then?

Berent. Of course. (*A pause.*) If we are to assist the sound firms and leave the others to their fate, the best way will certainly be for all alike to disclose their actual position.

Tjælde. Is that Mr. Holst's opinion too?

Berent. It is. (*A pause.*) I have advised him for the present—at all events till we have all the balance-sheets— to say " no " to every request for an advance, without exception.

Tjælde. (*with a look of relief*). I understand!

Berent. Only a temporary measure, of course—

Tjælde. Quite so!

Berent. —but one that must apply to every one impartially.

Tjælde. Admirable!

Berent. Not to treat every one alike would be to run the danger of throwing premature suspicion on individuals.

Tjælde. I quite agree.

Berent. I am delighted to hear it. Then you will not misunderstand me if I ask you also to prepare a balance-sheet which shall show the actual position of your firm.

Tjælde. With the greatest pleasure, if by doing so I can assist the general welfare.

Berent. I assure you, you can. It is by such means that public confidence is strengthened.

Tjælde. When do you want the balance-sheet? Of course, it can only be a summary one.

Berent. Naturally. I will give myself the pleasure of calling for it.

Tjælde. By no means. I can let you have it at once, if you like. I am in the habit of frequently drawing up summary balance-sheets of that kind—as prices rise and fall, you know.

Berent. Indeed? (*Smiles.*) You know, of course, what they say of swindlers—that they draw up three balance-sheets every day, and all different! But you are teaching me, apparently—

Tjælde (*laughing*). —that others too, may have that bad habit!—though I haven't actually got as far as three a day!

Berent. Of course I was only joking. (*Gets up.*)

Tjælde (*getting up*). Of course. I will send it to the hotel in an hour's time; for I suppose you are staying in our only so-called hotel! Would you not care, for the rest of your stay, to move your things over here and make yourself at home in a couple of empty spare rooms that I have?

Berent. Thank you, but the length of my stay is so uncertain; and the state of my health imposes habits upon me which are embarrassing to every one, and to myself most of all, when I am among strangers.

Tjælde. But at all events I hope you will dine with us to-day? I expect one or two friends. And perhaps a short sail afterwards; it is very pretty among the islands here.

Berent. Thank you, but my health won't allow me such dissipations.

Tjælde. Ha, ha!—Well, if I can be of any further service to you—?

Berent. I should be glad to have a talk with you before I leave, preferably as soon as possible.

Tjælde (somewhat surprised). You mean, after you have received all the balance-sheets?

Berent. I have already managed to get most of them quietly, through Mr. Holst.

Tjælde (more surprised). Oh—so you mean to-day—?

Berent. Would five o'clock suit you?

Tjælde. I am quite at your disposal! I will give myself the pleasure of calling upon you at five.

Berent. No, I will come here at five o'clock. (*Bows, and turns to go.*)

Tjælde (following him). But you are the invalid—the older man—and a distinguished man—

Berent. But you are at home here. Good-bye!

Tjælde. Let me thank you for the honour you have done me by calling upon me!

Berent. Please don't bother to see me out.

Tjælde. Allow me to escort you?

Berent. I can find the way quite well, thank you.

Tjælde. No doubt, no doubt—but I should feel it an honour!

Berent. As you please! (*As they are about to go down the verandah steps they are met by* SIGNE *and* HAMAR, *who are coming up arm in arm. Each couple draws aside to make room for the other.*)

Tjælde. Let me introduce—no, I am sure Mr. Berent needs no introduction. This is my youngest daughter—and her fiancé, Lieutenant Hamar.

Berent. I thought your regiment was at the manœuvres, Lieutenant?

Hamar. I have got furlough—

Berent. On account of urgent business, no doubt! Good day!

Tjælde. Ha, ha, ha! (*He and* BERENT *go down the steps.*)

Hamar. Insolent fellow! But he is like that to every one.

Signe. Not to my father, as far as I could see.

Hamar. Your father is insolent too.

Signe. You shan't say such things of father!

Hamar. What else do you call it, to laugh at such impertinence as Berent's.

Signe. I call it good spirits! (*Sits down in a rocking-chair and begins rocking herself.*)

Hamar. Oh, then, so you—. You are not very agreeable to-day.

Signe (*still rocking herself*). No; do you know, sometimes I get so bored with you.

Hamar. Yet you won't let me go away?

Signe. Because I should be still worse bored without you.

Hamar. Let me tell you this, I am not going to put up much longer with the way I am treated here!

Signe. Very well. (*Takes off her engagement ring and holds it between her finger and her thumb, as she rocks herself and hums a tune.*)

Hamar. Oh, I don't say anything about *you ;* but look at Valborg! Look at your father! He hasn't even as much as offered me a mount on his new horse!

Signe. He has had something else to think about— possibly something even more important than that. (*Goes on humming.*)

Hamar. Oh, do be nice, Signe! You must admit that my feelings are very natural. Indeed, to speak quite candidly—because I know I can say anything to you— it seems to me that, as I am to be his son-in-law and am in a cavalry regiment, and as he has no sons of his own,

I might almost expect that—that he would make me a present of the horse.

Signe. Ha, ha, ha!

Hamar. Does it seem so unreasonable to you?

Signe. Ha, ha, ha!

Hamar. Why do you laugh at what I say, Signe? It seems to me that it would reflect very well on your family if, when my friends admired my horse, I could say: " My father-in-law made me a present of it." Because, you know, there isn't a finer horse in the whole of Norway.

Signe. And that is the reason why you should have it? Ha, ha, ha!

Hamar. I won't stand it!

Signe. The peerless lieutenant on the peerless horse! Ha, ha, ha!

Hamar. Signe, be quiet!

Signe. You are so funny! (*Begins to hum again.*)

Hamar. Listen, Signe! No one has so much influence with your father as you.—Oh, do listen! Can't you talk seriously for a moment?

Signe. I should like to! (*Goes on humming.*)

Hamar. My idea was that, if that horse were mine, I would stay here for the summer and break it in thoroughly. (SIGNE *stops rocking herself and humming.* HAMAR *comes up to her chair and leans over her.*) In that case I would not go back till the autumn, and then you could come with the horse and me into town. Wouldn't that be delightful?

Signe (*after looking at him for a moment*). Oh, yes, my dear, you always have such delightful ideas!

Hamar. Don't I! But the whole thing depends, of course, on whether you can get the horse from your father. Will you try, darling?

Signe. And then you would stay here all the summer?

Hamar. All the summer!

Signe. So as to break in the horse.

Hamar. Just to break in the horse!

Signe. And I would go with you into town in the autumn—that was what you said, wasn't it?

Hamar. Yes; wouldn't it be jolly?

Signe. Shall you take the bay horse to stay with your Aunt Ulla too?

Hamar (laughing). What?

Signe. Well, you have spent your furlough here simply for the sake of that horse—I know that well enough—and you propose to stay here, just to break it in—and then you propose that the horse and I should go to your aunt's—

Hamar. But, Signe, what do you—?

Signe (beginning to rock herself furiously). Ugh! Go away!

Hamar. Jealous of a horse! Ha, ha, ha!

Signe. Go away to the stables.

Hamar. Is that meant for a punishment? Because it would be more amusing there than it is here.

Signe (throwing down her ring). There! Let your horse wear that!

Hamar. Every time you throw down that ring—

Signe. Oh, you have said that so often! I am tired of that too! (*Turns her chair round so as to turn her back on him.*)

Hamar. You are such a spoilt child that it would be absurd to take everything you say seriously—

Signe. I am sick of that too, I tell you—for the hundred and twentieth time! Go away!

Hamar. But can't you see how ridiculous it is of you to be jealous of a horse? Have you ever heard of any one else behaving like that?

Signe (jumping up). Oh, you make me want to shout and scream! I feel so ashamed of you! (*Stamps her foot.*) I despise you!

Hamar (laughing). And all on account of the horse?

Signe. No, on your own account—yours, yours! I feel so miserable sometimes, I should like to throw myself down on the floor and cry—or run away and never come back! Can't you let me alone! Can't you go away!

Hamar. Yes—and I have not picked up the ring this time, either!

Signe. Oh, do go!—go, go, go! (*Bursts out crying and sits down.*)

Hamar. All right!—I see the steamer in the distance; I shall go home at once.

Signe. Oh, you know as well as I do that that steamer goes the other way! Oh! (*Cries. The masts and funnel of a steamer come into sight, and a trail of smoke passes over the sky.* TJÆLDE'S *voice is heard outside, calling:* "Hurry up! Take the lieutenant's boat; it is ready!" SIGNE *jumps up.*)

Hamar. They are going to fetch some one from the steamer! (TJÆLDE'S *voice is heard again:* "You get the boat out! He is coming here!" HAMAR *runs to pick up the ring and comes back hurriedly to* SIGNE.) Signe!

Signe. No, I won't!

Hamar. Signe, dear! What does this mean? What is it that I have done?

Signe. I don't know, but I am wretchedly unhappy! (*Bursts into tears.*)

Hamar. But you know that in the end I always do what you want? What more can you wish than that?

Signe. I can't help it, I wish I were dead! It is always the same thing! (*In tears again.*)

Hamar. But, Signe—you who have told me hundreds of times that you loved me!

Signe. And so I do. But sometimes our engagement seems horrible!—No, don't come near me!

Hamar. Signe! (TJÆLDE'S *voice is heard outside:* "Of course, put your best coat on!" *He calls louder:* "Sannæs!")

An answering voice is heard in the distance. TJÆLDE
continues : "Don't forget your gloves!") Dry your eyes,
Signe! Don't let him see you have been crying. (*He
tries to give her the ring, but she turns away, wiping her eyes.*
TJÆLDE *comes up the steps on to the verandah.*)

Tjælde. Oh, there you are! That's right.   Mr. Lind
is arriving by this steamer—I had a telegram from him
just now. (*Calls out over the verandah.*)   Come along with
those flags!   And get this boat out of the way and un-
step her mast!   She is moored up tight! (HAMAR *runs
to help him.*)   Yes, you cast her off! (HAMAR *does so,
and the boat is hauled away to the right.* TJÆLDE *comes
forward into the room.*)   Signe! (*Looks at her.*)   What?
Squabbling again?

Signe. Father!

Tjælde. Well, this is no time for tomfoolery of that
sort!   You must all do the honours of the house to-day.
Tell Valborg—

Signe. Tell her yourself, please!   You know Valborg
only does just what she likes.

Tjælde. Don't talk such rubbish!   This is an important
moment—and you will all do as *I* say!   Tell Valborg
that she is to make herself look nice and come to me here.
And you do the same. (*She goes.*)   Signe!

Signe (*stopping*). Yes?

Tjælde. We must ask five or six more people to dinner.
You must send word to Mr. Finne that we shall dine
punctually at three o'clock, instead of four.   Mr. Lind
has to go away again by the next boat, at five o'clock.
Do you understand?

Signe. But has mother enough in the house for so
many?

Tjælde. It is not a mere question of there being enough
—it must be a very good dinner.   I expect my larder to
be kept thoroughly well stocked all through the summer.
How often am I to repeat that?

I 696

Signe (trying to repress her tears). But mother is feeling so ill to-day—

Tjælde. Oh! don't begin about that everlasting " feeling ill." There is no time to-day to feel ill. Now, be quick! (SIGNE *goes out by the farther door.* TJÆLDE *turns to* HAMAR.) Get a pen and ink and some paper! We must draw up a list of guests, at once!

Hamar (looking about). There is none here.

Tjælde (impatiently). Fetch some, then! (HAMAR *goes into the next room.* TJÆLDE, *after a long sigh of relief, reads a telegram he has in his hand. His hand trembles as he reads it slowly, repeating some passages twice.*) " Letter received just as starting. Before taking charge of affairs, must have interview. Coming to-day earliest boat, return five o'clock. Have clear statement ready. Lind." I can hardly read it—but it is true! Yes, if I can only work this properly all doors will be open to me! (*To* HAMAR, *who has come back.*) Ah, there you are! It would take too long to write invitations. We will just draw up a list of names and one of my clerks shall run round to them all. Now then! (*Dictates.*) The Vicar—Oh, by the way, what is the champagne like?

Hamar. Do you mean the new lot?

Tjælde. Yes.

Hamar. The Vicar praised it highly.

Tjælde. Good. Well, then—

Hamar (writing). The Vicar.

Tjælde. Mr. Ring.

Hamar. Mr. Ring.

Tjælde. And—and—

Hamar. Mr. Holst?

Tjælde. No, not Holst. (HAMAR *appears greatly astonished.* TJÆLDE *says to himself :*) I can show him now that I have no need of him! (*Suddenly, to* HAMAR.) Mr. Holm. (*To himself.*) Holst's enemy!

Hamar. Mr. Holm.

Tjælde (to himself). Although Holm is a boor. Still, it will annoy Holst. *(Aloud.)* The Chief Constable.

Hamar. The Chief—

Tjælde. No, strike out the Chief Constable.

Hamar. Chief Constable struck out.

Tjælde. Have we got the Vicar down ?

Hamar. He is number one on the list.

Tjælde. Of course, yes.

Hamar. What about the Magistrate?

Tjælde. No, he lives too far off. Besides, unless he is the guest of honour and can talk shop all the time—. No! But, let me see. Mr. Knutzon—Knutzon with a " z."

Hamar. Knutzon with a " z."

Tjælde. Oh!—and— Knudsen, too! Knudsen with an " s."

Hamar. Knudsen with an " s."

Tjælde. How many have we got?

Hamar. The Vicar, Ring, Holm, the Chief—oh, no, the Chief Constable was struck out; Knutzon with a " z," Knudsen with an " s "—that is one, two, three, four, five, six.

Tjælde. And Finne, you, and I make nine. We must have twelve.

Hamar. What about some ladies?

Tjælde. No; ladies are out of place at a business dinner. They may do the honours afterwards, when we have got to the cigarette stage. But whom shall we—?

Hamar. That new lawyer fellow? He's a smart chap— I can't remember his name?

Tjælde. No, he always wants to be speechifying wherever he goes.—Ah, Mr. Pram, the custom-house officer!

Hamar. That man? He always gets drunk!

Tjælde. Yes, but he doesn't get noisy with it. He does no harm—quite the contrary! Yes, put down Pram.

Hamar. Mr. Pram.

Tjælde. It is a very difficult task, in such a small town, when you want to get a good set of people together. Ah! —Falbe! I forgot him. He is very neat, and has no opinions.

Hamar. Neat in his dress, do you mean?

Tjælde. Yes, in his dress too—but I meant it more generally. Now, for the twelfth—Morten Schultz?

Hamar. Morten Schultz! (*Gets up.*) No, really, I must take the liberty of protesting against him! Do you know what he did the last time he was here, when you had a lot of guests? In the middle of dinner he took out his false teeth and began showing them to his neighbours. He wanted to have them passed round the table! If that is your idea of a good set of people—well!

Tjælde. Yes, he is rather a rough diamond. But he is the richest man about here.

Hamar (*who has sat down again*). Well in that case he really ought to afford himself a new wig! It is far from pleasant to sit beside him, I can assure you!

Tjælde. Yes, I know he is a pig; but he is wide awake, and this would flatter him! You see, my young friend, when a man is very rich you must make certain allowances for him.

Hamar. I can't understand what *you* can hope to get out of him.

Tjælde. Hm, hm!—No, well, perhaps we had better leave him out?

Hamar. Certainly!

Tjælde (*to himself*). Although Lind would understand the significance of Morten Schultz's being here—

Hamar. And the things he says! Ladies have to leave the room!

Tjælde. Yes, you are right. (*Mutters to himself.*) And, after all, I don't need him any longer. (*Aloud.*) But what about our twelfth, then? Let me see—.

Hamar. Christopher Hansen?

Tjælde. Oh, Lord! no. We should have to talk politics. No, let me see—. Yes, I think I might risk it! Hm, hm—yes, just the man! Jakobsen, the brewery manager.

Hamar. Jakobsen?

Tjælde. Hm, hm! Jakobsen will do very well. I know Jakobsen.

Hamar. Oh, he is a very good fellow—we all know that, but in polite society—!

Tjælde. Hm, hm, hm!—Put him down!

Hamar (*writing*). Jakobsen. There, then! (*Gets up.*)

Tjælde. Now let Skogstad go with the list! Remember, three o'clock punctually! And be quick! (*Calls after* HAMAR, *who is going out.*) And come back when you have given him the list! There may be something more to do! (HAMAR *goes out by the nearer door.* TJÆLDE *takes a letter out of his pocket.*) Ah, of course! Shall I send the balance-sheet to Berent? I am independent of the banks now. Still, I am not out of the wood yet. And, anyway, it is a very pretty balance-sheet! Holst would be sure to see it, and that might be useful—and it might annoy him, too. Besides, if I don't send it, they will think that my promising to send it had put me into a hole, and that Lind had helped me out of it. I risk least by sending it. (HAMAR *comes back.*) Look here, let him take this letter, too. It is for Mr. Berent, at the Hotel Victoria.

Hamar. Is it an invitation? Because, if it is, we shall be thirteen at table.

Tjælde. It is not an invitation. Be quick, before he goes. (HAMAR *goes out again.*) Oh, if only it succeeds! Lind is the sort of man one can persuade—and I must, I must persuade him! (*Looks at his watch.*) I have four whole hours to do it in. I have never felt so hopeful —not for a long time. (*Is lost in thought ; then says quietly :*) After all, sometimes a crisis is a good thing—

like a big wave that carries one on!—They have all had
their suspicions aroused now, and are all ready to get into
a panic. (*Sighs.*) If only I could get safely out of my
difficulties without any one's suspecting it!—Oh, this
anxious fear, night and day!—all this mystery, these
shifts, these concealments, this farce I have to keep up!
I go about my business as if I were in a dream. (*Despairingly.*) This shall be the last time — my last performance of this sort! No more of it!—I only need a
helping hand now, and I have got it! But *have* I got it?—
that is the question. Oh! if only, after this, I could
know what it was to have a good night's sleep and to
wake in the morning free from anxiety!—to join them at
meals with an easy conscience!—come home in the evening
and feel that it was all done with! If only I had something to take my stand upon that I could call my own—
really and truly my own! I hardly dare to believe that
there is a chance—I have so often been disappointed!
(HAMAR *comes back.*)

Hamar. There—that's done!

Tjælde. Good Lord, what about a salute from our
cannon? We must give him a salute!

Hamar. We have powder.

Tjælde. Then send word up at once to Ole to see about
it! (*They hurry out. The curtain falls.*)

ACT II

Scene I

(Scene.—*The same room. The table, which has been drawn to one side, is covered with bottles of champagne and dishes of fruit.* Mrs. Tjælde *and* Signe, *with a man-servant and a maid, are busy preparing it. Through the door on the right a lively conversation can be heard, and occasional bursts of laughter.*)

Mrs. Tjælde (*in a tired voice*). Now I think it is all ready.

Signe. They are talking a long time over their dinner.

Mrs. Tjælde (*looking at her watch*). Yes, they will only have half an hour for their dessert, because Mr. Lind has to leave at five o'clock.

Signe. Ah, they have finished at last! Listen, they are getting up from the table. (*Amidst the loud noise of conversation the noise of chairs being pushed back is audible.*) Here they come!

Mrs. Tjælde. Yes; let us retreat. (*The maid goes out by the farther door;* Signe *helps* Mrs. Tjælde *out after her. The man-servant begins opening the champagne. The guests come in from the dining-room, headed by* Lind *escorted by* Tjælde, *whom he is assuring that the dinner was excellent, to which* Tjælde *replies that it is impossible to do much in a small country town. Both look at their watches, and observe that there is only half an hour left.* Tjælde *vainly endeavours to persuade* Lind *to stay longer. Close behind them come* Holm *and* Ring, *engaged in an animated dispute about timber prices, the former maintaining that they will fall still lower, the latter that they will rise speedily owing to the fall in the prices of coal and iron, a*

119

point of view which the former vigorously controverts.
Immediately behind them comes the VICAR, *escorted by*
HAMAR, *who is a little tipsy. The* VICAR *is assuring him*
that he has no objection to parishioners repudiating the
obligation to attend the services of their own priest, so long
as they are compelled to pay him for those services whether
they avail themselves of them or not ; because order, which is
an essential characteristic of the Heavenly Kingdom, must
be maintained. HAMAR *tries to get in a word or two about*
the bay horse, but without success. At the same time
KNUTZON *and* FALBE *are deep in a discussion about a*
dancer whom FALBE *has seen at Hamburg. He is main-*
taining that she can leap six feet into the air, which KNUTZON
ventures to doubt, but FALBE *says there is no doubt about it,*
and he knows because he has once sat at the same dinner-
table with her. FINNE, KNUDSEN, *and* JAKOBSEN *follow*
them. JAKOBSEN *is heard challenging any one to contradict*
him, while the others eagerly protest that he has entirely
misunderstood their meaning. He affirms stoutly that he
doesn't care a damn what they meant, but that his employer
is the greatest business man and the finest fellow in the
world, or at all events in Norway. PRAM *comes in by*
himself, wrapt in tipsy contemplation. They all talk at the
same time.)

Tjælde (rapping on a glass). Gentlemen! (*There is a*
sudden silence, except for the sound of the voices of FALBE
and JAKOBSEN, *who are hushed down by the others.*)
Gentlemen! I am sorry dinner has occupied such a long
time.

All (unanimously). No, no!

Tjælde. Our distinguished guest has, unfortunately,
to leave us in half an hour, so I should like to take the
opportunity of saying a few words. Gentlemen, we have
a prince among us to-day. I say a prince, because if it is
true that it is the financiers that rule the world—and it
is true, gentlemen—

Pram (who is standing well forward, supporting himself by the edge of the table, says solemnly :) Yes.

Tjælde. — then our friend here is a prince! There is not a single important undertaking that he has not initiated, or at any rate backed with his name.

Pram (lifting his glass). Mr. Lind, may I have the honour—?

Voices. Sh! Sh!

Tjælde. Yes, gentlemen, his name backs every enterprise. It would be impossible to carry one through that had not his backing.

Pram (solemnly). His backing.

Tjælde. Am I not right, then, in describing him as a prince?

Falbe (in a feeble voice). Yes.

Tjælde. Gentlemen, to-day his name is once more exercising its powerful, I might say its creative, influence upon circumstances. I may say that at this moment the country holds no truer benefactor than he.

Pram. Great man.

Tjælde. Let us drink his health! May prosperity attend him and his, and may his name be deathless in Norway! Mr. Lind!

All. Mr. Lind! Mr. Lind! (*They all drink his health effusively.*)

Tjælde (to HAMAR, whom he pulls forward somewhat roughly, as the others begin to help themselves to the dessert.) What has become of the salute?

Hamar (in consternation). Good Lord, yes! (*Rushes to the window, but comes back.*) I have no handkerchief. I must have laid it down in the dining-room.

Tjælde. Here is mine! (*Feels in his pocket for it.*) One cannot rely on you for the least thing. The salute will be too late now. It is disgraceful! (*HAMAR goes to the window and waves the handkerchief madly. At last the report of a cannon is heard. The guests are standing in a group, holding their dessert plates.*)

Holm. A little bit late!

Knutzon. Rather behind the moment—

Ring. A very important moment, however!

Holm. A very unexpected one, anyway!

Knutzon (jestingly). Allow me, amidst the cannon's roar, to introduce to you a man who has been led by the nose!

Ring. Oh, Tjælde knows what he is about!

Tjælde. Mr. Lind is kind enough to wish to propose a toast. (*They all compose themselves into respectful silence.*)

Lind. Our worthy host has proposed my health in most flattering terms. I would merely add this, that wealth is entrusted to those who have it precisely in order that they may support industry, genius, and great undertakings.

Pram (who has never changed his position). Nobly said.

Lind. I am only an administrator of a trust, and too often a weak and short-sighted one.

Pram. Beautiful.

Lind. But I shall not be mistaken if I say that Mr. Tjælde's many-sided activities, which we must all admire, rest upon a sound foundation; and of that fact no one, at the present moment, is better able to judge than I. (*The guests look at one another in surprise.*) Therefore I have no hesitation in saying that his activities are an honour to this town, to this district, to our whole country, and that therefore his genius and his energy deserve support. I propose the toast of " prosperity to the firm of Tjælde! "

All. Prosperity to the firm of Tjælde!

(HAMAR *signals again with the handkerchief, and a cannon shot is heard.*)

Tjælde. I thank you heartily, Mr. Lind! I am profoundly touched.

Lind. I said no more than I am convinced of, Mr. Tjælde!

Tjælde. Thank you! (*To* HAMAR.) What do you mean by signalling for a salute for the host?   Blockhead!

Hamar. You said there was to be a salute when a toast was proposed, didn't you?

Tjælde. Oh, you are a—!

Hamar (*to himself*). Well, if ever again I—!

Holm. Then it is an accomplished fact, I suppose?

Knutzon. Fait accompli ! That toast represents twenty thousand pounds, at least.

Ring. Yes, Tjælde knows what he is about! I have always said that! (FALBE *is seen drinking ceremoniously with* LIND. JAKOBSEN *comes forward, talking to* KNUDSEN.)

Jakobsen (*in a low voice*). There isn't a word of truth in what you say!

Knudsen. But, my dear Jakobsen, you misunderstand me!

Jakobsen (*louder*). Hang it, I know my people!

Knudsen. Don't talk so loud!

Jakobsen (*still louder*). What I say any one may hear!

Tjælde (*at the same moment*). The Vicar wishes to say a few words.

Knudsen (*to* JAKOBSEN). Hush! The Vicar wishes to say a few words.

Jakobsen. Have I got to hush because that damned—

Tjælde (*in a voice of authority*). The Vicar wishes to speak.

Jakobsen. I beg your pardon!

The Vicar (*in a feeble voice*). As the spiritual adviser of this household, I have the pleasing duty of invoking a blessing on the gifts that have been so richly showered upon our host and his friends.   May they be to their souls' present good and eternal welfare!

Pram. Amen.

The Vicar. I am going to ask you to drink the health of our host's dear children—those lovely girls whose welfare has been the object of my prayers ever since they were confirmed—ever since that memorable day when house-hold and religious duties began to walk side by side.

Pram. Ah, yes!

The Vicar. May they always in the future, as they have in the past, grow in the holy fear of God and in meekness and gratitude towards their parents!

All. Miss Valborg, Miss Signe!

Hamar (in a panic). Am I to signal?

Tjælde. Oh, go to—!

Hamar. Well, if ever again—!

Tjælde. Thank you very much, Mr. Vicar. Like you, I hope that the intimate relations between parent and child that exist here—

The Vicar. It has always been a pleasure to me to come into your most hospitable house.

Tjælde. May I have the honour of drinking a glass of wine with you? (*They drink to each other.*)

The Vicar. Excellent champagne, my dear sir!

Lind (to HOLM). It pains me to hear what you say. Is it possible that this town, which owes so much to Mr. Tjælde, repays him with such ingratitude?

Holm (in a low voice). One never can quite confidently rely on him.

Lind. Really? I have heard others sing his praises so loudly, you know.

Holm (as before). You misunderstand me. I mean his position—

Lind. His position? That must be merely envy! People are often so unjust towards those whose enterprise has lifted them above the heads of the crowd.

Holm. At any rate I assure you it was not from—

Lind (coldly). I don't doubt it. (*Walks away from him.*)

Jakobsen (with whom TJÆLDE *has just drunk).* Gentle-men!

Knutzon (to HOLM, *in passing).* Is that boor really going to be allowed to make a speech! (*Going up to* LIND.)

May I have the honour of drinking a glass of wine with you, Mr. Lind? (*Several of the guests begin to talk, ostentatiously indifferent to* JAKOBSEN *who is trying to begin his speech.*)

Jakobsen (*in a formidable voice*). Gentlemen! (*Silence ensues, and he continues in his usual voice.*) Permit a common man to say a word, too, on this festive occasion. I was a poor little boy when I entered Mr. Tjælde's employment; but he pulled me out of the gutter. (*Laughter.*) I am—what I am, gentlemen! And therefore if any here is qualified to talk about Mr. Tjælde, it is I; because I know him. I know he is a fine fellow.

Lind (*to* TJÆLDE). Children and drunken men—

Tjælde (*laughing*). —speak the truth!

Jakobsen. There are lots of people that will tell you one thing or another about him—and, of course, he may have his failings like all of us. But as I find myself in such fine company as this I am going to say that—that—devil take me if Mr. Tjælde isn't too good for the lot of you! (*Laughter.*)

Tjælde. That's enough, Jakobsen!

Jakobsen. No, it's not enough! Because there is one toast we have all forgotten, although we have all had such a splendid dinner. (*Laughter.* FALBE *claps his hands and cries:* "Bravo!") Yes, and it is nothing to laugh at; because it is the toast of Mrs. Tjælde's health that we have not drunk!

Lind. Bravo!

Jakobsen. There's a wife and mother for you! I can tell you—and it's true—she goes about the house attending to her duties and preparing for our entertainment when all the time she is ill, and she takes the whole thing on her shoulders and says nothing. God bless her, I say!—and that is all I have to say.

Several of the Guests (*raising their glasses*). Mrs. Tjælde! Mrs. Tjælde!

Pram (grasping JAKOBSEN *by the hand).* That was fine of you, Jakobsen! (LIND *joins them;* PRAM *steps aside respectfully.*)

Lind. Will you drink a glass of wine with me, Jakobsen?

Jakobsen. Thank you, very much. I am only a common man—

Lind. But a good-hearted one! Your health! (*They drink to each other. A boat is seen putting in to shore below the verandah. Its crew of six men stand up and toss their oars in naval fashion.* SANNÆS *is standing at the helm.*)

Holm (in a whisper, to KNUTZON). Tjælde knew what he was doing when he invited Jakobsen!

Knutzon (whispering). Just look at the boat!

Ring. Tjælde is a very clever fellow—a very clever fellow! (VALBORG, SIGNE *and* MRS. TJÆLDE *are seen coming up the verandah steps.*)

Tjælde. Gentlemen, the moment of departure is at hand; I see the ladies coming to take leave of our distinguished guest. Let us take this last opportunity of gathering around him—round our prince—and thanking him for coming! Let us cheer him with three times three! (*Cheers.*)

Lind. Thank you, gentlemen! There is so little time left that I must confine myself to merely bidding you all good-bye. (*To* MRS. TJÆLDE.) Good-bye, my dear madam! You should have heard how your health was proposed and drunk just now. My warmest thanks for your hospitality, and forgive me for the trouble I have caused you. (*To* SIGNE.) Good-bye, Miss Signe. I am sorry time has not permitted me to have the honour of becoming better acquainted with you; you seem so full of spirit! But if, as you said, you are soon coming to Christiania—

Signe. I shall then do myself the honour of calling upon your wife.

Lind. Thank you, thank you—you will be most welcome. (*To* VALBORG.) Are you not feeling well, Miss Valborg?

Valborg. Yes.

Lind. You look so serious. (*As* VALBORG *does not reply, he continues somewhat coldly :*) Good-bye, Miss Valborg. (*To* HAMAR.) Good-bye, Mr.—Mr.—

Tjælde. Mr. Hamar.

Lind. Ah, the young man that talked to me about a horse—your future son-in-law! Pray forgive me for not—

Hamar. Don't mention it!

Lind. Good-bye!

Hamar. A pleasant journey, sir!

Lind (*coldly, to* HOLM). Good-bye, Mr. Holm.

Holm (*imperturbably polite*). I wish you a very pleasant journey, Mr. Lind.

Lind (*to* PRAM). Good-bye, Mr. Pram.

Pram (*holds his hand, and seems as if he wanted to say something but could not. At last he finds his voice*). I want to thank you for—for—I want to thank you for—for—

Lind. You are an excellent fellow!

Pram (*in a relieved voice*). I am so glad to hear it! Thank you.

Lind (*to* KNUTZON). Good-bye, Mr.—

Knutzon (*hastily*). Knutzon.

Pram. With a " z."

Lind (*to* KNUDSEN). Good-bye, Mr.—

Knudsen. Knudsen, again.

Pram. With an " s."

Lind (*to* FALBE). Mr—?

Falbe. Falbe.

Lind. Good-bye, Mr. Falbe! (*To* RING.) I am delighted to see you looking so well, Mr. Ring.

Ring (*with a low bow*). The same to you, sir!

Lind. Good-bye, Mr. Vicar!

The Vicar (*holding his hand, impressively*). Let me wish you good luck and happiness, Mr. Lind—

Lind. Thank you.   (*Tries to get away.*)

The Vicar. —in your journey over the perilous seas to foreign lands!

Lind. Thank you.   (*Tries to get away.*)

The Vicar. Let me wish you a safe return, Mr. Lind—

Lind. Thank you very much.   (*Tries to get away.*)

The Vicar. —to our dear fatherland; a land, Mr. Lind, which possesses in you—

Lind. You must excuse me, Mr. Vicar, but time presses.

The Vicar. Let me thank you for the pleasure of our meeting to-day, Mr. Lind, for—

Lind. Indeed, there is no occasion! Good-bye! (*To* JAKOBSEN.) Good-bye, Jakobsen, good-bye!

Jakobsen. Good-bye, Mr. Lind! I am only a common man, I know; but that is no reason why I shouldn't wish you a pleasant journey too, is it?

Lind. Certainly not, Jakobsen.—Good-bye, Mr. Finne! By the way—just a word! (*In an undertone.*) You said that Mr. Berent—. (*Takes him aside.*)

Tjælde (*to* HAMAR). Now, remember the salute this time!—No, no, no! Don't be in such a hurry! Wait till the boat puts off! You want to make a mess of it again!

Hamar. Well, if ever again I—!

Tjælde (*to* LIND, *who holds out his hand to him*). Good-bye, Mr. Lind! (*In a low voice.*) No one has so much reason to thank you for your visit as I. You are the only one that can understand—.

Lind (*a shade coldly*). Don't mention it, Mr. Tjælde! Good luck to your business! (*In warmer tones.*) Good-bye everybody—and thank you all for your kindness! (*The footman, who has for some time been holding out his hat to him, gives it him, and his coat to* SANNÆS. LIND *steps on board the boat.*)

All. Good-bye, Mr. Lind, good-bye!

Tjælde. One cheer more! (*Cheers and a cannon salute are heard together. The boat glides away. They all wave their handkerchiefs.* TJÆLDE *hurries into the room.*) I have no handkerchief; that blockhead has—. (*Looks at* VALBORG.) Why are you not waving?

Valborg. Because I don't wish to. (TJÆLDE *looks at her, but says nothing. He goes into the other room and comes back with a table-napkin in each hand, and hurries on to the verandah.*)

Tjælde (*waving and shouting*). Good-bye! Good-bye!

Signe. Let us go out to the point and see the last of them!

All. Yes, yes! (*All but* TJÆLDE *and* VALBORG *hurry off to the right.*)

Tjælde (*coming into the room*). I saw Berent coming! (VALBORG *goes out by the door on the right.* TJÆLDE *comes forward, throws the napkins on to a table and himself into a chair.*) Oh—oh! But this must be the last time. —I shan't need this sort of thing any more! Never again! (*Gets up wearily.*) Ah, I had forgotten. Berent!

The Curtain falls.
*The interval between this scene and the next should
be as short as possible.*

SCENE II

(SCENE.—TJÆLDE'S *private office. On the left, a desk strewn with ledgers and papers. On the right, a stove. An easy chair by the stove. A table in the foreground to the right; on it an inkstand and pens. Two arm-chairs; one at the table facing the audience, the other at the side of the table. Windows on either side of the desk; a door beyond the stove. A door in the back-ground, leading to other offices. A bell-pull hangs*

*down the wall. A chair on either side of the door.
Quite at the back, on the left, a staircase leading direct
to* TJÆLDE'S *bedroom.* BERENT *and* TJÆLDE *come
in from the back.*)

Tjælde. You must excuse my receiving you here.
But the other rooms are all upside down; we have had
some people to dinner.

Berent. I heard you had guests.

Tjælde. Yes, Mr. Lind from Christiana.

Berent. Quite so.

Tjælde. Won't you sit down? (BERENT *lays down
his hat and coat on a chair by the door. He comes slowly
forward, sits down at the side of the table, and takes some
papers from his breast-pocket.* TJÆLDE *sits down at the
other chair by the table and watches him indifferently.*)

Berent. What we now want is some fixed standard by
which to make our valuations, especially of real estate.
Have you any objection to our making your business a
basis for arriving at that?

Tjælde. None at all.

Berent. Then may I make my comments on your own
figures, and ask you a few questions about them?

Tjælde. By all means.

Berent. Well, to begin with, let us take your properties
immediately round here; they will give us the best idea
of local values. For instance, take the Mjölstad forest;
you have put that down, I see, at £16,500.

Tjælde (indifferently). Have I?

Berent. You bought it for £10,000.

Tjælde. Yes, four years ago. Timber prices ruled low
then.

Berent. And since then you have cut down more than
£20,000 worth of timber there.

Tjælde. Who told you so?

Berent. Mr. Holst.

Tjælde. Holst knows nothing about it.

Berent. We must try to be very accurate, you know.

Tjælde. Well, of course, the whole valuation is not my concern; but those whom it does concern will protest.

Berent (*taking no notice of his objection*). So I think we will reduce the £16,500 to £10,000.

Tjælde. To £10,000! (*Laughs.*) As you please.

Berent. Calculating by the same standard, we can scarcely put down the Stav forest at more than £4000.

Tjælde. Allow me to say that, if that is the way you are going to make your valuation, everybody in the place will have to go bankrupt!

Berent (*with a smile*). We will risk that.   You have put down your wharf and its contents at £12,000.

Tjælde. Including two ships in course of construction—

Berent. —for which it would be difficult to find a purchaser, as they are so far from completion.

Tjælde. Indeed?

Berent. So I think we cannot put down the wharf and its contents at a higher figure than £8000—and I believe even that will turn out to be too high.

Tjælde. If you can find me another wharf as well stocked, and with the advantages that this one has, I will buy it whenever you like for £8000; I am certain I should be more than £4000 to the good over the bargain.

Berent. May I go on?

Tjælde. If you like! I even feel a certain curiosity to view my possessions under such an entirely new light.

Berent. As a matter of fact the items that are too highly valued are just those that comprise this property that you live on—its land, its gardens, its dwelling houses, warehouses, and quays—not to mention the brewery and the factory, which I shall come to later.   Even regarded as business premises they seem to me to be over-valued.

Tjælde. Well?

Berent. Moreover, the luxurious appointments of this

house of yours, which would very probably be superfluous for any one else, cannot possibly be counted upon to realise their full value in a sale. Suppose—as is indeed most likely—that it were a countryman that bought the place?

Tjælde. You are reckoning me as turned out of it already, then!

Berent. I am obliged to base all my calculations on what the property would fetch if sold now.

Tjælde (*getting up*). What may you happen to value it at then?

Berent. At less than half your valuation; that is to say at—

Tjælde. You must really forgive me if I use an expression which has been on the tip of my tongue for some time: this is scandalous! You force yourself into a man's house, and then, under pretext of asking for his opinion, you practically—on paper—rob him of his possessions!

Berent. I don't understand you. I am trying to arrive at a basis for values hereabouts; and you said yourself, did you not, that it is a matter that does not concern you alone?

Tjælde. Certainly ; but even in jest—if I may be allowed the expression—one does not take the statement that an honourable man has voluntarily offered and treat it as a mendacious document.

Berent. There are many different points of view from which valuations can be made, obviously. I see nothing more in it than that.

Tjælde. But don't you understand that this is like cutting into my living flesh? Bit by bit, my property has been brought together or created by my own work, and preserved by the most strenuous exertions on my part under terribly trying conditions—it is bound up with my family, with all that is dear to me—it has become a part of my very life!

Berent (*with a bow*). I understand that perfectly. You have put down the Brewery at—

Tjælde. No; I refuse to allow you to go on in this way. You must find some one else's property as a basis for your calculations—you must consult some one else, whose idea of business corresponds somewhat closer to your own ridiculous one.

Berent (*leaning back in his chair*). That is a pity. The banks were anxious to be acquainted with your answers to my observations.

Tjælde. Have you sent my statement to the banks?

Berent. With my remarks and comments on it, and Mr. Holst's.

Tjælde. This has been a trap, then? I believed I had to deal with a gentleman!

Berent. The banks or I, what is the difference? It comes to the same thing, as I represent them unreservedly.

Tjælde. Such impudent audacity is unpardonable!

Berent. I would suggest that we avoid hard words—at all events, for the moment—and rather consider the effect that will be produced by the balance-sheet sent in.

Tjælde. That some of us will see!

Berent. The banking house of Lind & Co., for instance?

Tjælde. Do you mean to say that my balance-sheet, ornamented with marginal notes by you and Holst, is to be submitted to Mr. Lind's firm too?

Berent. When the cannon-salutes and noise of your festivities enlightened me as to the situation, I took the liberty of making some inquiries of the banks.

Tjælde. So you have been spying here, too? You have been trying to undermine my business connections?

Berent. Is your position such, then, that you are afraid?

Tjælde. The question is not my position, but your behaviour!

Berent. I think we had better keep to the point. You have put down the Brewery at—

Tjælde. No; your conduct is so absolutely underhanded that, as an honest man, I must refuse all further dealings with you. I am, as I said before, accustomed to have to deal with gentlemen.

Berent. I think you misunderstand the situation. Your indebtedness to the banks is so considerable that a settlement of it may reasonably be required of you. But to effect that you must work with us in the matter.

Tjælde (after a moment's thought). Very well! But, no more details—let me know your conclusions, briefly.

Berent. My conclusions, briefly, are that you have estimated your assets at £90,800. I estimate them at £40,600.

Tjælde (quietly). That is to say, you make me out to have a deficit of about £30,000?

Berent. As to that, I must point out that your estimate of your liabilities does not agree with mine, either.

Tjælde (quietly). Oh, of course not!

Berent. For instance, the dividend that Möller's estate is to yield to you.

Tjælde. No more details! What do you put my total liabilities at?

Berent. Let me see. Your total liabilities amount, according to your calculations, to £70,000. I estimate them at £80,000—to be precise, at £79,372.

Tjælde. That puts my deficit at about—

Berent. At about £39,400—or, in round figures, £40,000.

Tjælde. Oh, by all means let us stick to round figures!

Berent. So that the difference between your views of your balance-sheet and mine is that, whereas you give yourself a surplus of about £20,000, I give you a deficit of about £40,000.

Tjælde. Thank you very much.—Do you know my

opinion of the whole matter? (BERENT *looks up at him.*)
That I am in this room with a madman.

Berent. I have had the same opinion for some time.—
The stock of timber you hold in France I have not been
able to deal with; you have forgotten to include it in
your account. Perhaps it may make a little difference.

Tjælde. It is of no consequence! I have often enough
heard people speak of your callousness and your heartlessness; but their account of you has come nowhere near the
truth. I don't know why I have not turned you out of
my house long before this; but you will have the goodness
to leave it now!

Berent. We shall both leave presently. But before we
do, we must discuss the question of handing over the house
to the Receiver in Bankruptcy.

Tjælde. Ha, ha, ha! Allow me to inform you that at
this very moment a sum is being telegraphed to me which
will be sufficient not only to cover my present liabilities,
but to set me straight in every direction!

Berent. The telegraph is a useful invention which is
open to every one.

Tjælde (after a moment's thought). What do you mean
by that?

Berent. One effect of the noise of your festivities was
that *I* used the telegraph also. Mr. Lind will receive,
on board the boat, a telegram from his firm—and I doubt
if the money you speak of will be forthcoming.

Tjælde. It is not true! You have not dared to do
that!

Berent. The facts are exactly as I state.

Tjælde. Give me my balance-sheet; let me look at it
again. (*Stretches out his hand to take it.*)

Berent (taking it up). Excuse me!

Tjælde. Do you presume to keep back my own balance-
sheet in my own writing?

Berent. Yes, and even to put it in my pocket. (*Does so.*)

A fraudulent balance-sheet, dated and signed, is a document of some importance.

Tjælde. You are determined to ruin my private and public reputation?

Berent. You have been working for that yourself for a long time. I know your position. For a month past I have been in correspondence with all the quarters in which you have business connections, both here and abroad.

Tjælde. What underhanded deceitfulness an honest man is exposed to! Here have I been surrounded by spies for the last month! A plot between my business acquaintances and the banks! A snake creeping into my house and crawling over my accounts! But I will break up the conspiracy! And you will find out what it means to try and ruin a reputable firm by underhand devices!

Berent. This is no time for fine phrases. Do you propose to surrender your property at once?

Tjælde. Ha, ha! I am to surrender it because you have made me out a bankrupt on your bit of paper!

Berent. You might conceal the facts for a month, I know. But for your own sake, and especially for the sake of others, I would urgently advise you to end the matter at once. That was the reason of my journey here.

Tjælde. Ah, now the truth is out! And you came here pretending a friendly concern that the tangle should be straightened out! We were to distinguish between the sound and unsound firms, and you requested me, most politely, to give you my assistance in the matter!

Berent. Exactly. But there is no question of anything unsound here except your own business and what is bound up with it.

Tjælde (when he has controlled himself). So you came into my house with the hidden design of ruining me?

Berent. I must repeat that it is not I that am responsible for your bankruptcy; it is yourself.

Tjælde. And I must repeat that my bankruptcy only exists in your imagination! Much may happen in a month; and I have shown that I can find a way out of difficulties before now!

Berent. That is to say, by involving yourself deeper and deeper in falsehood.

Tjælde. Only a man of business can understand such things. But, if you really understand them, I would say to you: "Give me £20,000 and I will save the situation entirely." That would be doing something worthy of your great powers; that would give you a reputation for penetration in discerning the real state of affairs; because by so doing you would safeguard the welfare of more than a thousand people, and ensure a prosperous future for the whole district!

Berent. I don't rise to that bait.

Tjælde (after a moment's reflection). Do you want me to explain to you how £20,000 would be sufficient to set the whole complicated situation straight? Within three months remittances would be coming in. I can make it as clear as daylight to you—

Berent. —that you would be falling from one disillusionment to another! That is what you have been doing for the last three years, from month to month.

Tjælde. Because the last three years have been bad years—horrible years! But we have reached the crisis; things must begin to improve now!

Berent. That is what every defaulter thinks.

Tjælde. Do not drive me to despair! Have you any idea what I have gone through in these three years? Have you any idea what I am capable of?

Berent. Of still further falsehood.

Tjælde. Take care!—It is quite true that I am standing on the edge of a precipice. It is true that for three years

I have done everything in mortal power to save the situation! I maintain that there has been something heroic in the fight I have made. And that deserves some reward. You have unrestricted powers; every one trusts you. Realise for yourself what your mission is; do not let it be necessary for me to teach it you! Let me tell you this, emphatically: it will be a dreadful thing for *you* if hundreds of people are to be ruined unnecessarily now!

Berent. Let us make an end of this.

Tjælde. No, devil take me if I give up a fight like this with a senseless surrender!

Berent. How do you propose to end it, then?

Tjælde. There is no issue to it that I have not turned over in my thoughts—thousands of times. *I* know what I shall do! I won't be a mark for the jeers of this wretched little town, nor triumphed over by those who have envied me all round the countryside!

Berent. What will you do, then?

Tjælde. You shall see! (*Speaking more and more excitedly.*) You won't help me under any conditions?

Berent. No.

Tjælde. You insist that I shall surrender my estate, here and now?

Berent. Yes.

Tjælde. Hell and damnation! You dare do that?

Berent. Yes.

Tjælde (*his agitation robbing him of his voice, which all at once sinks to a hoarse whisper*). You have never known what despair is!—You don't know what an existence I have endured!—But if the decisive moment has come, and I have a man here in my office who *ought* to save me but *will* not, then that man shall share what is in store for me.

Berent (*leaning back in his chair*). This is beginning to be impressive.

Tjælde. No more jesting; you might regret it! (*Goes*

*to all the doors and locks them with a key which he takes out
of his pocket; then unlocks his desk, and takes a revolver out
of it.*) How long do you suppose I have had this in here?

Berent. Since you bought it, I suppose.

Tjælde. And why do you suppose I bought it?—Do you
suppose that after I have been master of this town and
the biggest man in the district, I would endure the disgrace
of bankruptcy?

Berent. You have been enduring it for a long time.

Tjælde. It is in your power now either to ruin me or to
save me. You have behaved in such a way that you
deserve no mercy—and you shall have none! Report to
the banks that they may give me the use of £14,000 for a
year—I need no more than that—and I will save the
situation for good and all. Think seriously, now! Remember my family, remember how long my firm has been
established, remember the numbers that would be ruined
if I were! And do not forget to think of your own family!
Because, if you *don't* agree to what I ask, neither of us
shall leave this room alive!

Berent (pointing to the revolver). Is it loaded?

Tjælde (putting his finger on the trigger). You will find
that out in good time. You must answer me now!

Berent. I have a suggestion to make. Shoot yourself
first and me afterwards.

*Tjælde (going up to him and holding the revolver to his
head).* I will soon quiet your pretty wit.

*Berent (getting up, and taking out of his pocket a paper
which he unfolds).* This is a formal surrender of your estate
to the Receiver in Bankruptcy. If you sign it, you will be
doing your duty to your creditors, to your family, and to
yourself. Shooting yourself and me would only be adding
an acted lie to all your others. Put away your revolver
and take up your pen!

Tjælde. Never! I had resolved on this long ago. But
you shall keep me company, now!

Berent. Do what you please.   But you cannot threaten me into a falsehood.

Tjælde (who has lowered the revolver, takes a step back, raises the revolver and aims at BERENT*).* Very well!

Berent (walking up to TJÆLDE *and looking him straight in the eyes, while the latter reluctantly lowers the revolver).* Do you suppose I don't know that a man who has for so long shivered with falsehood and terror in his inmost heart has lots of schemes but no courage?   You *dare* not do it!

Tjælde (furiously). I will show you!   (*Steps back and raises the revolver again.*)

Berent (following him). Shoot, and you will hear a report—that is what you are longing for, I suppose!   Or, give up your plan of shooting, think of what you have done, confess, and afterwards hold your tongue!

Tjælde. No; may the devil take both you and me—

Berent. And the horse?

Tjælde. The horse?

Berent. I mean the magnificent charger on which you came galloping home from the sale of Moller's estate. You had better let some one shoot you on horseback—on what was your last and greatest piece of business duplicity!   (*Goes nearer to him and speaks more quietly.*)   Or —strip yourself of the tissue of lies which enfolds you, and your bankruptcy will bring you more blessing than your riches have ever done.   (TJÆLDE *lets the revolver drop out of his hand, and sinks into a chair in an outburst of tears.   There is silence for a moment.*)   You have made an amazing fight of it for these last three years.   I do not believe I know any one who could have done what you have done.   But you have lost the fight this time.   Do not shrink now from a final settlement and the pain that it must cost you.   Nothing else will cleanse your soul for you.

Tjælde (weeping unrestrainedly, with his face buried in his hands). Oh, oh!

Berent. You have blamed me for my method of proceeding in the matter. My answer to that is that I forgive you for yours. (*A pause.*) Try now to look the situation in the face, and take it like a man.

Tjælde (*as before*). Oh!

Berent. At the bottom of your heart you must be weary of it all; make an end of it all now!

Tjælde (*as before*). Oh!

Berent (*sitting down beside him, after a moment's pause*). Wouldn't you like to feel your conscience clear again—to be able really to live with your wife and children? Because I am sure you have not done that for many a day.

Tjælde (*as before*). Oh!

Berent. I have known many speculators in my time and have received many confessions. So I know what you have been robbed of for three years—never a good night's rest, never a meal eaten with a light heart. You have scarcely been conscious of what your children were doing or saying, except when accident brought you together. And your wife—

Tjælde. My wife!

Berent. Yes, she has slaved hard enough to prepare these banquets that were to conceal the nakedness of the land. Indeed, she has been the hardest worked servant in your house.

Tjælde. My patient, good wife!

Berent. I feel certain you would rather be the humblest labourer earning your daily bread than live through such suffering again.

Tjælde. A thousand times rather!

Berent. Then can you hesitate to do what will give every man his due, and bring you back to truthfulness again? Take the paper and sign it!

Tjælde (*falling on his knees*). Mercy, mercy! You do not know what you are asking me. My own children will curse me. I have just heard of a child doing that to her father! And my business friends, who will be ruined with me—numbers of them—think of their families! Oh! What is to become of my work-people? Do you know there are more than four hundred of them? Think of them and their families, robbed of their livelihood!— Be merciful! I cannot, I dare not, do it! Save me, help me! It was horrible of me to try and threaten you; but now I implore you, for the sake of all those that deserve more than I, but to whom I shall devote the rest of my life in loyal work!

Berent. I cannot save you, least of all with money that belongs to others. What you ask me to do would be disloyalty to them.

Tjælde. No, no! Publish my accounts openly—put me under trustees, if you like; but let me go on with the scheme that I believe will succeed! Every clear-headed man will see that it must succeed!

Berent. Come and sit down. Let us discuss it. (TJÆLDE *sits down.*) Isn't what you are now proposing exactly what you have been trying to do for the last three years? You *have* been able to borrow the means; but what good has it done?

Tjælde. Times have been so bad!

Berent (*shaking his head*). You have mixed up false-hood and truth for so long that you have forgotten the simplest laws of commerce. To speculate during bad times, on the chance of their becoming better, is all very well for those who can afford it. Others must leave such things alone.

Tjælde. But it is to the advantage of my creditors themselves, and of the banks too, that my estate should hold together!

Berent. It is of no advantage to sound firms to prop up unsound ones.

Tjælde. But, surely, to avoid losing their capital—?

Berent. Oh, perhaps in the Receiver's hands the estate may—

Tjælde (hopefully, half rising from his chair). Yes? Well?

Berent. But not till you have been removed from the control of it.

Tjælde (sinking down again). Not till I have been removed from the control of it!

Berent. On *its own* resources I dare say the estate can hold out until better times come, but not on borrowed money.

Tjælde. Not on borrowed money—

Berent. You understand the difference, of course?

Tjælde. Oh, yes.

Berent. Good. Then you must understand that there is nothing left for you to do but to sign this.

Tjælde. Nothing left but to sign—

Berent. Here is the paper. Come, now!

Tjælde (rousing himself). Oh, I cannot, I cannot!

Berent. Very well. But in that case the crash will come of itself in a short time, and everything will be worse than it is now.

Tjælde (falling on his knees). Mercy, mercy! I cannot let go of all hope! Think, after a fight like mine!

Berent. Tell the truth and say: " I haven't the courage to face the consequences."

Tjælde. Yes, that is the truth.

Berent. " I haven't the courage to begin an honest life."

Tjælde. Yes.

Berent. You don't know what you are saying, man!

Tjælde. No, I don't. But spare me!

Berent (getting up). This is nothing but despair! I am sorry for you.

Tjælde (getting up). Yes, surely you must be? Try me! Ask me to do anything you like! Tell me what you—

Berent. No, no! Before anything else, you must sign this.

Tjælde (*sinking back into his chair*). Oh!—How shall I ever dare to look any one in the face again?—I, who have defied everything and deceived every one!

Berent. The man who has enjoyed the respect which he did not deserve must some day undergo the humiliation which he has deserved. That is a law; and I cannot save you from that.

Tjælde. But they will be crueller to me than to any one else! I deserve it, I know; but I shall not be able to endure it!

Berent. Hm! You are remarkably tough; your fight, these last three years, proves that.

Tjælde. Be merciful! Surely your ingenuity—your influence—*must* be able to find some way out for me?

Berent. Yes. The way out is for you to sign this.

Tjælde. Won't you even take it over from me by private contract? If you did that, everything would come right.

Berent. Sign! Here is the paper! Every hour is precious.

Tjælde. Oh! (*Takes up a pen; but turns to* BERENT *with a gesture of supplication.*) Daren't you test me, after what I have just gone through?

Berent. Yes, when you have signed. (TJÆLDE *signs the paper, and sinks back in his chair with an expression of the keenest anguish.* BERENT *takes the paper, folds it, and puts it in his pocket-book.*) Now I will go to the Bankruptcy Court with this, and afterwards to the telegraph office. Probably the officials of the court will come this evening to make their inventory. So you ought to warn your family.

Tjælde. How shall I be able to do that? Give me a little time! Be merciful!

Berent. The sooner the better for you—not to speak of the interests of all concerned. Well, I have finished for the present.

Tjælde. Don't desert me like this! Don't desert me!

Berent. You would like your wife to come to you, wouldn't you?

Tjælde (resignedly). Yes.

Berent (taking up the revolver). And this—I will not take it with me. There is no danger from it now. But I will put it in the desk, for the sake of the others. Now, if you or yours should need me, send word to me.

Tjælde. Thank you.

Berent. I shall not leave the town until the worst is over.—Remember, night or day, if you need me, send word to me.

Tjælde. Thank you.

Berent. And now will you unlock the door for me?

Tjælde (getting up). Ah, of course. Excuse me!

Berent (taking his hat and coat). Won't you call your wife now?

Tjælde. No. I must have a little time first. I have the worst part of it before me now.

Berent. I believe you have, and that is just why—. (*Takes hold of the bell-pull and rings the bell.*)

Tjælde. What are you doing?

Berent. I want, before I go, to be sure of your wife's coming to you.

Tjælde. You should not have done that! (*An office-boy comes in.* BERENT *looks at* TJÆLDE.) Ask your mistress—ask my wife to come to me.

Berent. At once, please. (*The boy goes out.*) Good-bye! (*Goes out.* TJÆLDE *sinks down on to a chair by the door.*)

The Curtain falls.

ACT III

(SCENE.—*The same as in the preceding act.* TJÆLDE *is sitting alone, on the chair by the door, in the position he was in when the curtain fell on the last act. After sitting motionless for a considerable time, he suddenly gets up.*)

Tjælde. How am I to begin? After her, there are the children; after them, all my work-people—and then all the others! If only I could get away! But the Receiver's men will be here.—I must have some air! (*Goes to the nearest window.*) What a beautiful day!—but not for me. (*Opens the window and looks out.*) My horse! No, I daren't look at it. Why is it saddled? Oh, of course I meant, after my talk with Berent, to—. But now everything is different! (*Walks up and down once or twice, thinking; then says suddenly :*) Yes, on that horse I might reach the outer harbour before the foreign boat sails! (*Looks at his watch.*) I can do it! And I shall be able to put behind me all—. (*Stops, with a start, as he hears footsteps on the stair.*) Who is there? What is it? (MRS. TJÆLDE *comes down the stair into the room.*)

Mrs. Tjælde. You sent for me?

Tjælde. Yes. (*Watching her.*) Were you upstairs?

Mrs. Tjælde. Yes, I was resting.

Tjælde (*sympathetically*). Ah, you were sleeping, and I woke you up!

Mrs. Tjælde. No, I was not asleep. (*She has come slowly forward.*)

Tjælde. You weren't asleep? (*Apprehensively, to her.*) I suppose you didn't—? (*To himself.*) No, I daren't ask her.

Mrs. Tjælde. What did you want?

Tjælde. I wanted—. (*Sees her eyes fixed on the revolver.*) You are surprised at my having that out? I got it out because I am going on a journey.

Mrs. Tjælde (*supporting herself on the desk*). Going on a journey?

Tjælde. Yes. Mr. Berent has been here, as I dare say you know. (*She does not answer.*) Business, you know. I have to go abroad.

Mrs. Tjælde (*faintly*). Abroad?

Tjælde. Only for a few days. So I will only take my usual bag with a change of clothes and one or two shirts; but I must have it at once.

Mrs. Tjælde. I don't think your bag has been unpacked since you brought it home to-day.

Tjælde. So much the better. Will you get it for me?

Mrs. Tjælde. Are you going away now—at once?

Tjælde. Yes, by the foreign boat — from the outer harbour.

Mrs. Tjælde. You have no time to lose, then.

Tjælde. Are you not well?

Mrs. Tjælde. Not very.

Tjælde. One of your attacks?

Mrs. Tjælde. Yes! — but I must fetch your bag. (TJÆLDE *helps her over to the staircase.*)

Tjælde. You are not well, my dear—but you will be better some day.

Mrs. Tjælde. I only wish *you* looked better.

Tjælde. We all have our burdens to bear.

Mrs. Tjælde. If only we could bear more together!

Tjælde. But you don't understand my affairs—and I have never had time to talk about yours.

Mrs. Tjælde. No—that's it. (*Begins to go upstairs slowly.*)

Tjælde. Shall I help you?

Mrs. Tjælde. No, thank you, dear.

Tjælde (coming forward). Does she suspect? She is always like that—she takes all my courage away from me. But there is no other way! Now—about money? I surely have some gold here somewhere. *(Goes to his desk, takes some gold out of a drawer and counts it; then lifts his head and sees* MRS. TJÆLDE *who has sat down on the stair half-way up.)* My dear, are you sitting down?

Mrs. Tjælde. I felt faint for a moment. I will go up now. *(Gets up and climbs the stair slowly.)*

Tjælde. Poor thing, she is worn out. *(Pulls himself together.)* No—five, six, eight, ten—that is not enough. I must have some more. *(Searches in the desk.)* And when I run short I have my watch and chain. Twenty, twenty-four—that is all I can find. Ah, my papers! I must on no account forget them. The ground is falling away under me! Isn't she coming back? The bag was packed, surely?—Ah, how all this will make her suffer! But it will not be so bad for her if I am away. People will be more merciful, both to her and the children. Oh, my children! *(Collects himself.)* Only let me get away, away! Thoughts will follow me there, all the same!—Ah, here she is! (MRS. TJÆLDE *is seen coming down slowly, with a bag which is evidently heavy.)* Shall I help you, dear?

Mrs. Tjælde. Thanks, will you take hold of the bag?

Tjælde (takes it; she comes slowly down). It is heavier than it was this morning.

Mrs. Tjælde. Is it?

Tjælde. I have some papers to put in it. *(Opens the bag.)* But, my dear, there is money in this bag.

Mrs. Tjælde. Yes—some gold that you have given me at odd times. I thought it might be useful to you now.

Tjælde. There is a large sum.

Mrs. Tjælde. I don't believe you even know how much you have given me.

Tjælde. She knows everything!—My dear! (*Opens his arms.*)

Mrs. Tjælde. Henning! (*They both burst into tears and fall into each other's arms.* MRS. TJÆLDE *whispers to him :*) Shall I call the children?

Tjælde (*in a whisper*). No, say nothing—till later! (*They embrace again. He takes up the bag.*) Go to the window, so that I can see you when I mount. (*Shuts the bag and hurries to the door, but stops.*) My dear!

Mrs. Tjælde. Yes?

Tjælde. Forgive me!

Mrs. Tjælde. Everything! (TJÆLDE, *as he is hurrying out, meets in the doorway an office-boy who is bringing him a letter.* TJÆLDE *takes it, and the boy goes out.*)

Tjælde. From Berent! (*Opens the letter, stands in the doorway and reads it; then comes back into the room, with his bag in his hand, and reads it again.*) " When I left your house, I saw a horse standing saddled at your door. To prevent misunderstanding, let me inform you that your house is watched by the police."

Mrs. Tjælde (*supporting herself on the desk*). You can't go?

Tjælde. No. (*A pause. He puts down the bag and wipes his forehead.*)

Mrs. Tjælde. Henning, shall we pray together?

Tjælde. What do you mean?

Mrs. Tjælde. Pray—pray to God to help us? (*Bursts into tears.* TJÆLDE *is silent. She falls on her knees.*) Come, Henning! You see that all human ingenuity is of no avail!

Tjælde. I know that, only too well.

Mrs. Tjælde. Well, try once, in this hour of our greatest need! (TJÆLDE *appears to be struggling with his emotion.*) You never would! You have never confided in us, or in your God!—never opened your heart to any one!

Tjælde. Be quiet!

Mrs. Tjælde. But what you concealed by day, you used to talk of in the night. We mortals must talk, you know! But I have lain awake and listened to your distress. Now you know why I am no longer good for anything. No sleep at night, and none of your confidence in the daytime. I have suffered even more than you. (TJÆLDE *throws himself into a chair. She goes to him.*) You wanted to run away. When we are afraid of our fellow-men, we have only Him to turn to. Do you think I should be alive now, if it were not for Him?

Tjælde. I have thrown myself imploringly at His feet, but always in vain!

Mrs. Tjælde. Henning, Henning!

Tjælde. Why did He not bless my work and the fight I was making? It is all one now.

Mrs. Tjælde. Ah, there is more to come.

Tjælde (getting up). Yes, the worst is before us now—

Mrs. Tjælde. —because it is in our own hearts! (*A pause.* VALBORG *appears coming down the stair, but stops at the sight of the others.*) What do you want, dear?

Valborg (with suppressed emotion). From my room I can see the police watching the house. Are the Receiver's men coming now?

Mrs. Tjælde (sitting down). Yes, my child. After a terrible struggle—how terrible, his God and I alone know —your father has just sent in his declaration of bank-ruptcy. (VALBORG *takes a step or two forward, then stands still. A pause.*)

Tjælde (unable to control himself). Now I suppose you will say to me just what Möller's daughter said to him!

Mrs. Tjælde (getting up). You won't do that, Valborg! —God alone can judge him.

Tjælde. Tell me how cruelly I have wronged you! Tell me that you will never be able to forgive me—(*breaking down*)—that I have lost your respect and your love for ever!

Mrs. Tjælde. Oh, my child!

Tjælde. That your anger and your shame know no bounds!

Valborg. Oh, father, father! (*Goes out by the door at the back.* TJÆLDE *tries to cross the room, as if to follow her, but can only stagger as far as the staircase, to which he clings for support.* MRS. TJÆLDE *sinks back into her chair. There is a long pause. Suddenly* JAKOBSEN *comes in from the outer office, dressed as before except that he has changed his coat.* TJÆLDE *is not aware of his entrance until* JAKOBSEN *is close to him; then he stretches out his hands to him as if in entreaty, but* JAKOBSEN *goes right up to him and speaks in a voice choked with rage.*)

Jakobsen. You scoundrel! (TJÆLDE *recoils.*)

Mrs. Tjælde. Jakobsen! Jakobsen!

Jakobsen (*without heeding her*). The Receiver's men are here. The books and papers at the Brewery have been seized. Work is at a standstill—and the same thing at the factory.

Mrs. Tjælde. My God!

Jakobsen. And I had made myself responsible for twice as much as I possessed! (*He speaks low, but his voice vibrates with anger and emotion.*)

Mrs. Tjælde. Dear Jakobsen!

Jakobsen (*turning to her*). Didn't I say to him, every time he told me to sign, " But I don't possess as much as that! It's not right!"—But he used to answer, " It is only a matter of form, Jakobsen." " Yes, but not an honourable form," I used to say. " It is a matter of form in business," he would say; " all business folk do it." And all I knew of business, I had learnt from him; so I trusted him. (*With emotion.*) And he made me do it time after time. And now I owe more than I shall ever be able to pay, all my life. I shall live and die a dishonoured man. What have you to say to that, Mrs. Tjælde? (*She does not answer him. He turns angrily upon* TJÆLDE.) Do you hear? Even *she* can find nothing to say!—Scoundrel!

Mrs. Tjælde. Jakobsen!

Jakobsen (in a voice broken with emotion). I have nothing but the deepest respect for you, Mrs. Tjælde. But, you see, he has made me swindle other people! In his name I shall have ruined numbers of them. They trusted me, you see; just as I trusted him. I used to tell them that he was a benefactor to the whole countryside, and that therefore they ought to help him in these hard times. And now there will be many an honest family robbed of house and home by our treachery. And that is what he has brought me to! What heartless cruelty! (*To* TJÆLDE.) I can tell I feel inclined to—. (*Takes a threatening step towards him.*)

Mrs. Tjælde (getting up). For my sake, Jakobsen!

Jakobsen (restraining himself). Yes, for your sake, ma'am; because I have the deepest respect for you. But how am I to face all those poor creatures that I have ruined? It will do them no good to explain to them how it has happened; that won't help them to get their daily bread! How shall I face my own wife! (*With emotion.*) She has had such faith in me, and in those I trusted. And my children, too? It is very hard on children, because they hear so much talk in the street. It won't be long before they hear what sort of a father they have got; and they will hear it from the children of the men I have ruined.

Mrs. Tjælde. As you feel how hard it is yourself, that should make you willing to spare others. Be merciful!

Jakobsen. I have the deepest respect for you; but it is hard that in my home we should never again be able to eat a crust that we can properly call our own—for I owe more than I can ever live to repay! That is hard, Mrs. Tjælde! What will become of my evenings with my children now?—of our Sundays together? No, I mean that he shall hear the truth from me. (*Turns upon* TJÆLDE.) You scoundrel! You shan't escape me! (TJÆLDE *shrinks back in terror and tries to reach the office door, but at that moment the* RECEIVER *comes in, followed by two of his clerks and* SANNÆS. TJÆLDE *crosses the room, staggers to his desk, and leans upon it with his back turned to the newcomers.*)

The Receiver (*coming up behind Tjælde*). Excuse me! May I have your books and papers? (TJÆLDE *gives a start, moves away to the stove, and supports himself on it.*)

Jakobsen (*in a whisper, standing over him*). Scoundrel! (TJÆLDE *moves away from him and sits down on a chair by the door, hiding his face in his hands.*)

Mrs. Tjælde (*getting up and whispering to* JAKOBSEN). Jakobsen! Jakobsen! (*He comes towards her.*) He has never deliberately cheated any one! He has never been what you say, and never will be! (*Sits down again.*)

Jakobsen. I have the deepest respect for *you*, Mrs. Tjælde. But if *he* is not a liar and swindler, there is no truth in anything! (*Bursts into tears.* MRS. TJÆLDE *hides her face in her hands as she leans back in her chair. A short silence. Then a confused noise of voices is heard without. The* RECEIVER *and his men stop their work of sorting and inventorying papers, and all look up.*)

Mrs. Tjælde (*apprehensively*). What is that? (SANNÆS *and the* RECEIVER *go to one window, and* JAKOBSEN *to another.*)

Jakobsen. It's the hands from the quay and the brewery and the factory and the warehouse. All work is stopped until further orders; but this is pay-day—and there is no pay for them! (*The others resume their work.*)

Tjælde (*coming forward despairingly*). I had forgotten that!

Jakobsen (*going up to him*). Well, go out and face them, and they will let you know what you are!

Tjælde (*in a low voice, as he takes up his saddle-bag*).

Here is money, but it is all in gold. Go into the town and get it changed, and pay them!

Mrs. Tjælde. Yes, do, Jakobsen!

Jakobsen (in lower tones). If *you* ask me to, ma'am, I— So there is money in this bag? (*Opens it.*) And all done up in rolls. He meant to bolt, then!—and with the money his people had lent him. And yet you say he is not a scoundrel! (TJÆLDE *gives a groan. The noise of voices without grows louder.*)

Mrs. Tjælde (in a low voice). Be quick, or we shall have them in here.

Jakobsen. I will go.

The Receiver (interposing). Excuse me, but nothing must be taken away from here until it has been examined and inventoried.

Jakobsen. It is pay-day, and this is the money for the wages.

Mrs. Tjælde. Jakobsen is responsible for it, and will account for it.

The Receiver. Oh, that alters the case. Mr. Jakobsen is a man of integrity. (*Goes back to his work.*)

Jakobsen (to MRS. TJÆLDE, *in a low voice full of emotion*). Did you hear that, Mrs. Tjælde? He called me a man of integrity—and very soon not a single soul will call me that! (*Goes out past* TJÆLDE *to whom he whispers as he passes :*) Scoundrel! I shall come back again!

The Receiver (going up to TJÆLDE). Excuse me, but I must ask you for the keys of your private rooms and cupboards.

Mrs. Tjælde (answering for her husband). My house-keeper shall go with you. Sannæs, here is the key of the cupboard. (SANNÆS *takes it from her.*)

The Receiver (looking at TJÆLDE'S *massive watch-chain*). Whatever article of dress can be called a necessary, we have nothing to do with; but if it happens that it comprises jewellery of any great value—. (TJÆLDE *begins to take off the watch-chain.*) No, no; keep it on. But it will have to be included in the inventory.

Tjælde. I don't wish to keep it.

The Receiver. As you please. (*Signs to one of his clerks to take it.*) Good-day! (*Meanwhile* SIGNE *and* HAMAR *have appeared at the door of the outer office, and have seen what passed. The* RECEIVER, SANNÆS, *and the clerks try to open the door on the right, but find it locked.*) This door is locked.

Tjælde (*as if waking from a dream*). Ah, of course! (*Goes to the door and unlocks it.*)

Signe (*rushing to* MRS. TJÆLDE *and falling on her knees beside her*). Mother!

Mrs. Tjælde. Yes, dear, the day of our trial has come! And I am afraid—afraid that it may find us all too weak.

Signe. Mother, what is to become of us?

Mrs. Tjælde. We are in God's hands.

Signe. I will go with Hamar to his aunt's. We will go at once.

Mrs. Tjælde. It is possible that his aunt may not be willing to have you now.

Signe. Aunt Ulla! What do you mean?

Mrs. Tjælde. I mean that you have been the rich man's daughter; and you do not know what the world is.

Signe. Hamar, do you think Aunt Ulla would refuse to have me?

Hamar (*after a moment's thought*). I don't know.

Mrs. Tjælde. You hear that, my child. In the next few hours you will learn more than you have learnt in all your life.

Signe (*in a horrified whisper*). Do you mean that even—?

Mrs. Tjælde. Hush! (SIGNE *hides her face in her mother's lap. A loud burst of laughter is heard outside.*)

Hamar (*going to the nearest window*). What is that?

(SANNÆS *comes in through the right-hand door and goes to the other window.* TJÆLDE, SIGNE *and* MRS. TJÆLDE *get up.*) The bay horse! They have got hold of it.

Sannæs. They have led it up the steps, and are pretending to sell it by auction.

Hamar. They are ill-treating it! (SANNÆS *runs out.* HAMAR *snatches up the revolver from the desk and looks to see if it is loaded.*) I will—!

Signe. What are you going to do? (*As he starts to go out, she clings to him and prevents him.*)

Hamar. Let me go!

Signe. Tell me first what you are going to do! Do you mean to go out among all those men—alone?

Hamar. Yes.

Signe (*throwing her arms round him*). You shan't go!

Hamar. Take care, this is loaded!

Signe. What are you going to do with it?

Hamar (*in a determined voice, as he shakes himself free of her*). Put a bullet into the poor beast! It is too good for that crew. It shan't be put up for auction, either in joke or in earnest! (*Goes to the farther window.*) I shall get a better aim from here.

Signe (*following him, with a cry*). You will hit some one!

Hamar. No, I can aim too well for that. (*Takes aim.*)

Signe. Father! If they hear a shot from here now—

Tjælde (*starting up*). The house belongs to my creditors now—and the revolver too!

Hamar. No, I am past taking orders from you now! (TJÆLDE *snatches at the revolver, which goes off.* SIGNE *screams and rushes to her mother. Outside, but this time immediately below the window, two cries are heard :* "They are shooting at us! They are shooting at us!" *Then the noise of breaking glass is heard, and stones fly in through the windows, followed by shouts and ribald laughter.* VAL- BORG, *who has rushed in from the outer office, stands in*

front of her father to protect him, her face turned to the
*window.   A voice is heard : "*Follow me, my lads!*")*

Hamar (pointing the revolver at the window). Yes, just
you try it!

Mrs. Tjælde and Signe. They are coming in here!

Valborg. You shan't shoot! (*Stands between him and
the window.*)

Tjælde. It is Sannæs with the police! (*Cries of "Get
back, there!" are heard; then a renewed uproar and a
loud voice gradually dominating it; until at last the noise
gradually lessens and ceases.*)

Mrs. Tjælde. Thank God!   We were in great danger.
(*Sinks into a chair.   A pause.*) Henning, where are you?
(*TJÆLDE comes up behind her, and strokes her head with
his hand, but turns away immediately to hide his deep emotion.   A pause.*)

Signe (on her knees by her mother's side). But won't
they come back?   Hadn't we better go away from
here?

Mrs. Tjælde. Where to?

Signe (despairingly). What is to become of us?

Mrs. Tjælde. What God wills. (*A pause.   Meanwhile HAMAR, unobserved, has laid down the revolver on a
chair and slipped out of the room by the door at the back.*)

Valborg (softly). Signe, look! (SIGNE *gets up, looks
round the room, and gives a little cry.*)

Mrs. Tjælde. What is it?

Signe. I knew he would!

Mrs. Tjælde (apprehensively). What is it?

Valborg. Every rich family has its tame lieutenant—
and ours has just left us.   That's all.

Mrs. Tjælde (getting up). Signe, my child!

Signe (throwing herself into her arms). Mother!

Mrs. Tjælde. There will be no more pretence now.
Do not let us regret it!

Signe (in tears). Mother, mother!

Mrs. Tjælde. Things are better as they are. Do you hear, dear? Don't cry!

Signe. I am not crying! but I feel so ashamed—oh, so ashamed!

Mrs. Tjælde. It is I that ought to feel ashamed for never having had the courage to put a stop to what I saw was folly.

Signe (as before). Mother!

Mrs. Tjælde. Soon there will be no one else left to desert us; and we shall have nothing left that any one can rob us of, either.

Valborg (comes forward evidently labouring under great emotion). Yes, there is, mother; *I* mean to desert you.

Signe. You, Valborg? Desert us? You?

Valborg. Our home is going to be broken up, anyway. Each of us ought to shift for herself.

Signe. But what am I to do? I don't know how to do anything.

Mrs. Tjælde (who has sunk back into her chair). What a bad mother I must have been, not to be able to keep my children together now!

Valborg (impetuously). You know we cannot stay together now! You know we cannot put up with living on the charity of our creditors; we have done that too long!

Mrs. Tjælde. Hush, remember your father is in the room. *(A pause.)* What do you want to do, Valborg?

Valborg (after she has regained her self-control, quietly). I want to go into Mr. Holst's office, and learn commercial work—and keep myself.

Mrs. Tjælde. You don't know what you are undertaking.

Valborg. But I know what I am leaving.

Signe. And I shall only be a burden to you, mother, because I can't do anything—

Valborg. You *can!* Go out and earn a living; even if

it is only as a servant, what does that matter? Don't
live on our creditors—not for a day, not for an hour!

Signe. And what is to become of mother, then?

Mrs. Tjælde. Your mother will stay with your father.

Signe. But all alone? You, who are so ill?

Mrs. Tjælde. No, not alone! Your father and I will
be together. (TJÆLDE *comes forward, kisses the hand
she has stretched out to him, and falls on his knees by her
chair, burying his face in her lap. She strokes his hair
gently.*) Forgive your father, children. That is the
finest thing you can do. (TJÆLDE *gets up again and
goes back to the other end of the room. A messenger comes
in with a letter.*)

Signe (*turning round anxiously*). It is a letter from him!
I can't stand any more! I won't have it! (*The messenger hands the letter to* TJÆLDE.)

Tjælde. I accept no more letters.

Valborg (*looking at the letter*). It is from Sannæs?

Tjælde. He, too!

Mrs. Tjælde. Take it and read it, Valborg. Let us get
it all over at once. (VALBORG *takes the letter from the
messenger, who goes out. She opens the letter, looks at it,
and then reads it with emotion.*) " Sir,—I have owed you
everything since I entered your employment as a boy.
Therefore do not take what I am going to say amiss. You
know that about eight years ago I came into a little
legacy. I have used the money to some advantage, having
especially looked out for such investments as would not be
affected by the uncertainties of high finance. The total sum,
which now amounts to about £1400, I beg to offer to you
as a token of respectful gratitude; because, in the end, I
owe it to you that I have been able to make it that sum.
Besides, you will be able to make many times better use
of it than I could. If you need me, my dearest wish is to
remain with you in the future. Forgive me for having
seized just this moment for doing this; I could not do

otherwise.—Your obedient servant, J. SANNÆS." (*While* VALBORG *has been reading,* TJÆLDE *has come gradually forward, and is now standing beside his wife.*)

Mrs. Tjælde. Though out of all those you have helped, Henning, only one comes to your aid at a time like this, you must feel that you have your reward. (TJÆLDE *nods, and goes to the back of the room again.*) And you, children—do you see how loyally this man, a stranger, is standing by your father? (*A pause.* SIGNE *stands by the desk, crying.* TJÆLDE *walks up and down uneasily at the back of the room once or twice, then goes up the staircase.*)

Valborg. I should like to speak to Sannæs.

Mrs. Tjælde. Yes, do, dear! I couldn't, just now; and I am sure your father couldn't either. You speak to him! (*Gets up.*) Come, Signe, you and I must have a talk; you must open your heart to me now.—Ah, when have we ever had a real talk together? (SIGNE *goes to her.*) Where is your father?

Valborg. He went upstairs.

Mrs. Tjælde (*leaning on* SIGNE'S *arm*). So he did. I am sure he must be longing to rest—although he won't find it easy to do that. It has been a terrible day; but surely God will turn it to our good! (*Goes out with* SIGNE. VALBORG *goes to the back of the room and rings the bell. A messenger comes.*)

Valborg. If Mr. Sannæs is out there, please ask him to be so good as to come in here for a moment. (*The messenger goes out.*) Perhaps he won't come, when he hears it is I. (*Listens.*) Yes, he is coming!

(SANNÆS *comes in, but stops short when he sees* VALBORG, *and hurriedly puts his hands behind his back.*)

Sannæs. Is it you, Miss Valborg, that want me?

Valborg. Please come in. (SANNÆS *takes a few timid steps forward.* VALBORG *speaks in a more friendly tone.*) Come in, then! (SANNÆS *comes further into the room.*)

Valborg. You have written a letter to my father.

Sannæs (after a moment's pause). Yes.

Valborg. And made him a most generous offer.

Sannæs (as before). Oh, well—it was only natural that I should.

Valborg. Do you think so? It doesn't seem so to me. It is an offer that honours the man that made it. (*A pause.*)

Sannæs. I hope he means to accept it?

Valborg. I don't know.

Sannæs (sadly, after a moment's pause). Then he doesn't mean to? No—I suppose not.

Valborg. I honestly don't know. It depends on whether he dare.

Sannæs. Whether he dare?

Valborg. Yes. (*A pause.*)

Sannæs (evidently very shy of VALBORG). Have you any more orders for me, Miss Valborg?

Valborg (with a smile). Orders? I am not giving you orders.—You have offered also to stay with my father for the future.

Sannæs. Yes—that is to say, if he wishes me to.

Valborg. I don't know. In that case there would be only he and my mother and you; no one else.

Sannæs. Indeed? What about the others, then?

Valborg. I don't know for certain what my sister means to do—but I am leaving home to-day.

Sannæs. Then you are going to—

Valborg. —to try and get a clerkship somewhere. So that it will be a bit lonely for you to be in my father's employment now. (*A pause.*) I expect you had not thought of it in that light?

Sannæs. No—yes—that is to say, your father will have all the more need of me then.

Valborg. Indeed he will. But what sort of a prospect is it for you to bind up your fortunes with my father's? The future is so very problematical, you know.

Sannæs. What sort of a prospect—?

Valborg. Yes, a young man should have some sort of a prospect before him.

Sannæs. Yes—of course; that is to say, I only thought that at first it would be so difficult for him.

Valborg. But I am thinking of you. Surely you have some plans for the future?

Sannæs (embarrassed). Really I would rather not talk about myself.

Valborg. But I want to.—You have something else in reserve, then?

Sannæs. Well—if I must tell you—I have some well-to-do relations in America who have for a long time wanted me to go over there. I should soon be able to get a good situation there.

Valborg. Indeed?—But why haven't you accepted such a good offer long before this? (SANNÆS *does not answer.*) You must have been sacrificing your best interests by staying so long with us? (SANNÆS *is still silent.*) And it will be making a still greater sacrifice to stay with us now—

Sannæs (struggling with his embarrassment). I have never thought of it as being that.

Valborg. But my father can scarcely accept so much from you.

Sannæs (in alarm). Why not?

Valborg. Because it really would be too much.—And, in any case, *I* shall try to prevent him.

Sannæs (almost imploringly). You, Miss Valborg?

Valborg. Yes. You must not be misemployed any longer.

Sannæs. Misemployed? In what I *myself* desire so much?

Valborg. When I have talked it over with my father, I think he will see my point.

Sannæs (anxiously). What do you mean?

Valborg (after a moment's reflection). I mean, the reason of your having made such great sacrifices for us—and of your being willing to make still greater now. (*A pause.* SANNÆS *hangs his head, and is raising his hands to hide his face, when suddenly he puts them behind his back again.* VALBORG *continues, in gentle but firm tones :*) I have taught myself, all my life, to look behind deeds and words for their motives.

Sannæs (quietly, without raising his head). You have taught yourself to be cruelly bitter, hard and unjust.

Valborg (starts, but collects herself, and says gently :) Don't say that, Mr. Sannæs! It is not hard-heartedness or bitterness that makes me think of your future now— and makes me wish to spare you disappointment.

Sannæs (with a cry of pain). Miss Valborg!

Valborg. Be honest with yourself, and you will be able to take a fairer view of what I have just said.

Sannæs. Have you any more orders, Miss Valborg?

Valborg. I give you no orders, as I have told you already. I am only bidding you good-bye; and I do it with grateful thanks to you for all your goodness to me—and to us all. Good-bye and good luck, Mr. Sannæs. (SANNÆS *bows.*) Won't you shake hands? Ah, I forgot—I offended you. I beg your pardon for that. (SANNÆS *bows and turns to go.*) Come, Mr. Sannæs— let us at least part as good friends! You are going to America, and I am going among strangers. Let us go away wishing one another well.

Sannæs (moved). Good-bye, Miss Valborg. (*Turns to go.*)

Valborg. Mr. Sannæs—shake hands!

Sannæs (stopping). No, Miss Valborg.

Valborg. Don't treat me uncivilly; I have not deserved that. (SANNÆS *again turns to go.*) Mr. Sannæs!

Sannæs (stopping). You might soil your fingers, Miss Valborg! (*Walks proudly away.*)

Valborg (*controlling herself with an effort*). Well, we have offended each other now. But why should we not forgive each other as well?

Sannæs. Because you have just offended me for the second time to-day — and more deeply than the first time.

Valborg. Oh, this is too much! I spoke as I did, because I owed it to myself not to be put in a false position, and owed it to you to spare you future disappointment. And you call that insulting you! Which of us has insulted the other, I should like to know?

Sannæs. You have, by thinking such things of me. Do you realise how cruelly you have spoilt the happiest action of my life?

Valborg. I have done so quite unintentionally, then. I am only glad that I was mistaken.

Sannæs (*bitterly*). You are glad! So it really makes you glad to know that I am not a scoundrel!

Valborg (*quietly*). Who said anything of the kind?

Sannæs. You! You know the weak spot in my armour; but that you should on that account believe that I could lay a trap for you and try to trade on your father's misfortune, Miss Valborg—! No, I cannot shake hands with any one who has thought so badly of me as that! And, since you have so persistently insulted me that I have lost all the timidity I used to feel in your presence, let me tell you this openly; these hands (*stretching out his hands to her*) have grown red and ugly in loyal work for your father, and his daughter should have been above mocking at me for them! (*Turns to go, but stops.*) And, one word more. Ask your father for *his* hand now, and hold fast to it, instead of deserting him on the very day that misfortune has overtaken him. That would be more to the point than worrying about *my* future. I can look after that for myself. (*Turns again to go, but comes back.*) And when, in his service—which will be no easy service now—your hands bear the same honourable marks of work as mine do, and are as red as mine, then you will perhaps understand how you have hurt me! At present you cannot. (*He goes quickly towards the door of the outer office.*)

Valborg (*with a wry smile*). What a temper! (*More seriously.*) And yet, after all—. (*Looks after him. Just as* SANNÆS *gets to the door* TJÆLDE'S *voice is heard calling him from the top of the staircase.* SANNÆS *answers him.*)

Tjælde (*coming down the stairs*). Sannæs! Sannæs! I can see Jakobsen coming. (*Hurries across the room as if pursued by fear.* SANNÆS *follows him.*) Of course he will be coming back to look for me again! It is cowardly of me to feel that I cannot stand it; but I cannot—not to-day, not now! I cannot stand any more! Stop him! Don't let him come in! I shall have to drink my cup of misery to the dregs; but (*almost in a whisper*) not all at one draught! (*Hides his face in his hands.*)

Sannæs. He shan't come ; don't be afraid! (*Goes quickly out, with an air of determination.*)

Tjælde. It is hard—oh, it is hard!

Valborg (*coming to his side*). Father! (*He looks at her, anxiously.*) You may safely accept the money Sannæs offers you.

Tjælde (*in surprise*). What do you mean by that?

Valborg. I mean—that, if you do, I will not forsake you either, but stay here with you too.

Tjælde (*incredulously*). You, Valborg?

Valborg. Yes, you know I want to learn office work, and business; and I would rather learn in your office.

Tjælde (*shyly*). I don't understand what you—?

Valborg. Don't you understand, dear? I believe I could become of some use in the office. And in that way, you know, we might begin afresh—and try, with God's help, to pay your creditors.

Tjælde (happily, but shyly). My child! Who put such a happy idea into your head?

Valborg (putting an arm round his neck). Father, forgive me for all that I have neglected to do! You shall see how I will try and make up for it! How hard I shall work!

Tjælde (still half incredulous). My child! My child!

Valborg. I feel — I cannot tell you how deeply — a craving for love and for work! (*Throws both her arms round his neck*.) Oh, father, how I love you!—and how I shall work for you!

Tjælde. Ah, that is the Valborg I have waited for, ever since you were a little child! But we had drifted away from one another, somehow.

Valborg. No more about the past! Look forward, father, look forward! Concerns " that would not be affected by the uncertainties of high finance,"—weren't those his words?

Tjælde. So you were struck by that expression, too?

Valborg. That may mean a future for us now! We will have a home all to ourselves—a little house down on the shore—and I shall help you, and Signe will help mother— we shall know what it is to live, for the first time!

Tjælde. What happiness it will be!

Valborg. Only look forward, father! Look forward! A united family is invincible!

Tjælde. And to think that such help should come to me now!

Valborg. Yes, now we are all going to our posts—and all together, where formerly you stood alone! You will have good fairies round you; wherever you look, you will see happy faces and busy fingers all day long; and we shall all enjoy our meals and our evenings together, just as we did when we were children!

Tjælde. That, above everything!

Valborg. Ha, ha!—it is after the rain that the birds

sing blithest, you know! And this time our happiness can never miscarry, because we shall have something worth living for!

Tjælde. Let us go to your mother! This will cheer her heart!

Valborg. Ah, how I have learnt to love her! What has happened to-day has taught me.

Tjælde. It is for her that we shall all work now.

Valborg. Yes—for her, for her. She shall rest now. Let us go to her!

Tjælde. Kiss me first, my dear. (*His voice trembles.*) It is so long since you did!

Valborg (kissing him). Father!

Tjælde. Now let us go to your mother. (*The curtain falls as they go out together.*)

ACT IV

(SCENE.—*In the garden of* TJÆLDE'S *new home, on the shore of the fjord, three years later. A view of tranquil, sunlit sea, dotted with boats, in the background. On the left a portion of the house is seen, with an open window within which* VALBORG *is seen writing at a desk. The garden is shaded with birch trees; flower-beds run round the house, and the whole atmosphere is one of modest comfort. Two small garden tables and several chairs are in the foreground on the right. A chair standing by itself, further back, has evidently had a recent occupant. When the curtain rises the stage is empty, but* VALBORG *is visible at the open window. Soon afterwards* TJÆLDE *comes in, wheeling* MRS. TJÆLDE *in an invalid chair.*)

Mrs. Tjælde. Another lovely day!

Tjælde. Lovely! There was not a ripple on the sea last night. I saw a couple of steamers far out, and a sailing ship that had hove to, and the fisher-boats drifting silently in.

Mrs. Tjælde. And think of the storm that was raging two days ago!

Tjælde. And think of the storm that broke over our lives barely three years ago! I was thinking of that in the night.

Mrs. Tjælde. Sit down here with me.

Tjælde. Shall we not continue our stroll?

Mrs. Tjælde. The sun is too hot.

Tjælde. Not for me.

Mrs. Tjælde. You big strong man! It is too hot for me.

Tjælde (taking a chair). There you are, then.

Mrs. Tjælde (taking off his hat and wiping his forehead). You are very hot, dear. You have never looked so handsome as you do now!

Tjælde. That's just as well, as you have so much time to admire me now!

Mrs. Tjælde. Now that I find getting about so difficult, you mean? Ah, that is only my pretence, so as to get you to wheel me about!

Tjælde (with a sigh). Ah, my dear, it is good of you to take it so cheerfully. But that you should be the only one of us to bear such hard traces of our misfortune—

Mrs. Tjælde (interrupting him). Do you forget your own whitened hair? That is a sign of it, too, but a beautiful one! And, as for my being an invalid, I thank God every day for it! In the first place I have almost no pain, and then it gives me the opportunity to feel how good you are to me in every way.

Tjælde. You enjoy your life, then?

Mrs. Tjælde. Yes, indeed I do—and just as I should wish to.

Tjælde. Just to be spoiled, and yourself to spoil us?

Valborg (from the window). I have finished the accounts, father.

Tjælde. Doesn't it come out at about what I said?

Valborg. Almost exactly. Shall I enter it in the ledger at once?

Tjælde. Oho! You are glad then, as you seem in such a hurry?

Valborg. Certainly! Such a good stroke of business!

Tjælde. And both you and Sannæs tried your best to dissuade me from it!

Valborg. Such a pair of wiseacres!

Mrs. Tjælde. Ah, your father is your master, my dear!

Tjælde. Oh, it is easy enough to captain a small army

that marches on, instead of a big one that is in retreat. (VALBORG *goes on with her work.*)

Mrs. Tjælde. And yet it seemed hard enough for us to give it up.

Tjælde. Yes, yes—oh, yes. I can tell you, I was thinking of that last night. If God had given me what I begged for then, what state should we have been in now? I was thinking of that, too.

Mrs. Tjælde. It is the fact of the estate being at last wound up that has brought all these thoughts into your mind, dear?

Tjælde. Yes.

Mrs. Tjælde. Then I must confess that I, too, have scarcely been able to think of anything else since yesterday, when Sannæs went into town to settle it up. This is a red-letter day! Signe is wrestling with a little banquet for us; we shall see what an artist she has become! Here she is!

Tjælde. I think I will just go and look over Valborg's accounts. (*Goes to the window.* SIGNE *comes out of the house, wearing a cook's apron and carrying a basin.*)

Signe. Mother, you must taste my soup! (*Offers her a spoonful.*)

Mrs. Tjælde. Clever girl! (*Tastes the soup.*) Perhaps it would stand a little—. No, it is very good as it is. You are clever!

Signe. Am I not! Will Sannæs be back soon?

Mrs. Tjælde. Your father says we may expect him any moment.

Tjælde (*at the window,* **to** VALBORG). No, wait a moment. I will come in. (*Goes into the house, and is seen within the window beside* VALBORG.)

Mrs. Tjælde. My little Signe, I want to ask you something?

Signe. Do you?

Mrs. Tjælde. What was in the letter you had yesterday evening?

Signe. Aha, I might have guessed that was it! Nothing, mother.

Mrs. Tjælde. Nothing that pained you, then?

Signe. I slept like a top all night—so you can judge for yourself.

Mrs. Tjælde. I am so glad. But, you know, there seems to me something a little forced in the gay way you say that?

Signe. Does there? Well, it was something that I shall always be ashamed of; that is all.

Mrs. Tjælde. I am thankful to hear it, for—

Signe (interrupting her). That must be Sannæs. I hear wheels. Yes, here he is! He has come too soon; dinner won't be ready for half an hour yet.

Mrs. Tjælde. That doesn't matter.

Signe. Father, here is Sannæs!

Tjælde (from within). Good! I will come out! (SIGNE *goes into the house as* TJÆLDE *comes out.* SANNÆS *comes in a moment later.*)

Tjælde and Mrs. Tjælde. Welcome!

Sannæs. Thank you! (*Lays down his dust-coat and driving gloves on a chair, and comes forward.*)

Tjælde. Well?

Sannæs. Yes—your bankruptcy is discharged!

Mrs. Tjælde. And the result was—?

Sannæs. Just about what we expected.

Tjælde. And, I suppose, just about what Mr. Berent wrote?

Sannæs. Just about, except for one or two inconsiderable trifles. You can see for yourself. (*Gives him a bundle of papers.*) The high prices that have ruled of late, and good management, have altered the whole situation.

Tjælde (who has opened the papers and glanced at the totals). A deficit of £12,000.

Sannæs. I made a declaration on your behalf, that you

intended to try and repay that sum, but that you should be at liberty to do it in whatever way you found best. And so—

Tjælde. And so—?

Sannæs. —I preferred on the spot rather more than half the amount you still owed Jakobsen.

Mrs. Tjælde. Not really? (Tjælde *takes out a pencil and begins making calculations on the margins of the papers*.)

Sannæs. There was general satisfaction—and they all sent you their cordial congratulations.

Mrs. Tjælde. So that, if all goes well—

Tjælde. Yes, if things go as well with the business as they promise to, Sannæs, in twelve or fourteen years I shall have paid every one in full.

Mrs. Tjælde. We haven't much longer than that left to live, dear!

Tjælde. Then we shall die poor. And I shall not complain!

Mrs. Tjælde. No, indeed! The honourable name you will leave to your children will be well worth it.

Tjælde. And they will inherit a sound business, which they can go on with if they choose.

Mrs. Tjælde. Did you hear that, Valborg?

Valborg (*from the window*). Every word! (Sannæs *bows to her*.) I must go in and tell Signe! (*Moves away from the window*.)

Mrs. Tjælde. What did Jakobsen say? — honest old Jakobsen?

Sannæs. He was very much affected, as you would expect. He will certainly be coming out here to-day.

Tjælde (*looking up from the papers*). And Mr. Berent?

Sannæs. He is coming hard on my heels. I was to give you his kind regards and tell you so.

Tjælde. Splendid! We owe him so much.

Mrs. Tjælde. Yes, he has been a true friend to us. But,

talking of true friends, I have something particular to ask *you*, Sannæs.

Sannæs. Me, Mrs. Tjælde?

Mrs. Tjælde. The maid told me that yesterday, when you went into town, you took the greater part of your belongings with you. Is that so?

Sannæs. Yes, Mrs. Tjælde.

Tjælde. What does that mean? (*To his wife.*) You said nothing about it to me, my dear.

Mrs. Tjælde. Because I thought it might be a misunderstanding. But now I must ask what was the meaning of it. Are you going away?

Sannæs (*fingering a chair, in evident confusion*). Yes, Mrs. Tjælde.

Tjælde. Where to? You never said anything about it.

Sannæs. No; but I have always considered that I should have finished my task here as soon as the estate was finally wound up.

Tjælde and Mrs. Tjælde. You mean to leave us?

Sannæs. Yes.

Tjælde. But why?

Mrs. Tjælde. Where do you mean to go?

Sannæs. To my relations in America. I can now, without doing you any harm, withdraw my capital from the business by degrees and transfer it abroad.

Tjælde. And dissolve our partnership?

Sannæs. You know that at any rate you had decided now to resume the old style of the firm's name.

Tjælde. That is true; but, Sannæs, what does it all mean? What is your reason?

Mrs. Tjælde. Are you not happy here, where we are all so attached to you?

Tjælde. You have quite as good a prospect for the future here as in America.

Mrs. Tjælde. We held together in evil days; are we not to hold together now that good days have come?

Sannæs. I owe you both so much.

Mrs. Tjælde. Good heavens, it is we that owe you—

Tjælde. —more than we can ever repay. (*Reproachfully.*) Sannæs!

(SIGNE *comes in, having taken off her cooking apron.*)

Signe. Congratulations! Congratulations! Father—mother! (*Kisses them both.*) Welcome, Sannæs!—But aren't you pleased?—now? (*A pause.* VALBORG *comes in.*)

Valborg. What has happened?

Mrs. Tjælde. Sannæs wants to leave us, my children. (*A pause.*)

Signe. But, Sannæs—!

Tjælde. Even if you want to go away, why have you never said a single word to us about it before? (*To the others.*) Or has he spoken to any of you? (MRS. TJÆLDE *shakes her head.*)

Signe. No.

Sannæs. It was because—because—I wanted to be able to go as soon as I had told you. Otherwise it would be too hard to go.

Tjælde. You must have very serious grounds for it, then! Has anything happened to you to—to make it necessary? (SANNÆS *does not answer.*)

Mrs. Tjælde. And to make it impossible for you to trust any of us?

Sannæs (*shyly*). I thought I had better keep it to myself. (*A pause.*)

Tjælde. That makes it still more painful for us—to think that you could go about in our little home circle here, where you have shared everything with us, carrying the secret of this intention hidden in your heart.

Sannæs. Do not be hard on me! Believe me, if I could stay, I would; and if I could tell you the reason, I would. (*A pause.*)

Signe (to her mother, in an undertone). Perhaps he wants to get married?

Mrs. Tjælde. Would his being here with us make any difference to that? Any one that Sannæs loved would be dear to us.

Tjælde (going up to SANNÆS *and putting an arm round his shoulders).* Tell one of us, then, if you cannot tell us all. Is it nothing we can help you in?

Sannæs. No.

Tjælde. But can you judge of that alone? One does not always realise how much some one else's advice, on the experience of an older man, may help one.

Sannæs. Unfortunately it is as I say.

Tjælde. It must be something very painful, then?

Sannæs. Please—!

Tjælde. Well, Sannæs, you have quite cast a cloud over to-day's happiness for us. I shall miss you as I have never missed any one.

Mrs. Tjælde. I cannot imagine the house without Sannæs!

Tjælde (to his wife). Come, dear, shall we·go in again?

Mrs. Tjælde. Yes—it is not nice out here any longer. (TJÆLDE *takes her into the house.* SIGNE *turns to* VALBORG *to go in with her, but when she comes close to her she gives a little cry.* VALBORG *takes her arm, and their eyes meet.*)

Signe. Where have my wits been? (*She goes into the house, looking back at* VALBORG *and* SANNÆS. *The latter is giving way to his emotion, but as soon as his eyes fall on* VALBORG *he recovers himself.*)

Valborg (impetuously). Sannæs!

Sannæs. What are your orders, Miss Valborg?

Valborg (turning away from him, then turning back, but avoiding his eyes). Do you really mean to leave us?

Sannæs. Yes, Miss Valborg. (*A pause.*)

Valborg. So we shall never stand back to back at our desks in the same room again?

Sannæs. No, Miss Valborg.

Valborg. That is a pity; I had become so accustomed to it.

Sannæs. You will easily become accustomed to some one else's—back.

Valborg. Ah, some one else is some one else.

Sannæs. You must excuse me, Miss Valborg; I don't feel in the humour for jesting to-day. (*Turns to go.*)

Valborg (*looking up at him*). Is this to be our parting, then? (*A pause.*)

Sannæs. I thought of taking leave of you all this afternoon.

Valborg (*taking a step towards him*). But ought not we two to settle our accounts first?

Sannæs (*coldly*). No, Miss Valborg.

Valborg. Do you feel then that everything between us has been just as it ought?

Sannæs. God knows I don't!

Valborg. But you think I am to blame?—Oh, well, it doesn't matter.

Sannæs. I am quite willing to take the blame.   But, anyway, it is all finished with now.

Valborg. But if we were to share the blame? You cannot be quite indifferent as to which of us should take it?

Sannæs. I confess I am not.   But, as I said, I do not wish for any settling of accounts between us.

Valborg. But I wish it.

Sannæs. You will have plenty of time to settle it to your own satisfaction.

Valborg. But, if I am in difficulties about it, I cannot do it alone.

Sannæs. I do not think you will find any difficulty.

Valborg. But if *I* think so?—if I feel myself deeply wronged?

Sannæs. I have told you that I am willing to take all the blame upon myself.

Valborg. No, Sannæs—I don't want charity; I want to be understood. I have a question to ask you.

Sannæs. As you will.

Valborg. How was it that we got on so well for the first year after my father's failure—and even longer? Have you ever thought of that?

Sannæs. Yes. I think it was because we never talked about anything but our work—about business.

Valborg. You were my instructor.

Sannæs. And when you no longer needed an instructor—

Valborg. —we hardly spoke to one another.

Sannæs (softly). No.

Valborg. Well, what could I say or do, when every sign of friendship on my part went unnoticed?

Sannæs. Unnoticed? Oh no, Miss Valborg, I noticed them.

Valborg. That was my punishment, then!

Sannæs. God forbid I should do you an injustice. You had a motive which did you credit; you felt compassion for me, and so you could not help acting as you did. But, Miss Valborg, I refuse your compassion.

Valborg. And suppose it were gratitude?

Sannæs (softly). I dreaded that more than anything else! I had had a warning.

Valborg. You must admit, Sannæs, that all this made you very difficult to deal with!

Sannæs. I quite admit that. But, honestly, *you* must admit that I had good reason to mistrust an interest in me that sprang from mere gratitude. Had circumstances been different, I should only have bored you cruelly; I knew that quite well. And I had no fancy for being an amusement for your idle hours.

Valborg. How you have mistaken me! — If you will

N ⁶⁹⁶

think of it, surely you must understand how different a girl, who has been accustomed to travel and society, becomes when she has to stay at home and work because it is her duty. She comes to judge men by an altogether different standard, too. The men that she used to think delightful are very likely to appear small in her eyes when it is a question of the demands life makes on ability or courage or self-sacrifice; while the men she used to laugh at are transformed in her eyes into models of what God meant men to be, when she is brought into close contact with them in her father's office.—Is there anything so surprising in that? (*A pause.*)

Sannæs. Thank you, at all events, for saying that to me. It has done me good. But you should have said it sooner.

Valborg (*emphatically*). How could I, when you misjudged everything I did or said? No; it was impossible until mistakes and misunderstandings had driven us so far apart that we could not endure them any longer. (*Turns away.*)

Sannæs. Perhaps you are right. I cannot at once recall all that has happened. If I have been mistaken, I shall by degrees find the knowledge of it a profound comfort.—You must excuse me, Miss Valborg, I have a number of things to see to. (*Turns to go.*)

Valborg (*anxiously*). Sannæs, as you admit that you have judged me unjustly, don't you think you ought at least to give me—some satisfaction?

Sannæs. You may be certain, Miss Valborg, that when I am balancing our account you shall not suffer any injustice. But I cannot do it now. All I have to do now is to get ready to go.

Valborg. But you are not ready to go, Sannæs! You have not finished your work here yet! There is what I just spoke of—and something else that dates farther back than that.

Sannæs. You must feel how painful it is for me to prolong this interview. (*Turns to go.*)

Valborg. But surely you won't go without setting right something that I am going to beg you to?

Sannæs. What is that, Miss Valborg?

Valborg. Something that happened a long time ago.

Sannæs. If it is in my power, I will do what you ask.

Valborg. It is.—Ever since that day you have never offered to shake hands with me.

Sannæs. Have you really noticed that? (*A pause.*)

Valborg (*with a smile, turning away*). Will you do so now?

Sannæs (*stepping nearer to her*). Is this more than a mere whim?

Valborg (*concealing her emotion*). How can you ask such a question now?

Sannæs. Because all this time you have never once asked me to shake hands with you.

Valborg. I wanted you to offer me your hand. (*A pause.*)

Sannæs. Are you serious for once?

Valborg. I mean it, seriously.

Sannæs (*in a happier voice*). You really set a value on it?

Valborg. A great value.

Sannæs (*going up to her*). Here it is, then!

Valborg (*turning and taking his hand*). I accept the hand you offer me.

Sannæs (*turning pale*). What do you mean?

Valborg. I mean that for some time past I have known that I should be proud to be the wife of a man who has loved me, and me alone, ever since he was a boy, and has saved my father and us all.

Sannæs. Oh, Miss Valborg!

Valborg. And you wanted to go away, rather than offer me your hand; and that, only because we had accepted help from you—and you did not think we were free agents! That was too much; and, as you would not speak, I had to!

Sannæs (kneeling to her). Miss Valborg!

Valborg. You have the most loyal nature, the most delicate mind, and the warmest heart I have ever known.

Sannæs. This is a thousand times too much!

Valborg. Next to God, I have to thank you that I have become what I am; and I feel that I can offer you a life's devotion such as you would rarely find in this world.

Sannæs. I cannot answer because I scarcely realise what you are saying. But you are saying it because you are sorry for me, now that I have to go away, and feel that you owe me some gratitude. (*Takes both her hands in his.*) Let me speak! I know the truth better than you, and have thought over it far more than you. You are so immeasurably above me in ability, in education, in manners—and a wife should not be able to look down on her husband. At all events, I am too proud to be willing to be exposed to that. No, what you are feeling now is only the result of your beautiful nature, and the recollection of it will hallow all my life. All the pain and all the happiness I have known have come from you. Your life will be one of self-renunciation; but, God knows there are many such! And my burden will be lightened now, because I shall know that your good wishes will always be with me. (*Gets up.*) But part we must—and now more than ever! For I could not bear to be near you unless you were mine, and to make you mine would only mean misery for us both after a little while!

Valborg. Sannæs—!

Sannæs (holding her hands and interrupting her). I entreat you not to say anything more! You have too much power over me; do not use it to make me sin! For it would be that—a great sin—to put two honest hearts into a false position, where they would distress one another, even perhaps get to hate one another.

Valborg. But let me—

Sannæs (letting go her hands and stepping back). No, you must not tempt me. Life with you would mean perpetual anxiety, for I should never feel equal to what it would demand of me! But now I can part from you comforted. There will be no bitterness in my heart now; and by degrees all my thoughts of the past and of you will turn to sweetness. God bless you! May every good fortune go with you! Good-bye! (*Goes quickly towards the house.*)

Valborg. Sannæs! (*Follows him.*) Sannæs! Listen to me! (SANNÆS *takes up his coat and gloves, and, as he rushes out without looking where he is going, runs full tilt into* BERENT *who comes in at that moment followed by* JAKOBSEN.)

Sannæs. I beg your pardon! (*Rushes out to the right.*)

Berent. Are you two playing a game of blind man's buff?

Valborg. God knows we are!

Berent. You need not be so emphatic about it! I have had forcible evidence of it. (*Rubs his stomach and laughs.*)

Valborg. You must excuse me! Father is in there. (*Points to the left and goes hurriedly out to the right.*)

Berent. We don't seem to be getting a particularly polite reception!

Jakobsen. No, we seem to be rather in the way, Mr. Berent.

Berent (laughing). It looks like it. But what has been going on?

Jakobsen. I don't know. They looked as if they had been fighting, their faces were so flushed.

Berent. They looked upset, you mean?

Jakobsen. Yes, that's it. Ah, here is Mr. Tjælde!

(*To himself.*) Good Lord, how aged he looks! (*Withdraws into the background as* BERENT *goes forward to greet* TJÆLDE, *who comes in.*)

Tjælde (*to* BERENT). I am delighted to see you! You are always welcome in our little home—and this year more welcome than ever!

Berent. Because things are going better than ever this year! I congratulate you on your discharge—and also on your determination to pay everything in full!

Tjælde. Yes, if God wills, I mean to—

Berent. Well, things are going splendidly, aren't they?

Tjælde. So far, yes.

Berent. You are over the worst of it, now that you have laid the foundations of a new business and laid them solidly.

Tjælde. One of the things that have given me the greatest encouragement has been the fact that I have won your confidence—and that has gained me the confidence of others.

Berent. I could have done nothing unless you had first of all done everything. But don't let us say any more about it!—Well, the place looks even prettier than it did last year.

Tjælde. We do a little more to it each year, you know.

Berent. And you are still all together here?

Tjælde. So far, yes.

Berent. Ah, by the way, I can give you news of your deserter. (TJÆLDE *looks surprised.*) I mean your lieutenant!

Tjælde. Oh—of him! Have you seen him?

Berent. I was on the same boat coming here. There was a very rich girl on board.

Tjælde (*laughing*). Oh, I see!

Berent. All the same, I don't think it came to anything. It is rather like coming upon a herd of deer when

you are stalking; after your first shot, you don't find it
so easy to get another; they have grown wary!

*Jakobsen (who during this conversation has been screwing
up his courage to address* TJÆLDE). I—I am a pig, I am!
I know that!

Tjælde (taking his hand). Oh, come, Jakobsen!—

Jakobsen. A great blundering pig!—But I know it now!

Tjælde. That's all right! I can tell you I am delighted
to be able to set affairs straight between you and me.

Jakobsen. I don't know what to answer. It goes to
my heart! (*Shakes his hand heartily.*) You are a far
better man than I,—and I said so to my wife. " He's a
splendid fellow," I said.

Tjælde (releasing his hand). Let us forget everything
except the happy days we have had together, Jakobsen!
How do things go at the Brewery?

Jakobsen. At the Brewery! As long as folk ladle beer
into their stomachs at the rate they do now—

Berent. Jakobsen was kind enough to drive me out here.
We had a most amusing drive. He is a character.

Jakobsen (in an anxious undertone, to TJÆLDE). What
does he mean by that?

Tjælde. That you are different from most people.

Jakobsen. Ah!—I didn't feel sure, you know, whether
he wasn't sitting there making game of me, all the way
here.

Tjælde. How can you think such a thing? (*To*
BERENT.) Do come into the house. Excuse my going
first; but my wife is not always quite prepared to receive
visitors since she has been able to do so little for herself.
(*Goes into the house.*)

Berent. I don't think Mr. Tjælde seems to me to be
looking in quite as good form as I expected?

Jakobsen. Don't you? I didn't notice anything.

Berent. Perhaps I am mistaken. I think he meant us
to follow him in, didn't he?

184 The Bankrupt [ACT IV.

Jakobsen. So I understood.

Berent. Then, as you have brought me so far, you must take me in to Mrs. Tjælde.

Jakobsen. I am quite at your service, sir. I have the deepest respect for Mrs. Tjælde—(*hurriedly*)—and of course for Mr. Tjælde too. Of course.

Berent. Yes. Well, let us go in.

Jakobsen. Let us go in. (*He tries anxiously to keep in step with* BERENT'S *peculiar walk, but finds it difficult.*)

Berent. I think you had better not try. My step suits very few.

Jakobsen. Oh, I shall manage—! (*They go out to the left.* SANNÆS *comes hurriedly in from the right, and crosses the stage; looks around; then comes across to the foreground and leans with his back against a tree.* VALBORG *comes in a moment later, comes forward, sees him, and laughs.*)

Sannæs. There, you see, Miss Valborg; you are laughing at me.

Valborg. I don't know whether I want to laugh or to cry.

Sannæs. Believe me, you are mistaken about this, Miss Valborg. You don't see things as plainly as I do.

Valborg. Which of us was it that was mistaken to-day? —and had to beg pardon for it?

Sannæs. It was I, I know. But this is impossible! A real union of hearts needs to be founded on more than respect—

Valborg (*laughing*). On love?

Sannæs. You misunderstand me. Could you go into society with me without feeling embarrassed? (VALBORG *laughs.*) You see, the mere idea of it makes you laugh.

Valborg (*laughing*). I am laughing because you are magnifying the least important part of it into the most important.

Sannæs. You know how awkward and shy—in fact downright frightened I am amongst those who—.

(VALBORG *laughs again.*)   There, you see—you can't help laughing at the idea!

Valborg. I should perhaps even laugh **at** you when we were in society together!   (*Laughs.*)

Sannæs (*seriously*). But I should suffer horribly if you did.

Valborg. Believe me, Sannæs, I love you well enough to be able to afford to have a little laugh sometimes at your little imperfections.   Indeed, I often do!   And suppose we were out in society, and I saw you weighed down under the necessity for pretty manners that do not come easy to you; if I did laugh at you, do you think there would be any unkindness behind my laughter?   If others laughed at you, do you suppose I would not, the very next moment, take your arm and walk proudly down the room with you?   I know what you really are, and others know it too!   Thank God it is not only bad deeds that are known to others in this world!

Sannæs. Your words intoxicate me and carry me off my feet!

Valborg (*earnestly*). If you think I am only flattering you, let us put it to the test.   Mr. Berent is here.   He moves in the very best society, but he is superior to its littlenesses.   Shall we take his opinion?   Without betraying anything, I could make him give it in a moment.

Sannæs (*carried away*). I want no one's opinion but yours!

Valborg. That's right!   If only you feel certain of my love—

Sannæs (*impetuously*). —then nothing else will seem to matter; and that alone will be able to teach me all that I lack, in a very short time.

Valborg. Look into my eyes!

Sannæs (*taking her hands*). Yes!

Valborg. Do you believe that nothing would ever make me ashamed of you!

Sannæs. Yes, I believe that.

Valborg (with emotion). Do you believe that I love you?

Sannæs. Yes! *(Falls on one knee.)*

Valborg. Deeply enough for my love to last all our lives?

Sannæs. Yes, yes!

Valborg. Then stay with me; and we will look after the old folk—and replace them when, in God's good time, they are taken from us. (SANNÆS *bursts into tears.* TJÆLDE, *who has come to the window to show* BERENT *his ledgers, happens to look up and sees* VALBORG *and* SANNÆS.)

Tjælde (leaning out of the window, and speaking gently :) Valborg, what has happened?

Valborg (quietly). Only that Sannæs and I are engaged to be married.

Tjælde. Is it possible! *(To* BERENT, *who is immersed in the accounts.)* Excuse me! *(Hurries away from the window.)*

Sannæs (who, in his emotion has heard nothing). Forgive me! It has been such a long, hard struggle—and I feel overwhelmed!

Valborg. Let us go in to my mother.

Sannæs (shrinking back). I can't, Miss Valborg—you must wait a little—

Valborg. Here they come. (TJÆLDE *comes in wheeling* MRS. TJÆLDE *in her chair.* VALBORG *runs to her mother and throws herself into her arms.*)

Mrs. Tjælde (softly). God be praised and thanked!

Tjælde (going up to SANNÆS *and embracing him).* My son!

Mrs. Tjælde. So that was why Sannæs wanted to go away ! Oh, Sannæs ! (TJÆLDE *brings* SANNÆS *up to her.* SANNÆS *kneels and kisses her hand, then gets up and goes into the background, to recover himself.* SIGNE *comes in.*)

Signe. Mother, everything is ready now!

Mrs. Tjælde. So are things out here!

Signe (looking round). Not really?

Valborg (to SIGNE). Forgive me for never having told you!

Signe. You certainly kept your secret well!

Valborg. I kept long years of suffering secret—that was all! (SIGNE *kisses her and whispers to her; then turns to* SANNÆS.)

Signe. Sannæs! *(Shakes his hand.)* So we are to be brother and sister-in-law?

Sannæs (embarrassed). Oh, Miss Signe—

Signe. But you mustn't call me Miss Signe now, you know!

Valborg. You must expect that! He calls me " Miss " Valborg still!

Singe. Well, he won't be able to do that when you are married, anyway!

Mrs. Tjælde (to TJÆLDE). But where are our friends?

Tjælde. Mr. Berent is in the office. There he is, at the window.

Berent (at the window). Now I am coming straight out to congratulate you, with my friend Jakobsen. *(Comes out.)*

Valborg (going to TJÆLDE). Father!

Tjælde. My child!

Valborg. If we had not known those bad days we should never have known this happy one! *(He gives her a grip of the hand.)*

Tjælde (to BERENT). Allow me to present to you my daughter Valborg's *fiancé*—Mr. Sannæs.

Berent. I congratulate you on your choice, Miss Valborg —and I congratulate the whole family on such a son-in-law.

Valborg (triumphantly). There, Sannæs!

Jakobsen. May I too, though I am only a stupid sort of chap, say that this lad has been in love with you ever since he was in his teens—he hardly could be sooner than that.

But I can tell you, honestly, I should never have credited you with having so much sense as to take him. (*All laugh.*)

Mrs. Tjælde. Signe is whispering to me that our dinner is getting cold.

Signe. May I take my mother's place and ask you to take me in to dinner, Mr. Berent?

Berent (offering her his arm). I am honoured!—But our bridal pair must go first!

Valborg. Sannæs—?

Sannæs (whispers, as he gives her his arm). To think that I have you on my arm! (*They go into the house, followed by* BERENT *and* SIGNE, *and by* JAKOBSEN.)

Tjælde (bending over his wife, as he prepares to wheel her chair in). My dear, God has blessed our house now!

Mrs. Tjælde. My dear man!

Curtain.

THE KING

A PLAY IN A PROLOGUE AND FOUR ACTS

DRAMATIS PERSONÆ

The KING.
HARALD GRAN, a rich manufacturer.
KOLL, Chief Magistrate of the district.
FLINK.
CLARA ERNST.
The PRINCESS.
BARONESS MARC.
ANNA, a deaf and dumb girl.
FALBE.
The MAYOR.
NATHALIE, his daughter.
ALSTAD.
VILHELM, his son.
The PARISH PRIEST.
BANG, a rich trader.
VINÄGER.
COUNT PLATEN.
The GENERAL.
MATILDE.
A Ballad Singer.
A Young Beggar.
A Servant of the King's.

Ladies and Gentlemen, Masked Dancers, Work-people, Farmers, etc.

THE KING

PROLOGUE

(SCENE.—*A large gothic hall, brilliantly illuminated, in which a masked ball is taking place. At the rise of the curtain a ballet is being performed in the centre of the hall. Masked dancers are grouped around, watching it. Two of them, women, are conversing on the right of the stage.*)

First Mask. Have you heard that the King is to be here to-night?

Second Mask. Yes, and since I heard it I have been imagining I saw him everywhere.

First Mask (*pointing*). That is not he, is it?

Second Mask. He is taller than that.

First Mask. That one, then? Look, that one!

Second Mask. That one has spoken to me. He has too old a voice.

First Mask. Shall we see if we can find him?

Second Mask. Yes, come along!

    (*A number of girls, wearing similar costumes and all masked, have meanwhile collected on the left side of the stage.*)

First Girl. Are we all here?

Second Girl. All but Matilde.

Matilde. Here I am! Have you heard that the King is to be here?

All. Really?

Matilde. I don't know how he is dressed; but one of the masters of the ceremonies told me he was to be here.

Several of the Girls. The dear King! (*Two masked dancers, dressed as Cats, pass by.*)

Tom Cat. Do you hear that, my pet?

Puss. Miau!

Matilde. Let us try and discover him.

All. Yes, yes!

A Mask. And when we have discovered him—?

Matilde. Let us all dance round him!

All. Yes!

Tom Cat (*to Puss*). You had better look after your virtue, Miss!

Puss. Miau!

Tom Cat. Miau! (*They pass out of sight.*)

Matilde. Remember that we are all to meet here in a quarter of an hour!

All. Yes! (*They disperse. The ballet comes to a close amidst universal applause. Conversation among the dancers becomes general and animated. The* BARONESS MARC, *disguised as an Old Woman, comes forward, talking to another mask dressed as a Donkey.*)

Baroness. I will never forgive you for that, my lord chamberlain.

The Donkey. But you frighten me clean out of my part, Baroness!

Baroness. If only I could understand how it happened!

The Donkey. After all, my dear Baroness, you cannot be expected to take out all your schoolmistresses and their senior pupils on a leash!

Baroness. No, but I have particular reasons for wishing to look closely after *her*. (*All this time she has been persistently looking round the room.*) And in such a whirling crowd as this—

The Donkey. Let us lose ourselves in it, then! (*He brays as they go out. The* PRINCESS, *masked and dressed in a costume of the time of Louis XV., comes forward accompanied by a Cavalier in a costume of the same period.*)

Princess (continuing a discussion). And I say that if a king has such graces of mind and person as ours has, he may do anything he pleases.

Cavalier. Anything, Princess?

Princess. Anything that his mind prompts, provided that he do it beautifully. (*A* GENTLEMAN-IN-WAITING, *dressed in a costume of the same period, approaches them.*)

Gentleman-in-Waiting. I cannot discover him, your Royal Highness!

Princess. But he is here. He *is* here. And for a lady's sake. I am certain I am right.

Cavalier. But I asked one of the masters of the cere-monies, and he knew nothing about it.

Princess. Then it must have been one that has not been let into the secret.

Cavalier. But, your Royal Highness—

Princess. Don't keep calling me " your Royal High-ness," but get me a description of the costume he is wear-ing. (*The* GENTLEMAN-IN-WAITING *bows and goes away.*) And you and I will go on hunting—

Cavalier. —for the noble huntsman—

Princess. —who is being hunted himself! (*Moves away, but stops suddenly.*) Who is that? (CLARA ERNST, *masked and in peasant costume, comes forward followed by a masked figure wearing a domino. He is whispering to her over her shoulder. She keeps glancing about, as if looking for some one.*)

The Domino. —and there, in the enchanted castle, buried deep in the wooded park—

Clara. Let me alone!

The Domino. —there we shall be greeted by a babbling fountain of water—a nymph, holding the cup of joy high above her head—

Clara (anxiously). What can have become of her?

(*Meanwhile one of the masked dancers has been follow-ing them, and now turns back to join others.*)

A Masked Dancer (pointing to the DOMINO). That is the King!

Another (quickly). But who is *she?*

The Domino. —on both sides, shady alleys leading to the doors of a secret retreat; and there—

Clara (turning round). I despise you! (*The dancing and music suddenly stop. General consternation.*)

The Baroness (starting forward as she hears CLARA'S *voice.)* Clara!

The Domino (taking CLARA'S *hand and leading her apart from the others).* Do you know who it is that you despise?

Clara (greatly agitated). Yes, I know who you are!—and that is why, from the bottom of my heart, I despise you! (*The music begins afresh, covering the general consternation that has spread among the dancers. The* BARONESS *comes forward with a cry of* " Clara! " CLARA *bursts into tears, and throws herself into her arms. Curtain.*)

ACT I

SCENE I

(SCENE.—*A large hall in Gran's factory. The walls are bare. On the left, about half-way forward, is a small platform. A meeting of the shareholders of a railway company is in progress. Facing the platform are seated the gentry; the common herd, mainly farmers and work-people, are sitting and standing about wherever they can find room. On the right, large windows are standing open; through these another crowd can be seen, listening from outside.* GRAN *is standing in front of the platform, speaking to the meeting.*)

Gran. And, as it was found impossible for the main line of the railway to touch our town, we determined, rather than allow all our exertions to be wasted, to construct a branch line on our own account. I had the honour to be elected chairman of the board of directors of this undertaking. No directors ever had more unrestricted powers than were given to us—possibly because there were no two opinions as to the route the line should take; the natural formation of the ground indicated it unmistakably. It was only when we approached the question of the purchase of our rolling-stock that any dissension arose—not among the directors, but among the shareholders. As the majority of the latter are farmers and work-people, we had decided on buying only one class of railway carriage of a type slightly more comfortable than the ordinary third-class carriage. That is the extent of our misdeeds! To-day's meeting will probably show what the general sense on the matter is. Our powers being unlimited, we were under no obligation to consult any one in the matter; but, notwithstanding that, we decided to call a meeting of the shareholders and submit the question to them. And, on the directors' behalf, I must thank the shareholders for having attended in such numbers; young and old, men and women, I dare say quite a third of the total number of shareholders are present. The meeting will now proceed to elect a chairman. (*Sits down.*)

The Mayor (*after a pause*). I beg to move that Mr. Koll, our chief magistrate, whom it is a great pleasure to see honouring this meeting with his presence, have the further kindness to take the chair.

Gran. The motion before the meeting is that the Chief Magistrate shall take the chair. Shall I assume it to be carried? (*Silence follows.*)

The Mayor. Yes. (*Laughter.*)

Gran. The meeting should preferably elect some one who may be considered to be unaffected by considerations of party.

Alstad (*half rising, with his glasses in his hand*). Then we shall have to send for some one that does not live in these parts! There is no one of that sort left here! (*Sits down, amidst laughter.*)

The Priest. All authority springs from on high. Obedience to those set in authority over us is obedience to the Almighty. But it is against this very obedience that people are rebelling nowadays.

Gran. It is precisely some one to be in authority over us that we want to elect. At present we have no one.

The Priest. No, that's just it. Every meeting nowadays seems to claim authority on its own account. Let us rather show our respect to actual authority—such respect as we would show to our fathers. (*Sits down.*)

Gran. Then, as far as I can grasp the situation, the Chief Magistrate has been proposed and seconded?

The Priest. Yes.

Gran. Does any one wish to propose any one else? (*Silence.*)

Alstad. May I request the Chief Magistrate to take the chair?

Koll (*getting up*). I don't know that it is any great compliment to be elected in this way; but I will take the chair, for the sole reason of enabling the meeting to proceed to business. (*Takes his place on the platform, and raps on the table with a mallet.*) I declare the meeting open.

Gran (*getting up*). Mr. Chairman!

Koll. Mr. Gran will address the meeting.

Gran. The motion proposed by the directors is this: "That only one class of railway carriage shall be purchased, slightly more comfortable than the ordinary third-class carriage." (*Gives the motion in writing to the chairman, and sits down.*)

Koll. The following is the motion submitted to the meeting. (*Reads it out.*) Who wishes to speak on the motion? (*Silence.*) Come, some one must speak on it—or I shall have to put it to the vote forthwith. (*Silence, followed by laughter here and there.*)

The Priest. Mr. Chairman!

Koll. The Priest will address the meeting.

The Priest. I see, in this assembly, a number of young men, even a number of maidens; and I feel bound to ask whether young men, and even maidens, are to be allowed to take part in these proceedings?

Koll. Any shareholder that is of age has the right to.

The Priest. But St. Paul expressly tells us that women are not to speak in public places.

Koll. Well, they can hold their tongues, then. (*Laughter.*)

The Priest. But even the fact of voting at a railway meeting does not seem to me to be in accordance with the humility and modesty that both Nature and the Scriptures indicate as characteristic of woman. I believe it to be the first step on a wrong road. The apostle says—

Koll. We must leave them to decide the matter for themselves. Does any one wish to—?

The Priest (*interrupting him*). Mr. Chairman, if you will not permit me to quote the apostle, allow me at all events to say that the spectacle of a young man voting against his father, or a woman voting against her husband—

Koll. Will you tell me who could prohibit it? Does any one wish to speak—?

The Priest (*interrupting*). The Scriptures prohibit it, Mr. Chairman!—the Scriptures, which we are all bound to obey, even—

Gran (*getting up and interrupting him*). Mr. Chairman!

Koll. Mr. Gran will address the meeting.

Gran. I only want to ask whether—

The Priest. But *I* was addressing the meeting!

Koll. Mr. Gran will address the meeting.

The Priest. I protest against that ruling!

Alstad (*half rising*). Our worthy Priest must obey authority. (*Sits down amidst laughter.*)

The Priest. Not when it does an injustice! I appeal to the meeting!

Koll. Very good!—Will those in favour of the Priest's addressing the meeting kindly stand up? (*No one gets up; and those who were previously standing bob down. Laughter.*) Carried unanimously, that the Priest do not address the meeting. (*The* PRIEST *sits down.*) Mr. Gran will address the meeting.

Gran (*getting up*). I withdraw from my right! (*Renewed laughter.*)

The Mayor (*getting up*). Mr. Chairman!

Koll. The Mayor will address the meeting.

The Mayor. I am one of many to whom this proposal of the directors seems extraordinary, to say the least of it. Do they propose that the ladies of my family—I will leave myself out of the question, for as a public man I have to rub shoulders with all sorts of people—do they propose, I say, that ladies who have been delicately brought up shall travel with any Tom, Dick and Harry?—perhaps with convicts being conveyed to gaol, or with journeymen labourers? Is his honour the Chief Magistrate, who is a Commander of a noble Order of Knighthood, to travel side by side with a drunken navvy? Supposing the King were to pay a visit to this beautiful district, which has acquired such a reputation since so many of the best people from town have taken villas here; is his Majesty to make the journey in one of these third-class carriages, with the chance of travelling in company with tradesmen stinking of stale cheese?—with folk who, moreover—well, perhaps in common decency I ought not to go on, as ladies are present. (*Laughter.*) "Economy," I hear some one suggest. That word is in great favour nowadays. But I should like to know what economy there is getting your clothes soiled? (*Laughter.*) Does a first-class carriage wear out sooner than a third class? It costs more to build, no doubt, but that is soon made up by the higher fares charged. I can discover no reasonable ground for this proposal, look at it how you will from the commercial point of view. One has to look at the *political* aspect of the matter, to understand it; and I am reluctant to drag in politics.· I will only say, in conclusion, that it must be those who have framed this proposal that expect to derive some profit from it; the railway certainly would derive none. (*Sits down.*)

Koll. That last remark was a little like an accusation—

The Mayor (*getting up*). I only alluded to what is in every one's mind. (*Sits down.*)

Koll. A speaker is not in order in making accusations, even though they be assumed to be in every one's mind.— I see that Mr. Alstad wishes to speak.

Alstad. Human nature is frail. That seems to me a sufficient explanation of how such a proposal came to be laid before us. But honestly—for we all ought to be honest!—it seems to me that any material advantage it might bring would be more than counterbalanced by loss of esteem. (*Uproar.*) There has been quite a different spirit in the place of late years—what with the factories, and the stranger workmen, and the summer visitors. We never used to have so much unrest or to hear so much of this talk about " equality." And now, if we are to give the impression that there is only one social class here— and that a third class—I know that I shall be by no means alone in feeling offended. We certainly don't want to sit on our work-people's laps ; and, equally, we don't want to have them sitting on ours. (*Sits down.*)

Gran. Our friend the Mayor is very fond of talking of his loyalty; but I must say I am surprised at his dragging the King even into this matter. As for the matter of the railway carriage in which one of so high degree would travel here—well, if our carriages are not good enough, surely his Majesty's private saloon can be used on our line as well as on the main line. And as for any of us ordinary mortals who are afraid of mixing with the common herd, surely they can sit together in carriages by themselves. The carriages would be separate; they would only be of the same kind. I think there would be little fear of their being exposed to intrusion on the part of our country-folk. *They* are much more apt to be more timidly shy than is even desirable. On all small lines—even on many of the bigger ones—it is the less luxurious carriages, the second and third class, that pay for the cost of the more luxurious ones; it is the third class that pays for the first. But that some passengers should travel comfortably at the expense of those that travel less comfortably, is what we wish to avoid. (*Applause.*) An old resident of the yeoman class has reproached us with wishing to alter our customs. Well, if one of our old customs is the aristocratic one which makes the gulf that separates masters and men wider than it already is, all I can say is that the sooner it is abolished the better; for it is not a good custom; it is even a dangerous one. (*Murmurs.*) And as for the political aspect of the question—

Koll. Don't you think we should leave politics out of the question?

Gran (*bows, with a laugh*). That is just what I was going to say, Mr. Chairman; that we ought to leave politics out of the question. (*Sits down, amidst laughter and applause. The audience, first the younger men and then the older farmers, begin arguing the matter with one another, more and more loudly.*)

Koll. I must beg the meeting to keep quiet, as long as this business is under discussion. The Mayor wishes to speak.

The Mayor. I admit that I am loyal—

Koll. Those people outside must be quiet!

Alstad (going to the window). You must keep quiet!

The Mayor. I admit I am loyal! I count it a point of honour, as a native of the place, to show his Majesty that our first thought when we planned this railway was, at that important moment, that his Majesty might possibly be pleased to manifest a desire to pay us a visit. " Let him use his own private saloon," we are told! No, Mr. Chairman, that is not the way to speak when we are speaking of his Majesty! And what about his Majesty's suite? Are they to travel third class? What I say is that we are casting a slight on his Majesty if we cast a slight on his railway carriage—I should say, on his suite. And I go farther than that. I say that his Majesty's functionaries are his Majesty's representatives, and that it is casting an additional slight upon his Majesty not to show a proper respect for them. I know that this jars upon the ears of many present; they do not consider that a man who holds a public office should be shown any more respect than any one else. The majority rules, and the majority only thinks of its own interests and those of its servile supporters. But even in this community of ours there is a minority that bears the burden of its affairs and represents its honour; and we will never consent to be dragged down into the mire of this " equality " into which you want to plunge each and every one of us! (*Uproar.*)

Koll. The honourable speaker appears to me to be trenching upon politics—

The Mayor. Possibly I am, Mr. Chairman; but what honest man can shirk the truth? Only compare the present state of things in this community with what was the case when everything here was as it should be; when the King and his officials were respected; when public affairs were in the hands of those who knew how to direct them; when we used to have singing competitions, shooting competitions, and other festal meetings of that kind.

And—yes—well—compare, I say, the conditions in those days with our conditions to-day—that is to say, with all this talk of " the people; " as, for instance—

Koll. It is railway carriages that we are discussing.

The Mayor. Quite so! But what is it that is at the bottom of this proposal, Mr. Chairman? Does it not spring from that passion for destruction, for a universal levelling, which aims at abolishing the monarchy, at destroying all authority—

The Priest. And the Church too, my friend!

The Mayor. —and the Church, it is quite true! Yes, it is because they desire the Church and—

Koll. It is railway carriages that we are discussing.

The Mayor. Exactly. But an old public official like myself, who once was held in respect, when he sees the pillars of society tottering and feels the keenest pang of sorrow at—

Koll. For the last time, it is railway carriages that we are discussing!

The Mayor (*overcome by his feelings*). I have no more to say. (*Sits down.*)

Koll. Mr. Alstad wishes to speak.

Alstad (*getting up*). The question before the meeting is itself a small matter; but it is the consequences of it that I fear. We may expect any proposal of the same kidney now. Never let it be said that our community was eager to range itself under this banner of " equality! " It bears too old and honoured a name for that! But there is one thing I want to say. We have always, before this, felt it an honour and a privilege to have the richest man in these parts living amongst us. But when we see him one of the most eager in support of a " popular " proposal of this sort, then it appears, to me at all events, to be absolutely unaccountable how— oh, well, I won't run the risk of making what our chairman calls " accusations "; I will sit down and hold my tongue. I have the right to do that at all events. (*Sits down.*)

Koll. Mr. Gran will address the meeting.

Flink. Three cheers for Mr. Gran! (*Almost the whole meeting cheers lustily.* KOLL *shouts at them and hammers on the table with his mallet in vain.*)

Koll (*when peace is restored*). I must ask the meeting to show some respect for its chairman. If not, I will leave the chair.—Mr. Gran will address the meeting.

Gran. The plan that we are proposing is no new one. It has been in practice for a long time. In America—

The Priest, Alstad, and others. Yes, in America!

The Mayor (*getting up*). Mr. Chairman, are we to have politics, after all?

Koll. I cannot see that to mention America is to talk politics.

The Mayor. Then what is politics, if America isn't?

Koll. To talk politics is—for instance—to use the arguments your worship did. Mr. Gran will proceed.

Gran. I see that the Priest wishes to speak. I shall be happy to give way.

Koll. The Priest will address the meeting.

The Priest. I see here, in this assembly, a number of those whom I am accustomed to address in more solemn surroundings. My dear parishioners, it was for your sake that I came here. You have heard for yourselves—the whole question is a political one; and, dear fellow Christians, let me entreat you to shun politics! Did not our Lord Himself say: " My kingdom is not of this world " ? This freedom, this equality, of which they talk is not the soul's freedom, not that equality which—

Koll. I would suggest to the reverend speaker that he should postpone his remarks until the next time he gets into the pulpit. (*Slight laughter.*)

The Priest. One should be instant in season and out of season; therefore—

Koll. I forbid you to continue.

The Priest. It is written: " Thou shalt obey God rather than man " ! My dear parishioners, let us all leave this meeting! Who will follow his priest? (*Takes a few steps towards the door, but no one follows him. Laughter. He sighs deeply, and sits down again.*)

Koll. If no one else wishes to speak—

Vinäger. Mr. Chairman!

Koll. Mr. Vinäger wishes to speak.

Vinäger. These proceedings remind me of China, and of the Chinese mandarins who will not allow any one of lesser degree to come near them—although at moments I have felt as if I were still in Europe in the presence of a still greater power, greater even than the Grand Turk—I mean this democratic envy which grudges others what it has not got itself. To reconcile both parties I should like to make the following suggestion. Build the carriages, as is often done, in two stories. Then those who wish to ensure their privacy can do so by sitting upstairs; and the others will be satisfied too, because they will all be in the same carriage after all. (*Loud laughter.*)

Koll. If no one else wishes to speak (*looks at* GRAN, *who shakes his head*) I shall proceed to put the question to the vote. The motion submitted by the directors, which is now before the meeting, is as follows—

The Mayor. Excuse me, but what of my motion with regard to a saloon for his Majesty?

Koll. I did not understand your worship to mean your suggestion as a formal motion.

The Mayor. I did, though.

Koll. Then I will put it to the vote after the directors' motion has been voted upon.

The Mayor. A motion that concerns the King should take precedence of all others.

Koll. Even the King is subject to the rules of logic. The directors' motion is : " That only one class of railway carriage shall be purchased, of a type slightly more comfortable than the ordinary third-class carriage." Will those in favour of the motion kindly go to the left—on this side of the room; those against the motion, to the right. (*Nearly all go to the left. Cheers are heard outside, and are gradually taken up by those inside.* KOLL *hammers with his mallet.*) Order, please! (*The cheering ceases, but an animated conversation goes on.*) The directors' motion is carried!

The Mayor (*shouting*). I am sure every one did not understand the method of voting!

Koll (*hammering with his mallet*). Order, order. (*Quiet is gradually restored.*) What did your worship say?

The Mayor. That some people must have misunderstood the way of voting; because I see my daughter Natalie, who is a shareholder too, on the other side of the room. Of course she has made a mistake.

Natalie. Oh no, father, I haven't. (*Loud laughter, and applause.*)

The Priest. Ah, my poor deluded parishioners, I shall pray for you!

The Mayor. Order!—The Mayor's motion—

Alstad. I would suggest that the Mayor should withdraw it. We know what its fate would be in such a meeting as this.

Koll. As long as I occupy the chair, I shall not permit any derogatory expressions to be applied to the meeting. Does the Mayor still insist on his motion being put? (*Whispers to him :* " Say no! ")

The Mayor. No.

Koll. Then, as no one else wishes to speak, I declare the meeting at an end. (*Every one begins to move about and discuss affairs vigorously.*)

Alstad (*to his son* VILHELM). So you have the face to vote with these — these Americans, against your old father, have you?

Vilhelm. Well, father, I honestly think—

Alstad. Just you wait till I get you home!

Vilhelm. Oh, that's it, is it? Then I shan't go home—so there! I shall stay here and get drunk, I shall.

Alstad. Oh, come, come!

Vilhelm. Yes, I shall! I shall stay here and get drunk!

Alstad. But, Vilhelm, listen to me! (*Takes him by the arm. Meantime a* STRANGER *has taken* KOLL *and* GRAN *by the arm, to their manifest surprise, and brought them forward away from the crowd. He stands for a moment looking them in the face, till suddenly* KOLL *gives a start and cries out:* " The King! ")

The King. Hush!

Gran. It really is—!

The King (*to* GRAN). You are at home here; take us up into a room—and give us some champagne. My throat is as dry as a lime-kiln!

Curtain

SCENE II

(SCENE.—*A room built in Gothic style, comfortably furnished and decorated with trophies of the chase.* GRAN *ushers in the* KING *and* KOLL.)

Gran. We can be quite alone here. (ANNA, *a deaf and dumb girl of about fifteen, brings in some bottles of champagne, and, during the following dialogue, sets out glasses, refreshments, cigars, and pipes. She is quick and attentive to render the slightest service required of her ; when not so employed, she sits on a stool in the background. She talks to* GRAN *on her fingers, and receives orders from him in the same manner.*)

The King. Ah, this is like old times! I know the setting: " Gothic room in mediæval style, decorated with trophies of the chase. Furnished with an eye to bachelor comfort!" You always had bachelor habits, you know, even when you were quite a boy. (*To* KOLL.) We never called him anything but "the Bachelor" on board ship. He never had a love affair in all the three years our cruise lasted; but the rest of us had them in every port we touched at!

Koll. He is just the same in that respect now.

Gran (*offering the* KING *some champagne*). Allow me!

The King. Thanks; I shall be glad of it. (*To* KOLL.) Your health, my former tutor! (*To* GRAN.) And yours! (*They drink.*) Ah, that has done me good!—Well now, let me ask you this: isn't it true that, all through the meeting, you were talking nothing but republicanism, although you didn't actually mention the word?

Koll (*laughing*). You are not far wrong.

The King. And you, who in the old days were considered to be too advanced in your opinions to be retained as my tutor, are now not considered advanced enough! They nearly threw you over, didn't they?

Koll. Yes! That shows you, if I may say so, the result of government by a minority.

The King. And the result of mixing with such people as our excellent friend the millionaire here, I suppose?

Gran. It is always a mistake to lay the blame of public opinion on individuals.

The King. I quite agree with you. And now it is time you knew the reason of my coming here—in the strictest incognito, as you see. By the way, I hope no one recognised me?

Gran and Koll. Not a soul!

(FLINK *comes in.*)

Flink. Ah, here you are! (*Comes forward, rubbing his hands delightedly.*) Well, what did you think of the meeting, my boys?

The King (aside to GRAN). Who is that?

Gran (to the KING). We will get rid of him. (*To* FLINK.) Look here, old chap—!

Flink (catching sight of the KING). Oh, I beg your pardon, I thought we were—

Gran (obliged to introduce him). Let me introduce Mr. —? Mr. —? (*Looks at the* KING *inquiringly*.)

The King. Speranza.

Flink. An Italian?

The King. In name only.

Gran (completing the introduction). Mr. Flink.

The King. Surely not A. B. Flink?

Gran. Yes.

The King (interested). Our peripatetic philosopher? (*Shakes hands with him*.) I have read one or two of your books.

Flink (laughing). Really?

The King. Are you meditating another expedition?

Flink. That's it.

The King. And on foot?

Flink. Always on foot.

The King. Upon my word, I don't believe there is a man in the country that can gauge popular opinion as accurately as you! Let us sit down and have a chat. Do you drink champagne?

Flink. Yes—when I can't get anything better!

The King (lifting his glass to FLINK). Your health! (*They all drink, and then seat themselves.*) What part of the country were you in last?

Flink. I have just been shooting with our friend here.

The King. So he is your friend? He is mine, too! My best friend, ever since I was a boy. (*He stretches out his hand ;* GRAN *gets up and grasps it in both of his*.)

Koll (to FLINK, *who is looking astonished*). Mr. Speranza was a naval cadet at the same time as Gran.

Flink. Really! Were they on the same ship?

The King. Yes, we were on a cruise round the world together—

Flink. Do you mean the time when the Prince went on account of his lungs?—the present King, I mean?

The King. The Prince that afterwards became King— yes.

Flink. There is quite a royal flavour about our little gathering, then! Here is the King's shipmate, and here is his tutor in jurisprudence—

Koll. You are forgetting yourself! You are the King's tutor's tutor, you know—

The King. Were you Koll's tutor? Really?

Flink (with a laugh). Yes, I had that misfortune!

The King. You hadn't so great a misfortune in your pupil as he had in his!

Koll. The King was a very apt pupil.

Flink (jestingly). He has shown traces of it in his reign, hasn't he!

Koll. Don't speak ill of the King, please.

Flink (ironically). Heaven forbid! (*Takes a pinch of snuff.*) I know all about his talent—his great talent, his genial talent! (*Offers his snuff-box to the* KING.)

Gran. But it was public opinion we were talking about, Flink; is it very much like what we heard to-day?

Flink. I wouldn't say that; your opinions are rather advanced in these parts.

The King. Is the tendency republican, rather than monarchical?

Flink. That depends how you look at it. The King has just been paying some visits in the country districts; he is, so to speak, the commercial traveller for his firm— as all kings and crown princes are. Of course he was cheered everywhere. But go and ask the agricultural classes if they set great store by the pomp and circumstance of royalty; they will unanimously answer: "It costs an infernal lot to keep up!" Ha, ha, ha!

Gran. Your farmer is a realist.

Flink. A brutal realist! Ha, ha, ha! Self-government is cheaper. He has it all at his fingers' ends, the scoundrel!

The King. He is not a republican by conviction, then?

Flink. Not universally, no. At least, not *yet.* But things are moving that way; and our reactionary government is helping the movement—that, and the letters they get from America.

The King. The letters they get from America?

Koll. Letters from their relations in America.

Gran. There is scarcely a family in the country now that has not relations in America.

The King. And they write home about self-government?—about republican principles?

Flink. And republican institutions. That is the situation!

The King. Have you read any of these letters?

Flink. Lots!

The King. This is excellent champagne! (*Drinks.*)

Gran. Let me fill your glasses. (*They all drink.*)

Flink. It doesn't really agree with me.

The King. But suppose the King were to establish democratic government? Suppose he were to live like an ordinary citizen in every way?

Flink. In every way? What do you mean by that?

The King. Kept house like an ordinary citizen—were married like an ordinary citizen—were to be found in his office at regular hours like any other official?

Gran. And had no court, I suppose?

The King. No. (KOLL *and* GRAN *exchange glances.*)

Flink (*shrugging his shoulders*). It would be the last sensation left for him to try.

The King (*who did not observe his shrug, eagerly*). That is so, isn't it? You agree with me as to that? I am delighted to have had this talk with you, Mr. Flink.

Flink. The same to you, Mr.— Mr.—. (*In an undertone, to* KOLL.) Is he a republican?

The King (*who has overheard him*). Am I a republican? I have had too much experience not to be! Ha, ha! (*Takes up his glass.*) Devilish good champagne, this!

Flink (*drinking*). But, you know, Mr.— Mr. Republican—ha, ha!— (*smiles and whispers*)—the King simply would not be allowed to do what you suggest. Ha, ha!

The King. What do you mean?

Gran (*aside to* KOLL, *who gets up*). Are you sure this is right?

Koll. It will do him good, anyway, to hear all sides.

Flink (*who has got up and gone to the table on the other side to get a pipe*). He simply would not be allowed to, poor chap! What is monarchy, I ask you? Nothing more or less than an insurance business in which a whole crew of priests, officials, noblemen, landed proprietors, merchants and military men hold shares? And, goodness knows, *they* are not going to give their director leave to commit any such folly! Ha, ha, ha!

The King (*getting up*). Ha, ha, ha!

Flink (*vociferously, to him*). Don't you think that is true?

The King. Good Lord!—perfectly true! Ha, ha ha!

Flink (*who has cleaned and filled a pipe, but forgotten to light it, going up to the* KING). And what do they insure themselves again, these beauties? (*More seriously.*) Against the great mass of the people—against *his* people! (*The* KING *looks at him and makes a movement of dislike.*)

Gran. Look here, Flink; suppose we go out into the garden for a little? These spring evenings are so lovely.

Flink. Compared to a political talk, the loveliest spring evenings have no attraction for me—no more than warm water, offered me in place of fine cooling wine, would have. No, let us stay where we are. What is the matter with this pipe? (ANNA *signs that she will put it right for him, but he does not understand.*)

Gran Give her your pipe; she will put it right.

Koll. What I have always said is that, if the King had an opportunity of understanding the situation, he would interfere.

Flink. The King? He doesn't care a brass farthing about the whole matter! He has something else to do! Ha, ha!

The King. Ha, ha, ha!

Koll. The King is an unusually gifted man; he would not remain indifferent in the long run.

Flink. He has so many unusual gifts that have gone to the devil—!

The King. Tralalla! Tralalalalala! Tralala! It feels quite odd to be with you fellows again! (*Drinks.*)

Flink (*in an undertone, to* GRAN). Is he drunk?

The King (*sitting down*). Give me a cigar—! And let us discuss the matter a little more seriously. (KOLL *and* GRAN *sit down.*)

Gran. As a matter of fact, it is not a thing that can be discussed. It must be tried. If, one day, the King were to say: " I mean to live a natural life among my people, and to withdraw my name from the old-established royal firm, which has lost all its reputation for honesty "—that day everything else would follow of itself.

Flink. Yes, *that* day, I dare say!

Gran. Remember you are the guest of a man who is a friend of the King's!

The King. Don't play the domestic despot—you who are a republican! Let us have free discussion!

Flink. I certainly don't intend to insult the King. He has never done me any harm. But surely you will allow me to doubt whether he is really the shining light you make him out to be?

The King. That is true enough!

Flink (eagerly). You agree with me as to that, then?

The King. Absolutely! But—leaving him out of the question—suppose we *had* a king who made himself independent of others, and, as a necessary consequence, rose superior to questions of party—?

Flink (interrupting him). It is a vain supposition, my dear fellow! A king bound to no party? *(Puffs at his pipe.)* It wouldn't work! *(Puffs again.)* It wouldn't work!— It wouldn't work!— Falsehood is the foundation of constitutional monarchy. A king superior to questions of party? Rubbish!

Gran. It would be expecting something superhuman of him, too.

Flink. Of course it would!

The King. But the president of a republic is even less independent of party, isn't he?

Flink (turning to him). He doesn't make any pretence that he isn't. Haha! That's the difference! *(Comes forward, repeating to himself.)* It is the falsehood that makes the difference.

Koll. Oh, there are falsehoods enough in republics too, unfortunately!

Flink. I know; but they are not old-established institutions! Ha, ha!

The King. That is an idea you have got from Professor Ernst's writings.

Flink (eagerly). Have you read them?

The King. I have scarcely read anything else for the last few months. *(KOLL and GRAN exchange glances.)*

Flink. Indeed?—Then there is no need for me to say anything more.

Koll. But, after all this talk, we have got no further. Our friend *(pointing to the KING)* wants to know, I think, whether a real, serious attempt at what one might call " democratic monarchy " could not reckon on being understood and supported—

The King (breaking in, eagerly). **Yes,** that's just it!

Koll. —understood and supported by the most enlightened section of the people, who are weary of falsehood and long for a generous but secure measure of self-government.

The King. That's just it!

Flink (who was just going to sit down, jumps up again, lays down his pipe and stands with arms akimbo, as he says :) But what sort of ridiculous ideas are these? Aren't you republicans, then?

Koll. I am not.

Gran. I am; but that does not prevent my being of opinion that the change of government should be made gradually and gently—

Flink. That would be treason!

Gran. Treason!

Flink. Treason against the truth—against our convictions!

Koll. Don't let us use big words! Monarchy is strongly rooted in the existing order of things.

Flink (with a laugh). In the insurance company!

Koll. Well, call it so if you like. It *exists ;* that is the point. And, since it exists, we must make it as honest and as serviceable as we can.

The King. Your health, Koll! (*Drinks to him.*)

Flink (moving away from them). No true republican would agree with you.

Gran. You are wrong there. (FLINK *gives a start of surprise.*)

The King (who has seen FLINK'S *surprise, gets up).* Listen to me! Suppose we had a king who said: " Either you help me to establish a democratic monarchy—purged of all traces of absolutism, purged of falsehood—or else I abdicate—"

Flink. Bah!

The King. I only say, " suppose "! You know quite

well that the cousin of the present king, the heir apparent, is a bigoted—

Koll (who has been exchanging glances with GRAN *while the* KING *was speaking, breaks in hurriedly).* Don't go on!

The King (with a laugh). I won't!—And his mother, who rules him—

Flink. —is even worse!

The King. What would be your choice, then? Would you help the king to establish a democratic monarchy—or—?

Flink (impetuously). I would ten thousand times rather have the bigoted prince, with all his own and his mother's follies!—the madder the better!

Gran. No, no, no, no!

The King (to GRAN *and* KOLL*).* We see his true colours now! *(Moves away from them.)*

Koll (to FLINK*).* That is the way you republicans always ride your principles to death.

Gran. Patriotism ought to come before—

Flink. —before truth? No; a short sharp pang of agony is better than endless doubt and falsehood, my friend! That is true patriotism.

Koll. Oh, these theories!—these phrases!

Gran. I am a republican as well as you, and, I think, as sincere a one. But I should have no hesitation—

Flink. —in playing the traitor?

Gran. Why do you use such words as that?

Flink. Words! Do you think it is nothing but words? No, my friend, if you did what—what I did not allow you to say—I should come here one day to call you to account. And if you refused to fight me, I should shoot you like a dog!

Gran (gently). You would not do that.

Flink (heatedly). Not do it?—Have I given you the deepest affection of which my heart is capable, only for you to turn traitor to it? Am I to see the man whose character is the crowning achievement of my life, betraying our cause—and, by reason of his great personal prestige, dragging thousands down with him? On the head of all the disillusionments I have suffered, am I to have this one in the evening of my life—? (*Stops, overcome by his emotion. A pause.*) You shouldn't jest about such things you know. (*Walks away.* ANNA *has placed herself in front of* GRAN, *as if to protect him.*)

Koll. I think we had better change the subject, and go out for a little!

The King (*aside, to him*). Yes, get him away!

Flink (*in the background, as if he were addressing an invisible audience*). We must have discipline in the ranks!

Koll. Gran, ask your maid to hurry up with the supper.

Gran. Yes, I will.

Koll (*to the* KING). What do you say to a turn in the garden, meanwhile?

The King. By all means!

Flink (*coming forward to* GRAN). This friendship of yours with the King—to which I had attached no particular importance — I hope it has not altogether—. (*Stops short.*)

Gran. —not altogether corrupted me, you mean?

Flink. Exactly.

The King (*laughing*). Politically?

Flink. Politics are not unconnected with morals, sir!

The King. But why get so heated, sir? We know that the present King is a—

Koll (*breaking in hurriedly*). Don't say any more!

The King (*with a laugh*). You said yourself that he doesn't care a brass farthing about the whole matter—he has something else to do! And so the whole thing ends in smoke!

Flink (*more amiably*). I dare say you are right.

The King. Of course I am. You are all agreed that,

under his rule, republican sentiments are growing in real earnest.

Flink. You are right! He couldn't help things on better if he were a republican himself, I assure you!

The King. Perhaps he *is* a republican?

Flink (animatedly). Perhaps he *is!* Splendid! And works against his own interests—!

The King. A sort of commercial traveller working for the downfall of his own firm!

Flink (excitedly). For the downfall of his own firm! Splendid! Props up his reactionary rule by means of royal pronouncements, confidential communications, public speeches—

The King. —in a suicidal manner!

Flink. Splendidly suicidal! Ah, that makes you laugh, does it?

Koll. Hush, some one might hear us!

Flink. I don't care who hears us! (*The* KING *bursts out laughing.*) But you ought, as one of the King's officials, to stop *his* laughing! (*Points to the* KING.) It's shocking! —It's high treason!

Koll. Listen to me!

Flink. You ought to arrest him for laughing like that! Suppose the King—

Gran. That *is* the King! (*The* KING *goes on laughing.* FLINK *looks from him to the others, and from the others to him.*)

The King. This is too much for me! (*Sits down.* FLINK *rushes out.*)

Koll. That was very bad of you.

The King. I know it was; but forgive me! I couldn't help it! Ha, ha, ha, ha, ha!

Koll. For all his queer ways, he is too good a fellow to be made a fool of.

The King. Yes, scold me; I deserve it. But, all the same—ha, ha, ha, ha!

Gran. Hush!—he is coming back. (*The* KING *gets up as* FLINK *comes in again.*)

Flink. Your Majesty may be assured that I would never have expressed myself as I did in your Majesty's presence if I had been fairly treated and told whom I was addressing.

The King. I know. The fault is mine alone.

Flink. The fault is that of others—my so-called friends.

The King (*earnestly*). By no means! It is mine—mine alone. I have had a scolding for it!—And in your presence I ask my friends' pardon; I have put them in a false position. And, in the next place, I ask for your forgiveness. My sense of humour got the better of me. (*Laughs again.*)

Flink. Yes, it was extremely amusing.

The King. It really was! And, after all, what have you to complain of? You had an opportunity of speaking your mind, any way!

Flink. I certainly did!

The King. Very well, then!—And when you wanted to show any respect, *I* prevented you. So I think we are quits.

Flink. No, we are not.

The King (*impatiently*). Indeed?—What do you want from me, then?

Flink (*proudly*). Nothing!

The King. I beg your pardon! I did not mean to offend you.

Flink. You have done so to a degree that you are naturally incapable of appreciating. (*Goes out.*)

The King. This is a nice business! (*Laughs. Then notices* GRAN, *who is standing at his desk with his back to the* KING, *and goes up to him.*) You are angry with me.

Gran (*looking up slowly*). Yes.

The King. Why didn't you stop me?

Gran. It all happened too quickly. But to think that

you could have the heart to do it—in my own house—to a
man who was my father's oldest friend, and is mine—!

The King. Harald! (*Puts his arm round his shoulders.*)
Have I ever asked you for anything that you have not
given me?

Gran. No.

The King. Then I ask you now to admit that you know
that, if I had thought this would hurt *you*, I would never
have done it—not for worlds! Do you still believe as well
of me as that?

Gran. Yes.

The King. Thank you. Then I will admit to you, in
return, that for months past I have lived in a state of
horrible tension of mind; and that is why I jump too
easily from one extreme to the other. So, my friends, you
must forgive me! Or finish my scolding some other time!
Because now I must talk to you of the matter which induced me to come here. You are the only ones I can turn
to; so be good to me!—Shall we sit down again?

Koll. As you please.

The King (*moving towards the table*). I know you both
want to ask me the same question: why I have never come
before now. My answer is: because I have only now
arrived at a clear conception of my own position. Some
months ago some hard words that were used to me lit a
fire in my heart and burnt out a heap of rubbish that had
collected there. (ANNA *fills their glasses.*) Won't you
send that girl away?

Gran. She is deaf and dumb.

The King. Poor girl! (*Sits down.*) When I came back
from my cruise round the world, the old king was dead.
My father had come to the throne, and I was crown prince,
and I went with my father to the cathedral to attend a
thanksgiving service for my safe return.

Gran. I was there.

The King. The whole thing was a novelty to me, and a

solemn one. I was overcome with emotion. Seeing that, my father whispered to me: " Come farther forward, my boy! The people must see their future king praying." That finished it! I was not born to be a king; my soul was still too unsullied, and I spurned such falsehood with the deepest loathing. Just think of it!—to come back from three years at sea, and begin my life in that way—as if perpetually in front of a mirror! I won't dwell on it. But when my father died and I became king, I had become so accustomed to the atmosphere of falsehood I lived in that I no longer recognised truth when I saw it. The constitution prescribed my religion for me—and naturally I had none. And it was the same with everything—one thing after another! What else could you expect? The only tutor I valued—you, Koll—had been dismissed; they considered you to be too freethinking.

Koll (*smilingly*). Oh, yes!

The King. The only real friend that dated from my happier days—you, Harald,—had been sent to the right about; you were a republican. It was while I was in despair over that loss that I fell really in love for the first time—with your sister, Harald. Banishment, again. What then? Why, then the craving that every healthy youth feels—the desire for love—was turned into dissolute channels. (*Drinks.*)

Gran. I understand, well enough.

The King. Well, put all those things together. That was what my life was—until just lately. Because lately something happened, my dear friends. And now you must help me! Because, to make a long story short, either I mean to be the chief official in my country in a peaceful, citizenlike, genuine way, or—as God is above me—I will no longer be king! (*Gets up, and the others do so.*)

Koll. Ah, we have got it at last!

The King. Do you think I don't know that our republican friend there spoke what is every thoughtful man's verdict upon me? (*They are silent.*) But how could I possibly undertake my task, as long as I believed everything to be make-believe and falsehood, without exception? Now I know the root of the falsehood! It is in our institutions; he was quite right. And one kind of falsehood begets another. You cannot imagine how ludicrous it appeared to me—who up till then had led such a sinful, miserable existence—when I saw honourable men pretending that I was a being of some superior mould! I! (*Walks up and down, then stops.*) It is the state—our institutions—that demand this falsehood both on their part and on mine. And that for the security and happiness of the country! (*Moves about restlessly.*) From the time I became crown prince they kept from me everything that might have instilled truth into me—friendship, love, religion, a vocation—for my vocation is quite another one; and it was all done in the name of my country! And now that I am king, they take away all responsibility from me as well—all responsibility for my own acts—the system demands it! Instead of an individual, what sort of a contemptible creature do they make of me! The kingly power, too?—that is in the hands of the people's representatives and the government. I don't complain of that; but what I do complain of is that they should pretend that *I* have it, and that everything should be done in *my* name; that I should be the recipient of petitions, cheers, acclamations, obeisances—as if the whole power and responsibility were centred in *my* person! In me—from whom, in the interests of all, they have taken away everything! Is that not a pitiful and ludicrous falsehood? And, to make it credible, they endow me into the bargain with a halo of sanctity! "The King is sacred;" "Our Most Gracious Sovereign," "Your Majesty!" It becomes almost blasphemous!

Gran. Quite true.

The King. No, if that cannot be done away with, I can do away with myself. But it must be possible to do away with it! It cannot be necessary for a people, who are marching on the eternal path towards truth, to have a lie marching at the head of them!

Koll. No, it is not necessary.

The King (eagerly). And that is what you will help me to show them.

Koll. I have no objection! There is life in the country yet!

The King (to Gran). And you, my friend? Are you afraid of being shot by a mad republican if you help me?

Gran. I am not particularly afraid of death, any way. But the maid is telling us that supper is served.

The King. Yes, let us have supper!

Koll. And then, to our task!

Curtain

ACT II

(SCENE.—*A park with old lofty trees. In the foreground,
to the right, an arbour with a seat. The* KING *is sitting,
talking to* BANG, *who is a man of gross corpulence.*)

Bang. And I felt so well in every way that, I assure
your Majesty, I used to feel it a pleasure to be alive.

The King (*drawing patterns in the dust with his walking-
stick*). I can quite believe it.

Bang. And then I was attacked by this pain in my
heart and this difficulty in breathing. I run round and
round this park, on an empty stomach, till I am absolutely
exhausted.

The King (*absently*). Couldn't you drive round, then?

Bang. Drive?—But it is the exercise, your Majesty,
that—.

The King. Of course. I was thinking of something
else.

Bang. I would not mind betting that I know what your
Majesty was thinking of—if I may say so without impertinence.

The King. What was it, then?

Bang. Your Majesty was thinking of the socialists!

The King. Of the—?

Bang. The socialists!

The King (*looking amused*). Why particularly of them?

Bang. I was right, you see! Ha, ha, ha! (*His laughter brings on a violent fit of coughing.*) Your Majesty must
excuse me ; laughing always brings on my cough.—But,
you know, the papers this morning are full of their goings-
on!

The King. I have not read the paper.

Bang. Then I can assure your Majesty that the way they are going on is dreadful. And just when we were all getting on so comfortably! What in the world do they want?

The King. Probably they want to get on comfortably too.

Bang. Aren't they well off as it is, the beasts? Excuse me, your Majesty, for losing my temper in your Majesty's presence.

The King. Don't mention it.

Bang. You are very good. These strikes, too—what is the object of them? To make every one poor? Every one can't be rich. However, I pin my faith to a strong monarchy. Your Majesty is the padlock on my cash-box!

The King. I am what?

Bang. The padlock on my cash-box! A figure of speech I ventured to apply to your Majesty.

The King. I am much obliged!

Bang. Heaven help us if the liberals come into power; their aim is to weaken the monarchy.

(*A* Beggar Boy *comes up to them.*)

Beggar Boy. Please, kind gentlemen, spare a penny! I've had nothing to eat to-day!

Bang (*taking no notice of him*). Aren't there whispers of the sort about? But of course it can't be true.

Beggar Boy (*pertinaciously*). Please, kind gentlemen, spare a penny! I've had nothing to eat to-day.

Bang. You have no right to beg.

The King. You have only the right to starve, my boy! Here! (*Gives him a gold coin. The* Beggar Boy *backs away from him, staring at him, and gripping the coin in his fist.*)

Bang. He never even thanked you! Probably the son of a socialist!—I would never have opened this park to every one in the way your Majesty has done.

The King. It saves the work-people a quarter of an hour if they can go through it to get to their work.

(*The* GENERAL *appears, driving the* BEGGAR BOY *before him with his stick.*)

The General (*to the* BEGGAR). A gentleman sitting on a seat gave it you? Point him out to me, then!

Bang (*getting up*). Good morning, your Majesty!

The King. Good morning! (*Looks at his watch.*)

The General. That gentleman, do you say?

The King (*looking up*). What is it?

The General. Your Majesty? Allow me to welcome you back!

The King. Thank you.

The General. Excuse me, sir; but I saw this fellow with a gold coin in his hand, and stopped him. He says your Majesty gave it to him—?

The King. It is quite true.

The General. Oh—of course that alters the case! (*To the* BEGGAR.) It is the King. Have you thanked him? (*The boy stands still, staring at the* KING.)

The King. Are you taking a morning walk on an empty stomach because of a weak heart, too?

The General. Because of my stomach, sir—because of my stomach! It has struck work!

The Beggar Boy. Ha, ha, ha! Ho, ho, ho! (*Runs away.*)

The General. I am astonished at your Majesty's having thrown this park open to every one.

The King. It saves the work-people a quarter of an hour if they can go through it to get to their work.— Well, General, it seems you have become religious all of a sudden?

The General. Ha, ha, ha! Your Majesty has read my Order of the Day, then?

The King. Yes.

The General (*confidentially*). Well, sir, you see things couldn't go on any longer as they were. (*Whispers.*) Debauchery in the ranks! I won't say anything about

Q 696

the officers; but when the men take to such courses
openly—!

The King. Oho!

The General. My brother the bishop and I, between us,
composed an Order of the Day on the subject of the
necessity of religion—religion as the basis of discipline.

The King. As a matter of fact the bishop was the first
person I met here to-day.—Is he suffering from a dis-
ordered stomach, too?

The General. More so than any of us, sir! Ha, ha, ha!
(*The* KING *motions to him to sit down.*) Thank you, sir.—
But, apart from that, I have had it in my mind for some
time that in these troublous days there ought to be a
closer co-operation between the Army and the Church—

The King. In the matter of digestion, do you mean?

The General. Ha, ha, ha!—But seriously, sir, the time
is approaching when such a co-operation will be the only
safeguard of the throne.

The King. Indeed?

The General (*hurriedly*). That is to say, of course, the
throne stands firm by itself—God forbid I should hint
otherwise! But what I mean is that it is the Army and
the Church that must supply the monarchy with the
necessary splendour and authority—

The King. I suppose, then, that the monarchy has no
longer any of its own?

The General (*jumping up*). Heaven forbid that I should
say such a thing! I would give my life in support of the
monarchy!

The King. You will have to die some day, unfortunately.
(*Laughs as he gets up.*) Who is that coming this
way?

The General (*putting up his eyeglass*). That? It is the
Princess and Countess L'Estoque, sir.

The King. Is the Princess suffering from indigestion
too?

The General (confidentially). I fancy your Majesty knows best what the Princess is suffering from. (*The* KING *moves away from him.*) I made a mess of that! It comes of my trying to be too clever.—He is walking towards her. Perhaps there is something in it, after all? I must tell Falbe about it. (*Turns to go.*) Confound it, he saw that I was watching them! (*Goes out. The* KING *returns to the arbour with the* PRINCESS *on his arm. The* COUNTESS *and one of the royal servants are seen crossing the park in the background.*)

The Princess. This is a most surprising meeting! When did your Majesty return?

The King. Last night.—You look very charming, Princess! Such blushing cheeks!—and so early in the morning!

The Princess. I suppose you think it is rouge?—No, sir, it is nothing but pleasure at meeting you.

The King. Flatterer! And I went pale at the sight of you.

The Princess. Perhaps your conscience—?

The King. I am sorry to say my conscience had nothing to do with it. But this morning I have been meeting so many people that are suffering from indigestion that, when I saw your Highness walking quickly along—

The Princess. Make your mind easy! My reason for my morning walk is to keep my fat down. Later in the day I ride—for the same reason. I live for nothing else now.

The King. It is a sacred vocation!

The Princess. Because it is a royal one?

The King. Do you attribute your sanctity to me? Wicked Princess!

The Princess. Both my sanctity and any good fortune I enjoy. It is nothing but my relationship to your Majesty that induces the tradespeople to give me unlimited credit.

The King. You don't feel any awkwardness about it, then?

The Princess. Not a bit! The good folk have to maintain many worse parasites than me!—By the way, talking of parasites, is it true that you have pensioned off all your lords-in-waiting and their hangers-on?

The King. Yes.

The Princess. Ha, ha, ha! But why did you make the special stipulation that they should live in Switzerland?

The King. Because there is no court in Switzerland, and—

The Princess. And so they could not fall into temptation again! I have had many a good laugh at the thought of it. But it has its serious side too, you know; because your Majesty cannot dispense with a court.

The King. Why not?

The Princess. Well, suppose some day you are " joined in the bonds of holy matrimony," as the parsons so beautifully put it?

The King. If I were, it would be for the sake of knowing what family life is.

The Princess. Like any other citizen?

The King. Precisely.

The Princess. Are you going to keep no servants?

The King. As many as are necessary—but no more.

The Princess. Then I must secure a place as chambermaid in your Majesty's household as soon as possible. Because if my financial circumstances are inquired into there will be nothing else left for me but that!

The King. You have too sacred a vocation for that, Princess!

The Princess. How pretty! Your Majesty is a poet, and poets are allowed to be enthusiastic about ideals. But the people are poets too, in their way; they like their figure-head to be well gilded, and don't mind paying for it. That is their poetry.

The King. Are you certain of that?

The Princess. Absolutely certain! It is a point of honour with them.

The King. Then I have to weigh my honour against theirs! And my honour forbids me—for the honour of my people and their poetry—to keep up my palaces, my guards, and my court any longer! *Voila tout!*

The Princess. My dear King, certain positions carry with them certain duties!

The King. Then I know higher duties than those!— But, Princess, here are we two seriously discussing—

The Princess. Yes, but there is something at the bottom of it that is not to be laughed away. All tradition and all experience proclaim it to be the truth that a king— the kingly majesty—should be a dignity apart; and should be the ultimate source of law, surrounded with pomp and circumstance, and secure behind the fortified walls of wealth, rank, and hereditary nobility. If he steps out of that magic circle, the law's authority is weakened.

The King. Has your Royal Highness breakfasted yet?

The Princess. No. (*Bursts out laughing.*)

The King. Because, if you had, I should have had great pleasure is giving you a lesson in history; but on an empty stomach that would be cruel.

The Princess. Do you know—you used to be such an entertaining king, but this last year you have become so tedious!

The King. Most beautiful of princesses! Do you really mean to say that I rise and fall in your estimation according as I have my pretty royal gew-gaws on or not?

The Princess. In my estimation?

The King. Or in any one's? You know the story of " The Emperor's New Clothes "?

The Princess. Yes.

The King. We don't keep up that pretence any longer.

The Princess. But will every one understand?

The King. You understand, don't you?

The Princess. The people or I—that is all the same, I suppose! You are very flattering.

The King. Heaven forbid that I should lump your Royal Highness together with the common herd; but—

The Princess. We have already had proof of the fact that your Majesty does not hold the same place in *every one's* estimation that you do in mine, at all events!

The King. If I occupy a place of honour in your Royal Highness's heart, your Royal Highness may be certain that—

The Princess. I will interrupt you to save you from speaking an untruth! Because the way to attain to a place of honour in your Majesty's heart is not to admire you as I do, but, on the contrary, to shout out: "I despise you!"—Au revoir!

The King. You wicked, terrifying, dangerous—

The Princess. —omniscient and ubiquitous Princess! (*Makes a deep curtsey, and goes away.*)

The King (*calling after her*). In spite of everything, my heart goes with you—

The Princess. —to show me the door! I know all about that! (*To the* COUNTESS.) Come, Countess! (*Goes out.* FALBE, *an old gentleman in civilian dress, has come in from the side to which the* KING'S *back is turned.*)

The King. How the devil did she—?

Fable (*coming up behind him*). Your Majesty!

The King (*turning quickly*). Ah, there you are!

Falbe. Yes, sir—we have been walking about in the park for some time; your Majesty was engaged.

The King. Not engaged—I was only deadening my thoughts by gossiping. My anxiety was too much for me. So they have come?—both of them?

Falbe. Both of them.

The King. Can I believe it! (*Appears overcome.*)

But—you must wait a moment! I can't, just at this moment—. I don't know what has come over me!

Falbe. Are you unwell, sir? You look so pale.

The King My nerves are not what they should be. Is there any water near here?

Falbe (*pointing, in astonishment*). Why, there is the fountain, sir!

The King. Of course! Of course!—I don't seem able to collect my thoughts. And my mouth is as dry as—. Look here, I am going that way (*points*); and then you can—you can bring the ladies here.—She is here! She is here! (*Goes out to the left, and turns round as he goes.*) Don't forget to lock the gates of the inner park!

Falbe. Of course not, sir. (*Goes out to the right, and returns bringing in the* BARONESS MARC *and* CLARA.) His Majesty will be here in a moment. (*Goes out to the right.*)

Clara. You must stay near enough for me to be able to call you.

Baroness. Of course, my dear. Compose yourself; nothing can happen.

Clara. I am so frightened.

Baroness. Here is the King! (*The* KING *comes in and bows to them.*)

The King. Excuse me, ladies, for having kept you waiting. I am very grateful to you both for coming.

Baroness. We only came upon your Majesty's solemn promise—

The King. —which shall be inviolable.

Baroness. I understand that you wish to speak to Miss Ernst alone?

The King. Your ladyship need only go up to the top of that little slope. (*Points.*) I can recommend the view from there.

Baroness. The interview will not be a long one, I suppose?

The King. If it is, I give your ladyship permission to

come and interrupt us. (*The* Baroness *goes out. The* King *turns to* Clara.) May I be permitted to thank you again—you especially—for having been so good as to grant me this interview?

Clara. It will be the only one.

The King. I know that. You have not condescended to answer one of my letters—

Clara. I have not read them.

The King. —so there was nothing left for me but to address myself to the Baroness. She was *obliged* to listen to me, Miss Ernst.

Clara (trembling). What has your Majesty to say to me?

The King. Indeed, I can't tell it you in a single sentence. Won't you sit down? (Clara *remains standing.*) You must not be afraid of me. I mean you no harm; I never *could* mean you any harm.

Clara (in tears). Then what do you call the persecution that I have endured for more than a year?

The King. If you had condescended to read a single one of my long and many letters you would have known. I call it a passion that is stronger than—. (Clara *turns to go. The* King *continues anxiously.*) No, Miss Ernst, by everything you hold dear, I beg you not to leave me!

Clara. Then you must not insult me!

The King. If that is an insult your terms are very hard.

Clara. Hard? No, but what you have done to me is hard! (*Bursts into tears.*)

The King. Don't cry, Miss Ernst! You don't know how you hurt me!

Clara (angrily). Do you know what it means to try and ruin a young girl's reputation?

The King. I repeat that you are doing me an injustice.

Clara. An injustice?—Good God! Do you know who I am?

The King (taking off his hat respectfully). You are the woman I love.

Clara (quietly and with dignity). Your Majesty has solemnly promised not to insult me.

The King. As sure as there is a heaven above us I will not, and could not, insult you! But I will obey your wishes.

Clara. When a king says such a thing as—as you did just now, to a poor little governess, it is more than an insult! It is so cowardly, so base! And to think that you could have the heart to do it after what you have done to my father!

The King. Your father?—I?

Clara. Do you really not know who I am?

The King. I don't understand—

Clara. Whose daughter I am, I mean?

The King. I only know that your father's name is Ernst. (*Suddenly.*) Surely your father is not—?

Clara. Professor Ernst.

The King. The republican?

Clara (slowly). Yes. (*A pause.*) I may remind your Majesty that he was sentenced for high treason. And why? Because he warned the young men at the university against the bad example set by the King! (*A pause.*) He was sentenced to a long term of imprisonment. In escaping from his prison he broke both his legs; and now he lives in exile—a cripple—supported by what money I am able to earn. (*A pause.*) You have ruined his life —and now you are trying to ruin mine too!

The King. I beg of you—!

Clara. I am ashamed of my tears. It is not compassion for myself or for my father that makes them flow; it is the heartless injustice of it all that overcomes me.

The King. God knows, if only I could atone for the injustice—! But what can I do?

Clara. You can let me alone, so that I may do my work in peace; that is what you can do! Neither he nor I ask for more than that—of you!

The King. I must do more than that!

Clara. No! Can you not understand that a girl who is persecuted by the king's attentions cannot be a governess? All you will achieve will be to rob me and my father of our bread!—Oh, God!

The King. But my intention is not to—

Clara (*interrupting him*). And you are not even man enough to be ashamed of yourself!

The King. Yes, you may say what you please to me!

Clara. I have nothing more to say to you. I have said what I have to say. (*Turns to go.*)

The King. No, don't go! You have not even heard me yet. You don't even know what I want to beg of you!

Clara. My dishonour.

The King (*vehemently*). You misunderstand me utterly! If you had only read a single one of my letters you would have known that there is standing before you a man whom you have humbled. Ah, don't look so incredulous! It is true, if there is any truth in anything. You don't believe me? (*Despairingly.*) How am I to—! A man who has risked your contempt for more than a year, and has been faithful to you without even being allowed to see you or exchange a word with you—who has had no thought for anything or any one else—is not likely to be doing that out of mere idleness of heart! Do you not believe that, either?

Clara. No.

The King. Well, then, there must surely be some general truths that you, as Ernst's daughter, cannot refuse to believe! Let me ask you if you can understand how a man becomes what I was at the time when I repeatedly insulted you. You must know, from your father's books, in what an unnatural atmosphere a king is brought up, the soul-destroying sense of self-importance which all his surroundings foster, until, even in his dreams, he thinks himself something more than human; the doubtful channels into which his thoughts are forced, while any virtues that he has are trumpeted abroad, and his vices glossed over with tactful and humorous tolerance. Don't you think that a young king, full of eager life, as I was, may plead something in excuse of himself that no other man can?

Clara. Yes, I admit that.

The King. Then you must admit that the very position he has to assume as a constitutional monarch is an acted lie. Think what a king's vocation is; *can* a vocation of that sort be hereditary? Can the finest and noblest vocation in the world be that?

Clara. No!

The King. Then suppose that he realises that himself; suppose that the young king is conscious, however dimly and partially, of the lie he is living—and suppose that, to escape from it, he rushes into a life of pleasure. Is it not conceivable that he may have some good in him, for all that? And then suppose that one morning, after a night of revelling, the sun shines into his room; and he seems to see upon the wall, in letters of fire, some words that were said to him the night before— true words (CLARA *looks up at him in surprise*)—the words: "I despise you!" (CLARA *gives a start.*) Words like that can burn out falsehood. And he, to whom they are said, may long to hear again the tones of the voice that spoke them. No man has ever hated what has given him new life. If you had read a single one of the letters which I felt impelled to write even if they were refused acceptance—you would not have called it persecution. (CLARA *does not answer.*) And, as for my persecution of your father—I am not going to make any excuses for myself; I will only ask you to remember that a king has no control over the law and its judgments. I feel the sincerest respect for your father.

Clara. Thank you.

The King. And it is just part of the falsehood I was speaking of, that he should be condemned for saying of me what I have said a thousand times of myself!

Clara (softly). Dare I believe that?

The King. Ah, if only you had read one of my letters! Or even the little book of poems I sent you last! I thought that, if you would not receive my letters, perhaps a book—

Clara. I do not accept anonymous gifts.

The King. I see you are on your guard—although I don't admit that the poems were mine! May I read it to you?

Clara. I don't understand—.

The King. One that I marked—for you. It will prove to you what you refuse to believe.

Clara. But if the poem is not yours?

The King. The fact that I have marked it shows that its sentiments apply to me. Will you let me read it to you? (CLARA *looks up.*) Do not be too much surprised, Miss Ernst! (*Takes a slim volume from his pocket.*) I found this somewhere. (*Turns over the leaves.*) It won't take long to read. May I?

Clara. If only I understood—

The King. —why I want to read it? Simply for the reason that you have forbidden me to speak to you—or to write to you; but not, as yet, to read to you! (CLARA *smiles. A pause.*) Do you know—a little event has just happened in my life?—and yet not such a little one, after all!

Clara. What is that?

The King. I have seen you smile for the first time.

Clara. Your Majesty!

The King. But, Miss Ernst, is it an insult, too, to see you smile?

Clara (smiling). If I consent to hear the poem, shall not the Baroness—

The King. —hear it also? With pleasure; but not at the same time! Please! Because I am a very bad reader. You can show it to the Baroness afterwards, if you like. (CLARA *smiles.*) May I?

Clara. You are sure there is nothing in it that—

The King. You can interrupt me, if you think fit. It is called " The Young Prince;" and it is about—no, I won't tell you what it is about unless you will be so good as to sit down, so that I can sit down too. If I stand up I shall be sure to begin declaiming, and I do that shockingly badly!—You can get up again when you like, you know! (CLARA *smiles and sits down. The* KING *sits down beside her.*) Now, then! " The Young Prince." (*To himself.*) I can scarcely breathe. (*He begins to read.*)

Full fed with early flattery and pride—

(*Breaks off.*) Excuse me, Miss Ernst! I don't feel—

Clara. Is your Majesty not well?

The King. Quite well! It is only—. Now, then!

> Full fed with early flattery and pride,
> His sated soul was wearied all too young;
> Honour and kingly pomp seemed naught to him
> But whimsies from the people's folly sprung.
>
> From such pretence he fled to what was real—
> Fair women's arms, laughter and love and pleasure,
> All the mad joy of life; whate'er he craved,
> He found was given him in double measure.
>
> Whate'er he craved—until one day a maiden
> To whom he whispered, like a drunken sot,
> " I'd give my life to make thee mine, my sweeting! "
> Turned from him silently and answered not.
>
> He sought by every means to win her to him;
> But when his love with cold *contempt* was met,
> It was as if a judgment had been spoken
> Upon his life, and doom thereon were set.
>
> His boon companions left him; in his castles
> None seemed to be awake but he alone,
> Racked with remorse, enshrouded in the darkness
> Of dull despair, yet longing to atone.

Then through the darkness she appeared! and humbly,
Emboldend by her gentleness of mien,
He sued once more: " If only thou wouldst listen!
If still 'twere not too late—"

(*His emotion overcomes him, and he stops suddenly, gets up,
and walks away from* CLARA. *She gets up, as he comes back
to her.*) Excuse me! I had no intention of making a
scene. But it made me think of—. (*Breaks off again
overcome by emotion, and moves a little way from her.
There is a pause as he collects himself before returning to her.*)
As you can hear, Miss Ernst, it is nothing much of a poem
—not written by a real poet, that is to say; a real poet
would have exalted his theme, but this is a common-
place—

Clara. Has your Majesty anything more to say to me?
(*A pause.*)

The King. If I have anything more to say to any one,
it is to you.

Clara. I beg your pardon.

The King. No, it is I should beg yours. But I am sure
you do not wish me to lie to you.

Clara (*turning her head away*). No.

The King. You have no confidence in me. (*Controls
his emotion.*) Will you ever, I wonder, come to understand that the only thing I crave for now is—one person's
confidence!

Clara. Any one who speaks as your Majesty has done
to-day surely craves for more than that.

The King. More than that, yes; but, first of all, one
person's confidence.

Clara (*turning away*). I don't understand—

The King (*interrupting her, with emotion*). Your life
has not been as empty and artificial as mine.

Clara. But surely you have your task here to fill it
with?

The King. I remember reading once about the way

a rock was undermined, and the mine filled with gun-powder with an electric wire leading to it. Just a slight pressure on a little button and the great rock was shattered into a thousand pieces. And in the same way everything is ready here; but the little pressure—to cause the explosion—is what I am waiting for!

Clara. The metaphor is a little forced.

The King. And yet it came into my mind as unconsciously as you broke off that twig just now. If I do not get what I lack, nothing can be accomplished—there can be no explosion! I shall abandon the whole thing and let myself go under.

Clara. Go under?

The King. Well, not like the hero of a sensational novel —not straight to the bottom like a stone—but like a dreamer carried off by pixies in a wood, with one name ever upon my lips! And the world would have to look after itself.

Clara. But that is sheer recklessness.

The King. I know it is; but I am reckless. I stake everything upon one throw! (*A pause.*)

Clara. Heaven send you may win.

The King. At least I am daring enough to hope that I may—and there are moments when I almost feel certain of victory!

Clara (*embarrassed*). It is a lovely morning—

The King. —for the time of year; yes. And it is lovelier here than it is anywhere else!

Clara. I cannot really understand a course of action which implies a want of all sense of responsibility—

The King. Every one has their own point of view. A scheme of life, to satisfy me, must have its greatest happiness hidden away at its core; in my case that would be to have a house of my own—all to myself, like any other citizen—from which I should go away to my work, and come back to as to a safe refuge. That is the button on the electric wire, do you understand? It is the little pressure on it that I am waiting for. (*A pause.*)

Clara. Have you read my father's book, *Democratic Monarchy* ?

The King. Yes.

Clara. He wrote it when I was a child; and so I may say that I grew up amongst ideas like—like those I have heard from you to-day. All the friends that came to our house used to talk to me about it.

The King. Then no doubt you heard the crown prince talked about, too!

Clara. I think I heard his name oftener mentioned at home than any one's. I believe the book was written expressly for you.

The King. I can feel that when I read it. If only I had been allowed to read it in those days! Do you remember how in it your father maintains, too, that all reform depends on the beating down of the hedge that surrounds royalty?—on a king's becoming, as he says, " wedded to his people " in the fullest sense of the word, not irregularly or surreptitiously ? No king can share his people's thoughts if he lives apart from them in a great palace, married to a foreign princess. There is no national spirit behind a complicated court life of outlandish ceremonial.

Clara (*turning away her head*). You should have heard how vehemently my father used to assert those ideas.

The King. And yet he abandoned them.

Clara. Became a republican, you mean?

The King. Yes.

Clara. He was so disappointed. (*A pause.*)

The King. I sometimes wonder every one isn't a republican! It must come to that in the end; I can see that. If only royalties nowadays thought seriously enough about it to realise it!

Clara. It is made so difficult for them by those who surround them.

The King. Yes, you see, that is another reason why any such reform must begin at home. Do you think that a king, who went every day to his work from a home that was in every respect like that of one of his people, could fail in the long run?

Clara. There are so many different kinds of homes.

The King. I mean a home that holds love instead of subservience—comfort instead of ceremony—truth instead of flattery; a home where—ah, well, I need not teach a woman what a home means.

Clara. We make them what they are.

The King. Surely; but they are especially what women make them. (*A pause.*)

Clara. The sun is quite strong now.

The King. But it can scarcely pierce through the screen of leaves here.

Clara. When the sun shines down like this and the leaves tremble—

The King. The sunshine seems to tremble too.

Clara. Yes, but it makes one feel as if everything were trembling—even deep down into our hearts!

The King. That is true.—Yes, its homes are the most precious things a nation makes. Their national characteristics mean reverence for their past and possibilities for their future.

Clara. I understand better now what you meant.

The King. When I said I wanted to begin at the beginning?

Clara. Yes. (*A pause.*)

The King. I cannot do otherwise. My heart must be in my work.

Clara (smiling). My father had his heart in his work, too.

The King. Forgive me—but don't you think it was just

R 696

the want of an object in his life that led your father to push his theories too far?—an object outside himself, I mean?

Clara. Perhaps. If my mother had lived—. (*Stops.*)

The King. —he might have taken it differently; don't you think so?

Clara. I have sometimes thought so. (*A pause.*)

The King. How still it is! Not a sound!

Clara. Yes, there is the fountain.

The King. That is true; but one ends by hardly hearing a continuous sound like that.

Clara. There is a tremulousness in *that* too. (*Looks round her.*)

The King. What are you looking for?

Clara. It is time to look for the Baroness.

The King. She is up on that slope. Shall I call her? Or—perhaps you would like to see a fine view?

Clara. Yes.

The King. Then let us go up to her together! (*They go.*)

ACT III

SCENE I

(SCENE.—*An open place in the town. It is evening, and the square is badly lit. On the right is the club, a large building, standing alone; lights are shining from all its windows. Steps lead from the door, above which is a balcony. The square is full of people. In the background, standing on the lowest step of the pedestal of an equestrian statue, is a* BALLAD SINGER, *singing to the accompaniment of his guitar. Cigars, oranges, and other wares are being sold by hawkers. The singer's voice is heard before the curtain rises. The crowd gradually joins him in the refrain which he repeats after each verse of his ballad.*)

The Ballad Singer (sings).

> The Princeling begged and begged and begged
> Her love, on bended knee.
> The Maid said craftily, " Nay, nay,
> I doubt your high degree! "

> *Refrain.*

> She knew the might, the might, the might
> Of love's distracting hour;
> How royalty, with all its pomp,
> Will curtsey to its power.

> The Princeling said: " Consent, my dear,
> And you shall marry me."
> The Maiden answered mockingly,
> " Over the left, maybe! "

> " Nay, as my Queen, enchanting maid,
> And that this very day! "
> The Maiden answered him, " Gadzooks! "
> And fainted right away.

243

Recovering, she sighed, " My Lord,
Princesses will be wroth;
On every side they sit and wait
To plight to you their troth."

He answered, " Bosh! "—" But what of those
Who counselled you before? "
" Whom do you mean? "—" Your ministers! "
" I'll show them to the door! "

" But think, my dear—your generals,
Your nobles, court, and priest;
They'll try to drag you from my side
Or shun us as the pest."

" Nay, be not feared! I'll make you more
By dozens at a word,
Who'll bow and grovel if they be
To rank and place preferred."

" But think of the republicans!
My father!—what if he——? "
" The cock that crows the loudest, then,
Prime minister shall be! "

" Suppose the people stoutly swear
They'll none of me? "—" Nay, nay,
An order here, a title there,
And all will homage pay."

" Then I am yours! "—" Hurrah! " He holds
Her tight his arms between;
" Nay, not so fast, my kingly love!
Not till I am your Queen! "

> She knew the might, the might, the might
> Of love's distracting hour;
> How royalty, with all its pomp,
> Will curtsey to its power.

An Old Gentleman (to another). What is going on here?

Second Old Gentleman. I don't know. I have only just come.

A Workman. Why, the King is coming past here with her!

First Old Gentleman. Coming past here with her? To hold a court at the palace?

The Workman. Yes.

Second Old Gentleman (taking a pinch of snuff). And

I suppose those fellows in the club mean to make a demonstration?—hiss them, or something of that sort?

The Workman. So they say.

First Old Gentleman. Have they decided not to attend the court then?

A Dandy. Unanimously decided.

A Woman. It's filthy!

The Dandy. I beg your pardon?

The Woman. I say that those fellows in there will condescend to seduce our daughters, right enough; but they won't condescend to marry them. But, you see, the King does.

The Workman. I am not sure it wouldn't be better if he didn't.

The Woman. Well, I know people who say that she is quite a respectable person.

The Dandy. I imagine that you have not read the newspapers?

First Old Gentleman. Hm!—one has to be a little careful as to how far one believes the newspapers.

Second Old Gentleman (offering him his snuff-box). I am delighted to hear you say that! There is such a lot of slander flying about. That bawdy ballad just now, for instance.

The Woman. Yes, that's poking fun at *him*—I know that.

The Dandy. You had better take care what you are saying, my good woman!

The Woman. Ah, I only say what I know.

(FLINK *appears on the steps of the statue beside the* BALLAD SINGER.)

Flink. Stop your stupid songs! I want to speak!

Voice in the Crowd. Who is that?

Flink. You don't know me. I have never made public speeches—and least of all to street mobs.

Voice in the Crowd. Why are you doing it now, then?

Flink. Because I have been charged with a message to you! (*The members of the club rush to the windows and on to the balcony and steps. Uproar.*)

Voice in the Crowd. Be quiet! Let us hear him!

Flink. Listen to me, good people! You don't know me. But you used to know a tall chap, with long white hair and a big hat, who often made speeches to you. I mean Professor Ernst.

Voice in the Crowd. Three cheers for Professor Ernst. (*Cheers.*)

Flink. He was sent to prison, as you know, for high treason; escaped from prison, but broke his legs. Now he is living in exile, hopelessly crippled.

Voice in the Crowd. He got a pardon.

Another. No one knows where he is.

Flink. I know where he is. He has charged me to deliver a message to you to-day.

Voices from the Club. Bravo!

Voices from the Crowd. Has he! Bravo, Ernst!

Voices from the Club. Be quiet, down there!

Flink. He made me promise that, on the day on which his daughter was to be presented at the palace as the King's betrothed, I would stand up in some public place where she would pass by, and say that it was being done against her father's will and in spite of his urgent entreaties and commands. (*Loud cries of* "Bravo!" *from the club. A voice in the crowd:* "That is just what we thought!") I am charged to announce publicly that he despises her for it and sends her his curse! (*Fresh cries of* "Bravo!" *from the club. Voices in the crowd:* "That's shocking!"—"No, he was quite right;" *etc., etc. Uproar.*) Quiet, good people!

A Young Man in the Crowd. May I be allowed to ask a question? (*Shouts of* "Yes!" *and* "No!" *and laughter are heard.*)

Flink. By all means.

The Young Man. Did not Professor Ernst himself advocate a king's doing just what our King has done?

Voices in the Crowd. Hear, hear!

Flink. Yes, and in return was thrown into prison and is now an incurable cripple. No one has been more cruelly treated by the King's hirelings. And now here is his daughter willing to become Queen!

Count Platen (from the club balcony). I don't see why you want to blame *her!* No; what I say is, that it is our dissolute King's fault altogether! (*Renewed uproar. Cries of :* " Turn him out! " *from the club.*)

Flink. I had something more to say about those who—. But make those fellows at the club be quiet first.

A Voice. They are fighting over there! (*Laughter. Wild uproar is heard from the club, amidst which* COUNT PLATEN'S *voice is heard shouting :* " Let me be! Let me alone! "—*and other voices :* " Don't let him go out! "— " He is drunk! " *Eventually* COUNT PLATEN *comes out on to the steps, hatless and dishevelled.*)

Count Platen. I'm going to make a speech to you! I am better than that crew in there! (*Cries of* " Bravo! ") What I say is, that the King is coming past here directly with a woman. (*Applause, and laughter. Every one crowds towards him. The police try to pull him down. A free fight ensues.*) Hiss them when they come! (*Cries of* " Throw him down! "—" Bravo! "—" Hurrah! ") I, Count Platen, tell you to do so! Hiss him, howl at him, make a regular hullabaloo when he comes! I, Count Platen, tell you to! (*Cries of* " Three cheers for Count Platen! " *are mingled with cries of* " Three cheers for the King! " *There is a general tumult.* COUNT PLATEN *is hustled up and down the steps, and tries to go on making his speech every time he comes up.*) He is defiling the throne! —He wants to marry a traitor's daughter! Shame!— I, Count Platen, say so! Here I stand—! (*A trumpet-call is heard ; then cries of* " Here is the King! "—" No, it's the cavalry!"— "The cavalry are coming!"— "Clear the square!" *A shot is heard, followed by a scream; the people take to their heels as another trumpet-call is heard. Curtain.*)

SCENE II

(SCENE.—*A room in the* BARONESS' *house. The* BARONESS *is sitting reading. A* MAID *enters and brings her a card.*)

Baroness (*looking at the card*). The Minister of the Interior!—Show him in! (GRAN *comes in.*) I am glad to see you back, your Excellency!—You have found him, then?

Gran. Yes, we have discovered him.

Baroness. And spoken to him?

Gran. Yes.

Baroness. May I send for his daughter?

Gran. For heaven's sake—

Baroness. What is the matter?

Gran. He is a dying man.

Baroness. What!

Gran. The King desires me to tell you that he has ordered a special train to be ready at 10 o'clock, so that as soon as the court is over she can go to her father. The King will accompany her.

Baroness. That is kind of him!

Gran. Then you will get ready everything that she needs for a night's journey?

Baroness. Yes.

Gran. And without her being aware of it? The King does not wish her to know anything of her father's condition till after the court.

Baroness. The court is to be held, then?

Gran. The court is to be held. After it is over, His Majesty will tell her the news himself.

Baroness. I am thankful for that.—But what did

Professor Ernst say? Why has he not answered his daughter's letter? Why has he hidden from her? Is he really irreconcilable?

Gran. Irreconcilable? He hates her!

Baroness. Good heavens!

Gran. And not only her, but every one that has made common cause with the King—every one!

Baroness. I suppose it was to be expected.—But won't you sit down?

Gran (bows, but remains standing). I had a talk with his doctor before I saw him. He had some hesitation about letting me in. It was a fortnight since his patient had been able to move. But when I told him my errand, and that I had come from the King, he let me see him.

Baroness. How did he look? He was a fine man once.

Gran. He was sitting in a big chair, a mere paralysed wreck of a man. But when he saw me and realised who I was—and probably, too, what my errand was—he found the strength not only to move, but to seize both his crutches and raise himself on them! I shall never forget his gaunt ashen-grey face, the feverish gleam in his sunken eyes, his unkempt hair and beard—

Baroness. He must have looked terrible!

Gran. He was like a creature from beyond the grave—with an eternity of hatred in his eyes!

Baroness. Oh, my God!

Gran. When at last I could find my voice, I gave him his daughter's greeting, and asked if she might come and see him. A dark look came into his eyes, and his face flushed for a moment, as he gasped out: "May she be—." He could not finish the sentence. His crutches slipped from his grasp and he fell down, blood pouring from his mouth. The doctor rushed to him; and for a long time we thought he was dead.

Baroness. But he came round?

Gran. I waited an hour or two before I started back.

Then the doctor told me that he had recovered consciousness, but that the end could certainly not be far off—perhaps not twenty-four hours.

Baroness. It must have been a shock to you.

Gran. It was.

Baroness. But what did he mean by: " May she be—"?

Gran. That is what I have been wondering.

Baroness. He cannot do her any harm, can he?

Gran. He may give her the same reception that he gave me, if she goes.

Baroness. Even if the King is with her?

Gran. All the more then!

Baroness. Oh, that would be horrible! But it won't prevent her going.

Gran. Let us hope so!

Baroness. I am certain of it! She has extraordinary strength of character—just like her father's.

Gran. Yes, that is the one thing I rely on.

Baroness. What do you mean? Your words sound so despondent!

Gran. I mean what is perfectly true—that everything will depend upon her strength of character.

Baroness. What about the King, then?

Gran. I could say a great deal on that topic, Baroness; but (*bows*) you must excuse me—I haven't time now.

Baroness. How are the elections going?

Gran. They are going well—if nothing happens now?

Baroness. What could happen?

Gran. The situation is very strained; one must expect anything.

Baroness. Are you anxious, your Excellency?

Gran. I must beg leave to retire now. (*A* MAID *comes in.*)

Maid (*to* GRAN). The Inspector of Police, who came with your Excellency, wishes to know if he may speak to your Excellency.

Gran. I will come at once. (*To the* BARONESS.) There is rioting going on in the town, not far from here—in front of the club.

Baroness (*in alarm*). What?—Isn't the King coming along that way?

Gran. Don't be afraid! We have taken our precautions—Good-bye! (*Goes out.*)

Baroness.—He has quite alarmed me—everything seems to come at the same time! She has had a suspicion that there was something amiss with her father; I have noticed that, but she hasn't wanted to speak about it. (CLARA *comes in, dressed for the court.*) Ah, there you are, my dear! Quite ready?

Clara. Quite.

Baroness (*looking at her*). Well, I daresay there have been royal brides more elaborately dressed, but I am sure there has never been one more charming. (*Kisses her.*)

Clara. I think I hear a carriage?

Baroness. I expect it is the King!

Clara. I am afraid it is too early yet—but all the same I hope it is he!

Baroness. Do you feel afraid?

Clara. No, no—it is not that at all; it is something— something that you don't—a kind of feeling as if—as if some one were haunting me; and I know who it is. I only feel secure when the King is with me. I hope it may be he coming. (*Goes to the window.*)

(*The* MAID *comes in.*)

Maid. A lady wishes to speak to you, Miss Ernst—

Baroness. A lady?

Clara. Didn't she give her name?

Maid. She is veiled—and very handsomely dressed.

Clara (*with decision*). No! I can see no one.

Baroness. No one that we do not know. (*To the* MAID.) You ought to know that.

Maid (*hesitatingly*). But I think it is—. (*The door opens and the* PRINCESS *comes in.*)

Baroness. What does this mean? Clara! leave us, my dear.

Princess (*drawing aside her veil*). Do you know me?

Clara.
Baroness. } The Princess!

Princess. Are you Clara Ernst?

Clara. Yes.

Princess (*haughtily, to the* BARONESS). Leave us alone! (*The* BARONESS *goes out.*) Before going to the palace I wanted to come here—even at the risk of meeting the King.

Clara. He has not come yet. (*A long pause.*)

Princess. Have you thought well over what you are going to do?

Clara. I think so.

Princess. I don't think you have. Have you read what the papers say about it—every one of them—to-day?

Clara. No. The King has advised me not to.

Princess. But the letters that have been sent to you? I know letters have been written to you.

Clara. The King has advised me not to read them either. He takes all the letters.

Princess. Do you know that they are rioting in the streets close to here?

Clara (*in alarm*). No!

Princess. You will be received with hisses, hooting— perhaps with stone throwing. You didn't expect anything like that, did you?

Clara. No.

Princess. What shall you do?

Clara (*after a moment, quietly*). I shall go with the King.

Princess. A nice road you are dragging him along, truly! And I assure you that the farther you go along it, the worse it will become. You cannot possibly have prepared yourself for all that you will have to go through.

Clara. I think I have.

Princess (in surprise). What do you mean?   How?

Clara (bending her head). I have prayed to God.

Princess. Pshaw!   I mean that you cannot have considered the misery into which you are dragging the King —and the disgrace and trouble you are bringing upon all his people. (CLARA *is silent.*) You are young still; your heart cannot be altogether hardened yet, whatever your past may have been.

Clara (proudly). I have no reason to be ashamed of my past.

Princess. Indeed?   What sort of a past has it been, then?

Clara. One full of suffering, princess—and of work. (*A pause.*)

Princess. Do you know what the King's past has been?

Clara (drooping her head). Ah, yes.

Princess. Yours will be tarred with the same brush— no matter what it really has been.

Clara. I know that.   He has told me so.

Princess. Really!—After all, is it a sacrifice you are making for his sake?   Do you love the King?

Clara (faintly). Yes.

Princess. Then listen to me.   If you loved the King, you would have made a *real* sacrifice for him.   We are women, you and I; we can understand these things without many words.   But such a sacrifice does not consist in consenting to be his queen.

Clara. It is not I that wished it.

Princess. You have allowed yourself to be persuaded? —Well, you are either deceiving yourself, my girl, or you are deceiving him.   Perhaps you began with the one and are ending with the other.   Anyway, it is time you had your eyes opened as to which of you it is that is making the sacrifice. Do you not know that, on your account, he is already the target for general contempt? (CLARA *bursts into tears.*) If that makes you repent, show it—show it by your deeds!

Clara. I repent of nothing.

Princess (*in astonishment*). What state of mind are you in, then?

Clara. I have suffered terribly. But I pray God for strength to bear it.

Princess. Don't talk nonsense! The whole thing is a horrible confusion of ideas—half remorse and half cant—the one so mixed up with the other in your mind that you cannot disentangle them. But, believe me, others feel very sure that sacred things and—and what I won't call bluntly by its name, go very ill together! So don't waste those airs on me; they only irritate me!

Clara. Princess, don't be cruel to me. I *am* suffering, all the same.

Princess. Why on earth do you want to go any farther with the affair? If you aren't clear about it, take advice! Your father is opposed to it, isn't he?

Clara. Yes. (*Throws herself into a chair.*)

Princess. He has hidden himself away from you. You don't know where he is, or how he is—though you know he is crippled and ill. And, meanwhile, here you are in full dress, with a rose in your hair, waiting to set out to a court at the palace! Are you willing to pass through contemptuous rioting crowds, and over your sick father's body, to become queen? What callous levity! What a presumptuous mixture of what you think is love, duty, sacrifice, trial—with an unscrupulous ambition—! The King? Are you depending on him? He is a poet. He loves anything unusual or sensational. Resistance stimulates him; and that is what drives him into believing that his love will be unending. When you have been married a week, it will be all over. If he had not met

with resistance, it would have been all over before this. I
know the King better than you; for I know his faithlessness. It is like his love—unending! It hurts you to
hear that, does it? Well, it hurts one's eyes to look at
the sun. But I can tell you about these things. The
only reason I had for coming was to tell you what I know.
And now that I have seen you, I can tell you that I know
one thing more—and I will tell you what it is. If you
actually allow the King, with his ardent temperament, to
stray into a path which will lead to the ruin of his career,
your action will, in the fullness of time, recoil so appal-
lingly upon your own head that it will kill you. I know
you are one of those that faithlessness, remorse and contempt *would* kill.—Don't look so beseechingly at me; I
cannot retract a word of what I have said. But I can
tell you now what I had decided upon before I came. *I*
will look after your future. I am not rich; but, as sure
as I stand here before you, you shall live free from care—
you shall have everything that you need—for the rest of
your life. I want no thanks! I do it for the sake of the
King, and for the sake of the country to which I belong.
It is my duty. Only get up now and come with me to
my carriage. (*Offers* CLARA *her hand.*)

Clara. If it were as easy as that, I should have done it
long, long ago.

Princess (*turns away. Then comes back*). Get up.
(*Pulls her on to her feet.*) Do you love the King?

Clara. Do I love him? I am a motherless child, and
have lived alone with a father who has been constantly
persecuted on account of his principles; I shared his
ideals from a very early age, and I have never abandoned
them since. Then one day I was given the chance of
making these ideals real. " What *I* long to do, *you* shall
accomplish! " he said. There is something great about
that, Princess—something all-powerful—a call from God
Himself. Of that I am certain.

Princess. It is merely a rhapsody of the King's—nothing else!

Clara. Then I will make it real and live it! I have given my whole soul to it, and have strengthened his to the same end. It has been my ideal all my life.

Princess. And you believe that it will last?

Clara. Yes.

Princess. Then let me beg you to believe this, too—it will last until he has attained his end.

Clara. If you mean our marriage, let me tell you that *that* is not our end.

Princess (in surprise). What is, then?

Clara. Our end is to accomplish something together. That task shall be consecrated and ennobled by our love. Yes, you may look at me! Those were his own words.

Princess. That answer! — That thought! — But what certainty have you?

Clara. Of what?

Princess. That you did not put the thought into his mind?—and that the fire in his soul may not flicker out?

Clara. If I needed any assurance, I should find it in the fact that he changed his whole life for my sake; he waited for me for more than a year. Has he ever done that for any one before? I am sure he has never needed to! (*The* PRINCESS *winces.*) It is those who have seduced that " ardent " temperament of his—you called it that yourself—that are to blame, and not I, Princess! (*A pause.*) I checked him to the best of my power when he came to me as he was wont to go to others. (*A pause.*) Indeed it is no sacrifice to become his wife. When one loves, there is no question of sacrifice. But the position in which I now stand exposes me to more suspicion than the humblest of his subjects, to more scorn than if I were his mistress. Think how you have spoken to me to-day yourself, Princess! (*A pause.*) It is no sacrifice to endure such things for the man one loves. It was not I that used the word " sacrifice," either; and as for the sacrifice you implied that I ought to have made, I don't wish to understand what you meant by that, even though I am a woman as well as you! But if you knew, Princess, how hard a fight I have been through before I found the strength to cast in my lot with his, against my father's wish and against you all—you would not have spoken to me about making a sacrifice. At all events you would not have spoken to me as you have done to-day; because you are not cruel, and I know that at bottom you mean me well. (*A longer pause.*)

Princess. This is more serious than I knew.—Poor child, your disappointment will be all the more serious.

Clara. Not with him!

Princess (half to herself). Is it possible he can be so changed? Was that what was needed to secure a hold on him—? (*To* CLARA.) Is he coming here to fetch you?

Clara. Yes.

Princess. What does he want to hold this court for? What is the good of throwing down this challenge to all the dignitaries of his kingdom?—especially if, after all, he means to live the life of an ordinary citizen?

Clara. He wished it.

Princess. An exciting episode in his rhapsody! Why did you not dissuade him?

Clara. Because I agree with him.

Princess. Perhaps you don't fully realise what it means? —what humiliation the King will have to undergo?

Clara. I only know that it seems to me that these things should be done openly, and that he has plenty of courage.

Princess. That is mere bravado. Are you going in that dress?—to court in that dress? (CLARA *is silent.*) I say it is mere bravado.

Clara. I have no better dress.

Princess. What do you mean? Surely the King can—? Are you jesting?

Clara (*shyly*). I do not allow the King to give me anything; not until—.

Princess. Doesn't he pay your expenses here, then? (*Looks round the room.*)

Clara. No.

Princess. It is the Baroness?

Clara. She and I. We are both poor.

Princess. Ah, yes—she has lost her post now, hasn't she?

Clara. On my account—yes. And you, Princess, who have known her—for she was once your governess—can you really suppose that she would have been faithful to me if she did not trust me and feel that this was right? You treated her so contemptuously when you came in.

Princess. I seem to have broken in upon the most incomprehensible romance!—Then you love the King? (CLARA *nods her head.*) He knows how to love, and make a woman happy! He is a dazzling creature!—We shall see now whether you are to suffer for all the hearts he has broken. You are not the first woman he has loved.

Clara. Princess!

Princess. Yes, let that sink into your mind! Your happiness is embroidered with tears!

Clara. It is cruel of you to reproach me with it.

Princess. Forgive me! I really did not mean that.— But there is still time to put on a more suitable dress. If you dare accept no gifts from the King—you might from some one else? A King's bride is a King's bride after all, you know!

Clara. He told me I should not need anything more than this.

Princess. Not in his eyes, I dare say. But we women know a little better!—If it were only a necklace? Will you accept this one? (*Begins to unfasten hers.*)

Clara. I knew you were kind.—But I daren't.

Princess. Why not?

Clara. Because—because people would think that—.
(*Bursts into tears. A pause.*)

Princess. Listen, my child. The whole thing is sheer
lunacy; but—as it cannot be altered—as soon as the
court assembles I shall take my place at your side and
not leave you till it is all over. Tell the King that!
Good-bye!

Clara (*going towards her*). Princess!

Princess (*kisses her, and whispers*). Haven't you allowed
him to kiss you, either?

Clara (*in a whisper*). Yes, I have.

Princess (*kissing her once more*). Love him! (*The
sound of carriage wheels is heard. The* BARONESS
comes in.)

Baroness. I hear the King's carriage.

Princess. I don't wish to meet him. (*Stretches out her
hand to the* BARONESS.) Baroness! (*Points to the door
through which the* BARONESS *has come in.*) Can I get out
that way?

Baroness. Yes. (*She takes the* PRINCESS *out. A moment
later the* MAID *ushers in the* KING, *who is dressed in plain
clothes and wearing no decorations.*)

The King. Clara!

Clara. My friend! (*They embrace.*)

The King. What does it mean?

Clara. What?

The King. The Princess's carriage here?

Clara. She told me to greet you. She has just gone,
and—

The King. And—?

Clara. She said that as soon as the court assembled
she would take her place beside me and stay there till we
left the palace.

The King. Is it possible?

Clara. It is *true.*

The King. You have conquered her! I knew she

could be conquered—she has a heart, as well as a head! It is a good omen!—So she offered to do *that!* What will our precious nobility have to say to that?

Clara. They are about the streets, aren't they?

The King. Ah, then you know?

Clara. I know, too, that there has been rioting outside the club.

The King. You know that too?—and are not afraid?

Clara. Perhaps I might have been—but there is something else that I am more afraid of. (*Draws closer to the* KING.)

The King. What is that?

Clara. You know. (*A pause.*)

The King. Have you been uneasy about him to-day too?

Clara. All day — incessantly. Something must have happened.

The King. Well, now I can tell you where he is.

Clara (*eagerly*). At last! Have you found him?

The King. Gran has been to see him.

Clara. Thank God! Is it far from here?

The King. This evening, immediately after the court, you and I will both start for there in a special train. We shall be there early to-morrow.

Clara (*throwing her arms round his neck*). Thanks, thanks! How good you are! Thanks! How is he? Is he ill!

The King. Yes.

Clara. I knew it? And implacable?

The King. Yes.

Clara. I feel it! (*Nestles closer in his arms.*)

The King. Are you afraid?

Clara. Yes!

The King. Dear, when you see him perhaps your fear will go.

Clara. Yes, only let me see him! Whatever he says, let me see him!

The King. Within twelve hours from now you shall! And I shall be with you.

Clara. The finest thing about you is your kindness. Oh, I am so glad you have come! I could not endure my fears any longer.

The King. There are dissensions going on about you!

Clara. Oh!— (*Nestles in his arms again.*)

The King. Bear up!—It will soon be over.

Clara. I believe it will. Yes, I know it will.—Let me walk about a little! (*The* KING *walks up and down with her.*)

The King. And turn our thoughts to something else! Do you know where I have come from?

Clara. Where?

The King. From our little house in the park.

Clara. Why, we drove past it yesterday!

The King. You will feel only *one* person's presence there! Wherever you go, you will be surrounded by the thoughts I have had of you there. If you look out of the window, or go out on to the balcony—on every rock, by each turn of the stream—on the lawns, under the trees, among the bushes—everywhere you will find a thousand thoughts of you hidden. Breathe the words " my darling girl," and they will all come clustering round you!—Let us sit down.

Clara. It is all like a fairy tale.

The King. And I am the latest fairy prince! (*He sits down and draws her on to his knee.*) And you are the little maid who comes, led by good fairies, to the enchanted castle to wake him. He has been kept asleep by wicked spells for many, many years.

Clara. For many, many years!

The King. I am not really *I*, nor you *you*. The monarch

was bewitched long ago. He was turned into a wild beast who gave reign to his passion by night and slept by day. And now the maiden of humble degree has become a woman and freed him from the spells.

Clara. Really! Ah, you are so clever at inventing things to cheat my fears away from me. And you always succeed. But after all, you know, I have no strength and no courage; I am so weak.

The King. You have more strength than I!—more than any one I have ever known.

Clara. No, don't say that; but—you may be sure of this!—if I did not feel that I had *some* strength I would never try to throw in my lot with yours.

The King. I will explain to you what you are! Some people are tremendously more spiritual, more delicately constituted than others; and they are a hundred times more sensitive. And they fancy that is weakness. But it is just they who draw their strength from *deeper* sources, through a thousand imperceptible channels. You will often find them with heads erect and valiant when others have gone under; they merely bend before the storm, with supple strength, when others break under it. You are like that!

Clara. You are very ingenious when you start explaining me!

The King. Well, listen to this! At the time when I was behaving so badly to you, your terror, every time I approached you, was so piteous that it was always before my eyes and rang in my ears like a cry of agony from a wounded heart. It is true! It filled me with terror, too. Do you call that weakness, to feel things so intensely that another person is influenced by your feelings against his will?

Clara. No.

The King. And then, when I found you again—the way you listened to me—

Clara (stopping him with a kiss). Don't let us talk about it now!

The King. What shall we talk about, then? It is a little too early to start yet.—Ah, I have it! We will talk about the impression you will make this evening when you come forward through the brightly lit rooms, radiant against the background of ugly calumny! That was prettily put, wasn't it? "Is *that* she?" they will think. And then something will come into their eyes that will cheat them into thinking that pearls and gold are strewn over your hair, over your dress, over your—

Clara (putting her hand over his mouth). No, no, no! Now I am going to tell you a little story!

The King. Tell away!

Clara. When I was a child, I saw a balloon being filled one day, and there was a horrible smell from the gas. Afterwards, when I saw the gleaming balloon rising in the air, I thought to myself: "Ah, that horrid smell was something burning; they had to burn it for the balloon to be able to rise." And after that, every time I heard anything horrid said about my father, I felt as if something was burning inside me, and I thought of the balloon and imagined I could smell the smell. And then all at once I imagined I saw it rising; the horrid part was burnt, and it was able to mount aloft! I assure you that balloon was a good genius to me. And now, years afterwards, when I have been a target for calumny myself —and you for my sake—I have felt just the same thing. Every word has burned; but I have got over it in a moment, and risen high, high above it all! I never seem to breathe so pure an atmosphere as a little while after something cruel has been said of me.

The King. I shall certainly set to work and abuse you at once, if it has such delightful results! I will begin with a selection from to-day's papers: "You Aspasia! You Messalina! You Pompadour! You Phylloxera, that are eating into our whole moral vine-crop! You blue-eyed curse of the country, that are causing panics in the money - market, overthrowing ministries, and upsetting all calculations in the elections! You mischievous hobgoblin, who are pouring gall into the printers' ink and poison into the people's coffee, filling all the old ladies' heads with buzzing flies, and the King's Majesty with a million lover's follies! Do you know that, besides all the harm you are doing to-day, you are hastening a revolution by ten years? You are! And no one can be sure whether you haven't been pursuing the same wicked courses for the last hundred years or more! All our royal and noble ancestors are turning in their graves because of you! And if our deceased queens have any noses left—

Clara (interrupting him). The Baroness! (*They get up. The* BARONESS *comes in wearing a cloak over her court dress and carrying* CLARA'S *cloak over her arm.*)

Baroness. I must take the liberty of disturbing you. Time is up!

The King. We have been killing it by talking nonsense.

Baroness. And that has put you in a good humour?

The King (taking his hat). In the best of humours! Here, my darling (*fastens* CLARA'S *cloak about her shoulders*), here is the last scandalous bit of concealment for you! When we take it off again, you shall stand radiant in the light of your own truth. Come! (*Gives her his arm, and they go trippingly up to the back of the room. Suddenly the phantom of an emaciated figure leaning on crutches appears in their path, staring at them. His hair and beard are in wild disorder, and blood is pouring from his mouth.* CLARA *gives a terrified scream.*)

The King. In Heaven's name, what is it?

Clara. My father!

The King. Where? (*To the* BARONESS.) Go and see! (*The* BARONESS *opens the doors at the back and looks out*).

Baroness. I can see no one.

The King. Look down the corridor!

Baroness. No—no one there, either! (CLARA *has sunk lifelessly into the* KING'S *arms. After one or two spasmodic twitchings of her hands, her arms slip away from him and her head falls back.*)

The King. Help, help!

The Baroness (*rushing to him with a shriek*). Clara!

Curtain.

ACT IV

(SCENE.—*A room in* GRAN'S *house; the same as in Act I, Scene II.* GRAN *is standing at his desk on the right.* FLINK *comes in carrying a pistol-case, which he puts down upon the table.*)

Gran. You?

Flink. As you see. (*Walks up and down for a little without speaking.*)

Gran. I haven't seen you since the day the King was here.

Flink. No.—Have you taken your holidays?

Gran. Yes; but, anyway, I am likely to have perpetual holidays now! The elections are going against us.

Flink (*walking about*). So I hear. The clerical party and the reactionaries are winning.

Gran. That would not have been so, but for her unhappy death—. (*Breaks off, and sighs.*)

Flink. A judgment from heaven — that is what the parsons say, and the women, and the reactionaries—

Gran. —and the landlords. And they really believe it.

Flink (*stopping*). Well, don't you believe it?

Gran (*after a pause*). At all events I interpret it differently from—

Flink. —from the parson? Naturally. But can any one doubt the fact that it was the finger of fate?

Gran. Then fate assumed her father's shape?

Flink. Whether her father appeared to her at the moment of his death or not (*shrugs his shoulders*) is a matter in which I am not interested. I don't believe in such things. But that she was suffering pangs of con-

266

science, I do believe. I believe it may have brought
painful visions before her eyes.

Gran. I knew her pretty well, and I will answer for it
she had no guilty conscience. She was approaching her
task with enthusiasm. Any one that knew her will tell
you the same. With her the King was first and foremost.

Flink. What did she die of, then? Of enthusiasm?

Gran. Of being overwrought by the force of her emo-
tions. Her task was too great for her. The time was
not ripe for it. (*Sadly.*) Our experiment was bound to
fail.

Flink. You condemn it when you say that!—But with
her last breath she called out: "My father!" And,
just at that moment, he died, fifty miles away from her.
Either she *saw* him, or she *imagined* she saw him, standing
before her. But his bloodstained, maltreated, crippled
form standing in the way of her criminal advance towards
the throne—is that not a symbol of maltreated humanity
revolting against monarchy at the very moment when
monarchy wishes to atone! Its guilt through thousands
of years is too black. Fate is inflexible.

Gran. But with what result? Are we rid of monarchy
yet?

Flink. We are rid of that treacherous attempt to
reconcile it with modern conditions. Thank God it
emerges, hand in glove with the parsons and reactionaries,
none the worse for its temporary eclipse.

Gran. So everything is all right, I suppose?

Flink. For the moment — yes. But there used to
exist here a strong republican party, which enjoyed
universal respect, and was making extraordinary progress.
Where is it now?

Gran. I knew that was why you came.

Flink. I have come to call you to account.

Gran. If I had been in your place I would not have
acted so, towards a defeated and wounded friend.

Flink. The republican party has often been defeated—but never despised till now. Who is to blame for that?

Gran. None of us ever think we deserve contempt.

Flink. A traitor always deserves it.

Gran. It is but a step from the present state of things to a republic; and we shall have to take that step in the end.

Flink. But at least we can do so without treachery.

Gran. I honestly believe that what we did was right. It may have miscarried the first time, and may miscarry a second and a third; but it is the only possible solution.

Flink. You pronounced your doom in those words.

Gran (more attentively). What do you mean by that?

Flink. We must make sure that such an attempt will not be made again.

Gran. So that is it.—I begin to understand you now.

Flink. The republican party is broken up. For a generation it will be annihilated by contempt. But a community without a republican party must be one without ideals and without any aspirations towards truth in its political life—and in other respects as well! That is what you are responsible for.

Gran. You pay me too great a compliment.

Flink. By no means! Your reputation, your personal qualities and associations are what have seduced them.

Gran. Listen to me for a moment! You used to over-rate me in the hopes you had of me. You are overrating me now in your censure. You are overrating the effects of our failure—you never seem to be able to do anything but overshoot your mark. For that reason you are a danger to your friends. You lure them on. When things go well you lure them on to excess of activity; when things go ill, you turn their despondency into despair. Your inordinate enthusiasm obscures your wits. *You* are not called upon to sit in judgment upon any one; because you draw the pure truths that lie hidden in your soul into such a frenzied vortex of strife that you lose sight of them; and then they have so little of truth left in them that in your hands they can be answerable for crimes.

Flink. Oh, spare me your dialectics!—because any skill you have in them, *I* taught you! You cannot excuse your own sins by running over the list of mine; that is the only answer I have to make to you! I don't stand before you as the embodiment of truth; I am no braggart. No; but simply as one who has loved you deeply and now is as deeply offended by you, I ask this question of your conscience: What have you done with the love we had for one another? Where is the sacred cause we both used to uphold? Where is our honour— our friends—our future?

Gran. I feel respect for your sorrow. Can you not feel any for mine? Or do you suppose that I am not suffering?

Flink. You cannot act as you have done without bringing unhappiness upon yourself. But there are others to be considered besides you, and we have the right to call you to account. Answer me!

Gran. And is it really you—you, my old friend—that propose to do that?

Flink. God knows I would sooner some one else did it! But none can do it so fitly as I—because no one else has loved you as I have. I expected too much of you, you say? The only thing I wanted of you was that you should be faithful! I had so often been disappointed; but in you and your quiet strength I thought I had splendid security that, as long as you lived, our cause would bear itself proudly and confidently. It was your prestige that brought it into being; your wealth that supported it. It did not cry aloud for the blood of martyrs!— You were the happiness of my life; my soul renewed its strength from yours.

Gran. Old friend—!

Flink. I was old, and you were young! Your nature was a harmonious whole—it was what I needed to lean upon.

Gran. Flink, my dear old friend—!

Flink. And now, here you stand—a broken man, and our whole cause broken with you; all our lives broken—at least mine is—

Gran. Don't say that!

Flink. You have destroyed my faith in mankind—and in myself, for I see what a mistake I made; but it will be the last I shall make! I took you to my heart of hearts—and now, the only thing I can do is to call you to account!

Gran. What do you want me to do? Tell me!

Flink. We must stand face to face — armed! You must die! (*A pause.*)

Gran (*without seeming greatly surprised*). Of the two of us, it will go hardest with you, old friend.

Flink. You think your aim will be the surer of the two? (*Goes towards the table.*)

Gran. I was not thinking of that—but of what your life would be afterwards. I know you.

Flink (*opening the pistol-case*). You need not be anxious! My life afterwards will not be a long one. What you have done has robbed me of anything to live for in this generation, and I don't aspire to live till the next. So it is all over and done with! (*Takes up the pistols.*)

Gran. Do you mean *here*—?

Flink. Why not? We are alone here.

Gran. The King is asleep in the next room. (*Points to the door near his desk.*)

Flink. The King here?

Gran. He came here to-night.

Flink. Well, it will wake him up; he will have to wake up some time, any way.

Gran. It would be horrible! No!

Flink. Indeed? It is for his sake you have betrayed

me. You did that as soon as ever you met him again. He has bewitched you. Let him hear and see what he has done! (*Holds out the pistols.*) Here!

Gran. Wait. What you have just said brings a doubt into my mind. Is not revenge, after all, the motive for what you are doing?

Flink. Revenge?

Gran. Yes. Don't misunderstand me; I am not trying to shuffle out of it. If I were free to choose, I would choose death rather than anything else. The King knows that, too. But I ask because there ought to be some serious reason for anything that may happen. I am not going to stand up and face a sentiment of revenge that is so ill-grounded.

Flink (*laying the pistols down*). I hate the man who has led you astray—that is true. When I was giving you the reasons why I took upon myself the task of calling you to account, perhaps I forgot that. I hate him. But the instrument that carries out a sentence is one thing; the sentence itself is quite another. You are sentenced to death because you have betrayed our cause—and because you say that you were right to do so. The world shall learn what that costs. It costs a man's life.

Gran. So be it!

Flink. The pistols are loaded. I loaded them myself. I imagine that you still have trust in my honour?

Gran (*with a smile*). Indeed I have.

Flink. One of them has a blank cartridge in it; the other is fully loaded. Choose!

Gran. But what do you mean? Suppose I were to—?

Flink. Don't be afraid! Heaven will decide! *You* will not choose the fully loaded one!—We shall stand face to face.

Gran. You are settling everything—the sentence, the challenge, the choice of weapons, the regulations for the duel—!

Flink. Are you dissatisfied with that?

Gran. By no means! You are quite welcome! We are to have no seconds? So be it. But the place?

Flink. The place? Here!

Gran. Horrible!

Flink. Why? (*Holds out the two pistols to him. The door to the left is opened softly.* ANNA *looks in, sees what is going on, and rushes with a pitiful attempt at a scream to* GRAN, *putting her arms round him protectingly, and caressing him with every sign of the utmost terror.*)

Gran (*bending down and kissing her*). She is right! Why should I die for the sake of dull theories, when I can hold life in my arms as I do now? A man who is loved has something left, after all. I won't die!

Flink. If you were not loved, my friend, you might be allowed to live. A cry of sorrow will be heard throughout the land, from the King's palace to the meanest hovel, when you have been shot. And that is just why I must do it! The louder the cry of sorrow, the greater will be the silence afterwards. And in that silence is to be found the answer to the question " Why? " The people will not allow themselves to be cheated any longer.

Gran. Horrible! I won't do it! (*Lifts* ANNA *in his arms as if she were a child.*)

Flink (*going up to him*). It is no mere theory that you are facing. Look at me!

Gran. Old friend—*must* it be?

Flink. It *must.* I have nothing else left to do.

Gran. But not here.

Flink. Since it cannot be here, then come out into the park. (*Puts the pistols into their case.*) You owe me that.

Gran (*to* ANNA). You must go, my dear!

Flink (*putting the pistol-case under his arm*). No, let her stay here. But you come! (*They all three move towards the door.* ANNA *will not let* GRAN *go, and there is a struggle until he, half commanding and half entreating, persuades her to stay behind. The two men go out, shutting the door after them. She throws herself against the door, but it has been locked on the outside. She sinks down to the floor in despair, then gets up, as if struck by a sudden idea, rushes into the room on the right, and almost immediately re-appears, dragging the* KING *after her. He is only half-dressed and has no shoes on.*)

The King. What is it? (*A shot is heard.*) What is it? (ANNA *pulls him to the door. He tries to open it, but in vain. She rushes to the window, with the* KING *after her. Meanwhile the door is opened from outside, and* FALBE *comes in, evidently overcome with emotion.*) What is it, Falbe? (ANNA *runs out.*)

Falbe. His Excellency the Minister of the Interior—

The King. Well, what of him?

Falbe. —has been assassinated!

The King. The Minister of the Interior?—Gran?

Falbe. Yes.

The King. Gran?—What did you say?

Falbe. He has been assassinated!

The King. Gran? Impossible!—Where? Why? I heard his voice only just now, here!

Falbe. That fellow shot him—the grey-haired fellow—the republican—

The King. Flink? Yes, I heard his voice here too!

Falbe. It was in the park! I saw it myself!

The King. Saw it yourself? Wretch! (*Rushes out.*)

Falbe. How could I prevent a madman—? (*Follows the* KING. *The door stands open, and through it a man is seen running past, calling out:* "Where?" *Others follow him, and amidst the sound of hurrying feet, cries are heard of* "Good God!"—"In the park, did you say?"—"A doctor! Fetch a doctor!"—"Who did it?"—"That fellow running towards the river!"—"After him! After him!"—"Fetch a barrow from the works!"—*After a while the* KING *returns alone, looking distracted. He stands motionless and silent for some time.*)

The King. What a happy smile there was on his face!—Just as she smiled!—Yes, it must be happiness! (*Hides his face in his hands.*) And he died for me too! My two only—. (*Breaks down.*) So that is the price they have to pay for loving me!—And at once! At once!—Of course! Of course! (*The sound of the crowd returning is heard, and cries of:* "This way!"— "Into the blue room!" *Women and children come streaming in, all in tears, surrounding* ANNA *and the men that are carrying* GRAN'S *body, and follow them into the room on the left. Cries are heard of:* "Why should *he* die?"—"He was so good!"—"What had he done to deserve it!"—"He was the best man in the world!")

The King. "He was the best man in the world!" Yes. And he died for my sake! That means something good of me!—the best possible! Are they two together now, I wonder? Oh, let me have a sign!—or is that too much to ask? (*The crowd come out again, sobbing and weeping, and cries are heard of:* "He looks so beautiful and peaceful!"—"I can't bring myself to believe it!" *When they see the* KING, *they hush their voices, and all go out as quietly as they can. When they have gone out, the* MAYOR'S *voice is heard asking:* "Is he in here?" *and an answer:* "No, in the blue room, over there." *Then the* GENERAL'S *voice:* "And the murderer escaped?"—*An answer:* "They are looking for him in the river!"—*The* GENERAL'S *voice:* "In the river? Did he jump into the river?"—*The* PRIEST'S *voice:* "Shocking!" *A few moments later the* GENERAL *with* BANG, *the* MAYOR, *and the* PRIEST *come in from the other room. They stop on seeing the* KING, *who is standing at the desk with his back to them, and whisper.*)

The General. Isn't that the King?

The Others. The King?

The Mayor. Is the King back? He must have come in the night!

Bang. Let me see!—I know him personally.

The General (*holding him back*). Of course it is the King.

The Mayor. Really?

Bang. I recognise him by his agitation! It is he.

The General. Hush! Let us go quietly out again! (*They begin to move off.*)

The Mayor. He is grieved. Naturally.

Bang. First of all her death; and then this—!

The Priest. It is the judgment of heaven!

The King (*turning round*). Who is that? What? (*Comes forward.*) Who said that? (*They all stop, take off their hats and bow.*) Come back! (*They come back hastily.*) Who said: " It is the judgment of heaven "?

The General. Your Majesty must forgive us—we were just taking a little stroll; I am here to spend Christmas with my friend Mr. Bang, who has a factory here—a branch of his works—and we happened to meet the Mayor and the Priest, and we joined company—and were strolling along when we heard a shot. A shot. We did not think anything more about it till we came nearer here and saw people running, and heard a great outcry and disturbance. Great disturbance—yes. We stopped, of course, and came to see what it was. Came to see what it was, of course. And they told us that the Minister of the Interior—

The King. What is all that to me! (*The* GENERAL *bows.*) Who said: " It is the judgment of heaven "? (*No one speaks.*) Come, answer me!

The Mayor. It was the Priest—I fancy.

The King (*to the* PRIEST). Haven't you the courage to tell me so yourself?

The General. Probably our reverend friend is unaccustomed to find himself in the presence of royalty.

The Priest. It is the first time that—that I have had

the honour of speaking to your Majesty—I did not feel self-possessed enough, for the moment, to—

The King. But you were self-possessed enough when you said it! What did you mean by saying it was " the judg-ment of heaven "?—I am asking you what you meant by it.

The Priest. I really don't quite know—it slipped out—

The King. That is a lie! Some one said: " First of all her death, and then this." And you said: " It is the judgment of heaven."

The Mayor. That is quite right, your Majesty.

The King. First of all *her* death? That meant the death of my betrothed, didn't it?

Bang. } Yes, your Majesty.
The Priest.

The King. " And then *this* " meant my friend—my dear friend! (*With emotion.*) Why did heaven condemn these two to death? (*A pause.*)

The General. It is most regrettable that we should, quite involuntarily, have disturbed your Majesty at a moment when your Majesty's feelings are, naturally, so overcome—

The King (*interrupting him*). I asked you why heaven condemned these two to death. (*To the* VICAR.) You are a clergyman; cudgel your brains!

The Priest. Well, your Majesty, I was thinking that— I meant that—that heaven had in a miraculous way checked your Majesty—

The General. "Ventured to check" would be more suitable, I think.

The Priest. —from continuing in a course which many people thought so unfortunate—I mean, so fatal to the nation, and the church; had checked your Majesty—

The General (*in an undertone*). Ventured to check.

The Priest. —by taking away from your Majesty the two persons who—the two persons who—in the first place the one who—

The King. The one who—?

The Priest. Who was—

The King. Who was—?   A harlot that wanted to sit on the throne?

The Priest. Those are your Majesty's words, not mine. (*Wipes his forehead.*)

The King. Confess that they express what you meant!

The Priest. I confess that I have heard—that people say—that—

The King. Pray to heaven that for a single day your thoughts may be as pure as hers were every day. (*Bursts into tears. Then says impetuously.*) How long have you been a clergyman?

The Priest. Fifteen years, your Majesty.

The King. Then you were already ordained at the time when I was leading a dissolute life.   Why did you never say anything to me then?

The Priest. My most gracious King—

The King. God is the only "most gracious King"! Do not speak blasphemy!

The Priest. It was not my duty to—

The General. Our friend is not a court chaplain.   He has merely a parish in the town here—

The Mayor. And his work lies chiefly among the factory hands.

The King. And so it is not your duty to speak the truth to me—but to attack my dear dead friends by prating about heaven's judgment and repeating vile lies?   Is that your duty?

The Mayor. I only had the honour to know one of the —the deceased.   Your Majesty honoured him with your friendship; the greatest honour a subject can enjoy.   I should like to say that one would rarely find a nobler heart, a loftier mind, or more modest fidelity, than his.

The General. I should like, if I may make so bold, to

make use of the opportunity chance has afforded me of associating myself with my sovereign's sorrow, a sorrow for which his whole people must feel the deepest respect, but especially those who, in consequence of their high position, are more particularly called upon to be the pillars of the monarchy; to use this opportunity, I say—and to do so, I know, as the representative of many thousands of your Majesty's subjects—to voice the sympathy, the unfeigned grief, that will be poured forth at the news of this new loss which has wrung your Majesty's heart —a loss which will reawaken consternation in the country and make it more than ever necessary to take the severest possible measures against a party to which nothing is sacred, neither the King's person nor the highest dignities of office nor the inviolability of the home—a party whose very existence depends on sedition and ought no longer to be tolerated, but ought, as the enemy of the throne and of society, to be visited with all the terrors of the law, until—

The King. What about compassion, my friend?

The General. Compassion?

The King. Not for the republicans—but for me!

The General. It is just the compassion which the whole nation will feel for your Majesty that compels me, in spite of everything, to invoke the intervention of justice at this particular crisis! Terror—

The King. —must be our weapon?

The General. Yes! Can any one imagine a more price-less proof of the care that a people have for their King, than for the gravely anxious tones of their voice to be heard, at this solemn moment, crying: Down with the enemies of the throne!

The King (turning away). No, I haven't thews and sinews for that lie!

The Mayor. I must say I altogether agree with the General. The feeling of affection, gratitude, esteem—

The General. — the legacy of devotion that your Majesty's ancestors of blessed memory—

The King (*to the Priest*). You, sir—what does my ancestors being " of blessed memory " mean?

The Priest (*after a moment's thought*). It is a respectful manner of alluding to them, your Majesty.

The King. A respectful lie, you mean. (*A pause. ANNA comes out of the room on the left and throws herself at the KING'S feet, embracing his knees in despairing sorrow.*) Ah, here comes a breath of truth!—And you come to me, my child, because you know that we two can mourn together. But I do not weep, as you do; because I know that for a long time he had been secretly praying for death. He has got his wish now. So you must not weep so bitterly. You must wish what he wished, you know.— Ah, what grief there is in her eyes! (*Sobs.*)

(*The GENERAL signs to the others that they should all withdraw quietly, without turning round. They gradually do so ; but the KING looks up and perceives what they are doing.*)

The General. Out of respect for your Majesty's grief, we were going to—

The King. Silence! With my hand on the head of this poor creature, who used to trust so unassumingly and devotedly to his goodness of heart, I wish to say something in memory of my friend. (*ANNA clings to him, weeping. The others come respectfully nearer, and wait.*) Gran was the richest man in the country. Why was it that *he* had no fear of the people? Why was it that he believed that its salvation lay in the overthrow of the present state of affairs?

Bang. Mr. Gran, with all his great qualities, was a visionary.

The King. He had not inherited all of his vast fortune; he had amassed a great part of it himself.

Bang. As a man of business, Mr. Gran was beyond all praise.

The King. And yet a visionary? The two things are absolutely contradictory.—You once called me " the padlock on your cash-box."

Bang. I allowed myself, with all respect, to make that jest—which, nevertheless, was nothing but the serious truth!

The King. Why did he, who has met his death, consider that the security for *his* cash-box came from those *below* him, as long as he did what was right, and not from those above him? Because he understood the times. No question of selfishness stood in the way of his doing that.—That is my funeral oration over him!—(*To* ANNA.) Get up, my dear! Did you understand what I was saying? Do not weep so! (*She clings to him, sobbing.*)

The Priest. He was a very great man! When your Majesty speaks so, I fully recognise it. But your Majesty may be certain that, though we may not have been so fortunate as to see so far ahead and so clearly—though our mental horizon may be narrow—we are none the less loyal to your Majesty for that, nor less devoted! It is our duty as subjects to say so, although your Majesty in your heaviness of heart seems to forget it—seems to forget that we, too, look for everything from your Majesty's favour, wisdom and justice. (*Perspires freely.*)

The King. It is very strange! My dear friend never said anything like that to me. (*A pause.*) He had the most prosperous business in the country. When I came to him and asked him to abandon it, he did so at once. And in the end he died for me. That is the sort of man he was. (*To* ANNA.) Go in to him, my dear! You are the very picture of dumb loyalty. Although I do not deserve to have such as you to watch by my side, still, for the sake of him who is dead, I shall have you to do so when I too—. (*Breaks off.*) Yes, yes, go in there now! I shall come. Do you understand? I shall come. (ANNA *moves towards the other room.*) There, that's it! (*He repeats*

his words to her every time she looks back as she goes.)
Yes, directly!—That's it!—In a very little while! Go
now!

Bang. Excuse me, your Majesty, but it is terribly hot
in here, and the affection of my heart which troubles me
is attacking me painfully. Will your Majesty be pleased
to allow me to withdraw?

The Mayor. With all respect, I should like to be
allowed to make the same request. Your Majesty is
obviously very much upset, and I am sure we are all
unwilling that our presence—which, indeed, was un-
intentional and unsought by us—should augment a distress of mind which is so natural in one of your Majesty's
noble disposition, and so inevitable considering the
deep sense of gratitude your Majesty must feel towards a
friend who—

The King (*interrupting him*). Hush, hush! Let us
have a little respect for the truth in the presence of the
dead! Do not misunderstand me—I do not mean to
say that any of you would lie wilfully; but the atmosphere
that surrounds a king is infected. And, as regards that—
just a word or two. I have only a short time. But as a
farewell message from me—

The Priest. A farewell message?

The King. —give my greeting to what is called Christianity in this country. Greet it from me! I have been
thinking a great deal about Christian folk lately.

The Priest. I am glad to hear it!

The King. Your tone jars on me! Greet those who
call themselves Christians—. Oh! come, come—don't
crane your necks and bend your backs like that, as if the
most precious words of wisdom were about to drop from
my lips! (*To himself.*) Is it any use my saying anything serious to them? (*Aloud.*) I suppose you are
Christians?

The General. Why, of course! Faith is invaluable—

The King. — in preserving discipline? (*To the Mayor.*) How about you?

The Mayor. I was taught by my parents, of blessed memory—

The King. Oh, so *they* are " of blessed memory " too, are they? Well, what did they teach you?

The Mayor. To fear God, honour the King—

The King. —and love the brotherhood! You are a public official, Mr. Mayor. That is what a Christian is, nowadays. (*To* BANG.) And you?

Bang. Of late I have been able to go so little to church, because of my cough. And in that unwholesome atmosphere—

The King. —you go to sleep. But you are a Christian?

Bang. Undoubtedly!

The King (*to the Priest*). And you are one, of course?

The Priest. By the grace of God I hope so!

The King (*snapping his fingers*). Yes, that is the regulation formula, my good fellow! You all answer by the card! Very well, then—you are a community of Christians; and it is not my fault if such a community refuses to take any serious interest in what really affects Christianity. Tell it from me that it ought to keep an eye on the monarchy.

The Priest. Christianity has nothing to do with such things. It concerns only the souls of men!

The King (*aside*). That voice. (*Aloud.*) I know—it does not concern itself with the air a patient breathes, but only with his lungs! Excellent!—All the same, Christianity ought to keep an eye on the monarchy. Ought to tear the falsehood away from it! Ought not to go in crowds to stare at a coronation in a church, like apes grinning at a peacock! I know what I felt at that moment. I had rehearsed it all once that morning already— ha, ha! Ask your Christianity if it may not be about time for it to interest itself a little in the monarchy? It seems to me that it scarcely ought any longer to allow monarchy, like a seductive harlot, to keep militarism before the people's eyes as an ideal—seeing that that is exactly contrary to the teachings of Christianity, or to encourage class divisions, luxury, hypocrisy and vanity. Monarchy has become so all-pervading a lie that it infects even the most upright of men.

The Mayor. But I don't understand, your Majesty!

The King. Don't you? You are an upright man yourself, Mr. Mayor—a most worthy man.

The Mayor. I do not know whether your Majesty is pleased to jest again?

The King. In sober earnest, I say you are one of the most upright of men.

The Mayor. I cannot tell your Majesty how flattered I am to hear your Majesty say so!

The King. Have you any decorations?

The Mayor. Your Majesty's government has not, so far, deigned to cast their eyes on me.

The King. That fault will be repaired. Be sure of that!

The General (to the Mayor). To have that from his Majesty's own mouth is equivalent to seeing it gazetted. I am fortunate to be able to be the first to congratulate you!

Bang. Allow me to congratulate you also!

The Priest. And me too! I have had the honour of working hand in hand with you, Mr. Mayor, for many years; I know how well deserved such a distinction is.

The Mayor. I feel quite overcome; but I must beg to be allowed to lay my thanks at your Majesty's feet. I trust I shall not prove unworthy of the distinction. One hesitates to make such confessions—but I am a candid man, and I admit that one of the chief aims of my ambition has been to be allowed some day to participate in—

The King (interrupting him). —in this falsehood. That just points my moral. As long as even upright men's thoughts run in that mould, Christianity cannot pretend to have any real hold on the nation. As for your decoration, you are quite sure to get one from my successor.—In a word, Christianity must tackle monarchy! And if it cannot tear the falsehood from it without destroying it, then let it destroy it!

The General. Your Majesty!

The King (turning to him). The same thing applies to a standing army, which is a creation of monarchy's. I do not believe that such an institution—with all its temptations to power, all its inevitable vices and habits—could be tolerated if Christianity were a living thing. Away with it!

The Priest. Really, your Majesty—!

The King (turning to him). The same applies to an established church — another of monarchy's creations! If we had in our country a Christianity worth the name, that salvation trade would stink in men's nostrils. Away with it!

The Mayor (reproachfully). Oh, your Majesty!

The King (turning on him). The same applies to the artificial disparity of circumstances that you prate about with tears in your eyes! I heard you once. Class distinctions are fostered by monarchy.

Bang. But equality is an impossibility!

The King. If *you* would only make it possible—which it can be made—even the socialists would cease to clamour for anything else. I tell you this: Christianity has destroyed ideals. Christianity lives on dogmas and formulas, instead of on ideals.

The Priest. Its ideals lead us away from earth to heaven—

The King. Not in a balloon, even if it were stuffed full of all the pages of the Bible! Christianity's ideals will lead to heaven only when they are realised on earth—never before.

The Priest. May I venture to say that Christianity's ideal is a pious life.

The King. Yes. But does not Christianity aim at more than that, or is it going to be content with making some few believers?

The Priest. It is written: " Few are chosen."

The King. Then it has given up the job in advance?

The Mayor. I think our friend is right, that Christianity has never occupied itself with such things as your Majesty demands of it.

The King. But what I mean is, could it not bring itself to do so?

The Priest. If it did, it would lose sight of its *inner* aim. The earliest communities are the model for a Christian people!

The King (turning away from him). Oh, have any model you like, so long as it leads to something!

The General. I must say I am astonished at the penetration your Majesty shows even into the deepest subjects.

Bang. Yes, I have never heard anything like it! I have not had the advantage of a university education, so I don't really understand it.

The King. And to think that I imagined that I should find my allies, my followers, in Christian people! One is so reluctant to give up *all* hope! I thought that a Christian nation would storm the strongholds of lies in our modern, so-called Christian communities—storm them, capture them!—and begin with monarchy, because that would need most courage, and because its falsehood lies deepest and goes farthest. I thought that Christianity would one day prove to be the salt of the earth. No, do *not* greet Christianity from me. I have said nothing, and do not mean it. I am what men call a betrayed

man — betrayed by all the most ideal powers of life.
There! Now I have done!

The General. But what does your Majesty mean?
Betrayed? By whom? Who are the traitors? Really—!

The King. Pooh! Think it over! — As a matter of
fact I am the only one that has been foolish.

Bang. Your Majesty, just now you were so full of
vigour—!

The King. Don't let that astonish you, my friend!
I am a mixture of enthusiasm and world-weariness; the
scion of a decrepit race is not likely to be any better than
that, you know! And as for being a reformer—! Ha,
ha! Well, I thank you all for having listened to me so
patiently. Whatever I said had no significance—except
perhaps that, like the oysters, I had to open my shell
before I died.—Good-bye!

The General. I really cannot find it in my heart to leave
your Majesty when your Majesty is in so despondent
a humour.

The King. I am afraid you will have to try, my gallant
friend!—Don't look so dejected, Mr. Mayor!—Suppose
some day serious-minded men should feel just as humili-
ated at such falsehoods existing as you do now because
you have not been allowed to participate in them. I
might perhaps be able to endure being king then! But
as things are now, I am not strong enough for the job.
I feel as if I had been shouldered out of actual life on to
this strip of carpet that I am standing on! That is what
my attempts at reform have ended in!

The Mayor. May I be allowed to say that the impression made on my mind by the somewhat painful scene
we have just gone through is that your Majesty is overwrought.

The King. Mad, you mean?

The Mayor. God forbid I should use such a word of my
King!

The King. Always punctilious!—Well, judging by the fact that every one else considers themselves sane, I must undoubtedly be the mad one. It is as simple as a sum in arithmetic.—And, in all conscience, isn't it madness, when all is said and done, to take such trifles so much to heart?—to bother about a few miserable superannuated forms that are not of the slightest importance?—a few venerable, harmless prejudices? — a few foolish social customs and other trumpery affairs of that sort?

The General. Quite so!

The Mayor. Your Majesty is absolutely right!

Bang. I quite agree!

The Priest. It is exactly what I have been thinking all the time.

The King. And probably we had better add to the list certain extravagant ideas—perhaps even certain dangerous ideas, like mine about Christianity?

The Priest (hastily and impressively). Your Majesty is mistaken on the subject of Christianity.

The Mayor. Christianity is entirely a personal matter, your Majesty.

The General. Your Majesty expects too much of it. Now, as a comfort for the dying—!

The King. And a powerful instrument of discipline.

The General (smiling). Ah, your Majesty!

Bang (confidentially). Christianity is no longer such a serious matter nowadays, except for certain persons—. (*Glances at the* PRIEST.)

The King. All I have to say on the head of such unanimous approval is this: that in such a shallow society, where there is no particular distinction between lies and truth, because most things are mere forms without any deeper meaning—where ideals are considered to be extravagant, dangerous things—it is not so *very* amusing to be alive.

The General. Oh, your Majesty! Really, you—! Ha, ha, ha!

The King. Don't you agree with me?—Ah, if only one could grapple with it!—but we should need to be many to do that, and better equipped than I am.

The General. Better equipped than your Majesty? Your Majesty is the most gifted man in the whole country!

All. Yes!

The General. Yes—your Majesty must excuse me—I spoke involuntarily!

The Mayor. There was a tone running through all your Majesty said that seemed to suggest that your Majesty was contemplating—. (*Breaks off.*)

The King. —going away? Yes.

All. Going away?

The General. And abdicating? For heaven's sake, your Majesty—!

Bang. That would mean handing us over to the crown prince—the pietist!

The Priest (*betraying his pleasure in spite of himself*). And his mother!

The King. You are pleased at the idea, parson! It will be a sight to see her and her son prancing along, with all of you in your best clothes following them! Hurrah!

The General. Ha, ha, ha! Ho, ho, ho!

Bang. Ha—ha—ha! (*Coughs.*) I get such a cough when I laugh.

The King (*seriously*). I had no intention of provoking laughter in the presence of death. I can hear the sounds of mourning through the open door.

The Mayor. With all due respect to the church—the vast majority of the nation have no desire for things to come to *that*—to the accession of a pietist to the throne. If your Majesty threatens to abdicate you will have us all at your feet.

The General (*with decision*). The accession of a new king just now would be universally considered a national calamity. I will wager my life on that!

Bang. And I too!

The King. My excellent friends—you must take the consequences of your actions!

The Mayor (despairingly). But *this!* Who ever imagined such a thing?

The General.
Bang. } No one—no one!

The King. So much the worse. What is it you are asking me to do? To stay where I am, so as to keep another man down? Is that work for a man? Shame!

The Mayor (in distress). We ask more than that! Your Majesty is making a fatal mistake! The whole of your Majesty's dissatisfaction springs from the fact that you believe yourself to be deserted by your people because the elections are going contrary to what your Majesty had hoped. Nothing is further from the truth! The people fight shy of revolutionary ideas; but they love their King!

Bang. They love their King!

The King. And that white dove, who came confidently to my hand—she had some experience of what their love was!

The Mayor. The King's associates may displease the people; ideas may alter; but love for their King endures!

The Others. Endures!

The King. Cease! Cease!

The General (warmly). Your Majesty may command us to do anything except refrain from giving utterance to a free people's freely offered homage of devotion, loyalty, and love for its royal house!

The Mayor (emotionally). There is no one who would not give his life for his King!

Bang.
The General. } No one!
The Priest.

The General. Try us! (*They all press forward.*)

The King. Done with you! (*Takes a revolver from his pocket.*) Since yesterday I have carried this little thing in my pocket. (*They all look alarmed.*)

The Priest. Merciful heavens!

The King (*holding out the revolver to him*). Will you die for me? If so, I will continue to be King.

The Priest. I? What does your Majesty mean? It would be a great sin!

The King. You love me, I suppose?

All (*desperately*). Yes, your Majesty!

The King. Those who love, believe. Therefore, believe me when I say this: If there is a single one of you who, without thinking twice about it, will die for his King now —here—at once—then I shall consider that as a command laid upon me to go on living and working.

The Mayor (*in a terrified whisper*). He is insane!

The General (*whispers*). Yes!

The King. I can hear you!—But I suppose you love your King, even if he is insane?

All (*in agitated tones*). Yes, your Majesty!

The King. Majesty, majesty! There is only One who has any majesty about Him—certainly not a madman!— But if I have been driven mad by the lies that surround me, it would be a holy deed to make me sound again. You said you would die for me. Redeem your words! That will make me well again!—You, General?

The General. My beloved King, it would be—as our reverend friend so aptly put it—a most dreadful sin.

The King. You have let slip a splendid opportunity for showing your heroism.—You ought to have seen that I was only putting you to the test!—Good-bye! (*Goes into the room on the left.*)

The General. Absolutely insane!

The Others. Absolutely.

The Mayor. Such great abilities, too! What might not have been made of him!

Bang. The pity of it!

The Priest. I got so alarmed.

Bang. So did I! (*A loud pistol-shot is heard.*)

The Priest. Another shot? (*A pitiful woman's cry is heard from the other room.*)

The Mayor. What on earth was that?

Bang. I daren't think!

The Priest. Nor I! (*An old woman rushes out of the room on the left, calling out:* " Help!—Help!—The King!" *and hurries out at the back, calling:* " The King!— Help, help!" *The* GENERAL *and the* MAYOR *rush into the other room. Voices are heard outside asking:* " The King?—Was it the King?" *The confusion and uproar grows. In the midst of it* ANNA *comes stumbling out of the other room, her hands stretched out before her, as if she did not know where she was going. The noise and confusion grows louder every minute, and crowds of people come rushing into the room from outside as the Curtain falls.*)